MW00585721

MAKING GREAT STRATEGY

MAKING GREAT STRATEGY

Arguing for Organizational Advantage

Jesper B. Sørensen

Glenn R. Carroll

Columbia Business School
Publishing

Columbia University Press
Publishers Since 1893
New York   Chichester, West Sussex
cup.columbia.edu
Copyright © 2021 Jesper B. Sørensen and Glenn R. Carroll
All rights reserved

Library of Congress Cataloging-in-Publication Data
Names: Sørensen, Jesper B., 1967– author. | Carroll, Glenn, author.
Title: Making great strategy : arguing for organizational advantage /
    Jesper B. Sørensen and Glenn R. Carroll.
Description: 1 edition. | New York City : Columbia University Press, 2021. |
    Includes bibliographical references and index.
Identifiers: LCCN 2020023410 (print) | LCCN 2020023411 (ebook) |
    ISBN 9780231199483 (hardback) | ISBN 9780231553155 (ebook)
Subjects: LCSH: Strategic planning. | Leadership. | Success in business.
Classification: LCC HD30.28 .S6277 2021 (print) | LCC HD30.28 (ebook) |
    DDC 658.4/012—dc23
LC record available at https://lccn.loc.gov/2020023410
LC ebook record available at https://lccn.loc.gov/2020023411

Columbia University Press books are printed
on permanent and durable acid-free paper.
Printed in the United States of America

Cover design: Lisa Hamm
Cover image: Adobe Stock

To

Patricia Chang and Nikolaj, Benjamin, and Chloe Chang Sørensen

Lihua Wang and Lishan Nan Carroll

CONTENTS

CONTENTS

PART VI
APPENDICES

PREFACE

S trategy is hard—really hard—to do well. Leaders of all organizations typically proclaim publicly that they have the right strategy, but these efforts often fall short of what's needed to guide an organization effectively through challenging times. Executives will admit to this embarrassing fact in anonymous surveys, but will never publicly question whether their firms have great strategies. Worse yet, they often don't know what to do about the dilemmas they find themselves in.

Why is making great strategy so difficult? At the top of the list is the exceedingly difficult nature of strategic decision making. Strategy involves undertaking major, interrelated, and often irreversible decisions to ensure long-run success in an uncertain future. Often it involves making and justifying bets that others think are foolish. More fundamentally, strategy involves trade-offs: saying no to some opportunities in the hope of realizing greater ones.

Yet when the time comes to confront upcoming challenges head-on and devise a strategic plan that allocates resources to address the wolf at the door, many executives deliver something short of what's needed. Instead of making great strategy, they produce what Richard Rumelt calls bad strategy: they describe trends, they articulate grand goals, and they make nice diagrams with pithy sayings, often using the help of outsiders.[1] In our view, they dodge.

How do you make strategy great? What leaders need is to develop and forcefully articulate the executive team's *argument* for how their chosen goals will be achieved. The argument might reference all kinds of resources, such as people, technology, finances, and even regulators. Above all, the argument must make sense to everyone. It must be logically valid, and it must be accessible to all members of the organization. Most importantly, the argument must realistically identify the various things that need to be true—the assumptions, conditions, or premises, if you will—for competitive success to happen. Such arguments are the core of great strategies and the centerpiece of successful strategic processes. The hardest part of strategic decision making involves choosing a direction and allocating resources on the basis of these assumptions and the arguments they support. Making such decisions can be terrifying, because the stakes are often very high and there are no guarantees. Clear, logical strategy arguments do not remove the need for choice or for making risky bets, but they allow leaders to approach them with confidence.

We wrote this book to aid current executives and future executives (MBA students, young managers, entrepreneurs) and their teams in developing strategy arguments, arguments that can be used to make tough strategic decisions for their organizations with confidence. We advocate a different mentality for thinking about strategy, one that celebrates the value of disciplined reasoning and places constructive argumentation at the center of the strategic process.

To help turn this mentality into practice, we offer a *flexible system of three core activities*: (1) iterative visualization, (2) logical formalization, and (3) constructive engagement and debate with others. We aim to make these activities practical and accessible for the working executive, as a means for developing the skills and habits of mind needed to develop and formulate strategy. That is, we explain and illustrate a system through which great strategy and its associated decisions can be actually formulated and managed on a day-to-day basis. We believe that the system demystifies strategy and makes it easier for executive teams to make their strategies great. While the system does not necessarily make placing risky strategic bets any easier, it does bring the important issues into sharper focus.

We wrote the book partly in reaction to conventional ways of teaching strategy and strategic management. It represents an attempt to do it differently, and better. Specifically, we aim to provide an approach to making strategy (and an associated set of managerial activities) that is more attuned to the needs of contemporary executives, especially as it concerns assessing and formulating organizational strategy for an uncertain future.

In teaching courses on strategy and organizational design, we discovered that many executives are highly conversant—even expert—in the recognition and analysis of the strategic actions and positions of firms and organizations.

Indeed, the central teaching material for a class session on strategy typically consists of a business case, wherein a firm and its competitors are described by their positions in a product market or larger environment. Like most strategy professors, we led discussions around these business cases, and we used basic economic and organizational theory to make sense of the firms' positions in the product market space. We facilitated fun and engaging discussions as the class identified likely winners and losers. We typically viewed our role as guiding the class participants as they applied theoretical ideas to support their views and to argue against the views of others.

In a typical case discussion, the class adopts the vantage point of a particular focal firm: its position gets analyzed in depth, and prescriptions are offered for how to improve its chances of success in the future. In a good class discussion, the students identify the key risks to the firm and specify the trade-offs inherent in decisions to be made. Additionally, class participants make sophisticated observations and analyses before stating what they would do if they were running the focal firm. A good strategy course takes the executives through a series of such cases, each chosen to emphasize a specific common strategic dilemma and an associated theoretical principle or two.

All that is fine—it's a very good, time-honored way to teach principles of strategy. Still, we often sensed a great deal of frustration from executives and students, and experienced even more ourselves, when using this approach. Why? What was missing?

Here's the problem. While the conventional approach does a good job of teaching the received wisdom of strategy theory and underlying research, it does little to teach *how* great strategy is actually made, or *how* it should be managed on a day-to-day basis in an organization that is performing well. Moreover, teaching this way simultaneously reifies strategy theory and mystifies the process by which it was created. It is akin to the traditional ways of teaching high school math. A math teacher may teach students the Pythagorean theorem, for example, by walking through the set of specific assumptions behind it and then—voila—deducing the conclusion. Of course, even for a hard-to-follow proof, the theorem contains useful knowledge, because it solves many puzzles. But the lesson plan tells you very little about how Pythagoras thought about the problem initially, what steps he took in trying to devise a solution, what criteria and process guided his work, and how many false leads he may have pursued before finally finding the correct solution.[2] It doesn't teach you how to think like Pythagoras. In the same way, conventional strategy texts do not teach you how to think like Sam Walton; instead they teach you the reasons behind Walmart's success. Similarly, while we recognize that dozens of books on strategy formulation and the strategy-making process exist, we find each sorely lacking for various reasons; but the main common reason is that they do not depict realistically how effective strategy gets made and at the same time offer practical tools for doing it.

In short, the process of discovering and creating knowledge often looks very different from how that knowledge is communicated to others after the discovery. The same holds true for strategic knowledge. The formulation process behind most successful strategies can often be, as the old adage goes, like making sausage—the end product is excellent, but those involved in its making describe the process as disorderly, chaotic, and messy. But does that mean strategy making must be hopeless?

As teachers and analysts, we are keenly aware that the challenge of formulating and changing strategy is almost always far more difficult than what our classroom discussions would suggest. We have long been dissatisfied with the idea that the existing approach reflects the best we can do. After all, for executives and other leaders, formulating and directing strategy making ranks as one of the most important things they do.

Executives come away from traditional strategy instruction knowing what happened in particular industries or markets, and why those outcomes occurred. So instructed, these executives could easily avoid the mistakes made by the case protagonists. But the next strategic dilemma never looks exactly the same. So, when taught the traditional way, executives will be ill prepared for a future in which they will be asked to craft and lead a strategy for new, unknown conditions—perhaps in markets that operate in different ways and with novel and often untested technologies. By contrast, teaching a positive and constructive system of activities to generate, evaluate, and revise strategies provides a missing critical component and may just be a better way on its own. The old cliché about teaching someone to fish rather than giving that person a fish comes to mind.

Despite its novelty, our approach to making strategy remains consistent with many widely used strategic theories of sustainable competitive advantage. That is, the book draws on familiar ways of thinking and problem solving—ways that are comfortable for most managers, but all too often not applied with discipline to strategic issues. The difference reflects a focus on the *activities* used to develop great strategy rather than actual strategic content. Our view says that it is hard, if not almost impossible, for the leaders of an organization to identify and pursue a strategy with good content if they do not have an effective well-honed system of activities for generating and evaluating it.

Who should read this book? We envision the primary audience for the book as current and future executives of businesses and other organizations, including entrepreneurial start-ups and nonprofits. We also think their strategy-making teams would benefit from reading and using the book. At some point in their careers, executives and entrepreneurs must lead and guide the strategy formulation and development process. We hope that the system of activities presented in this book will help them and their teams to do that in a disciplined and effective way. Strategy is too important to be treated in any less serious way.

Approaching strategy in this way can at times be challenging. We would be remiss if we did not mention the "technical" aspects of this book. By using logical syllogisms to articulate arguments, parts of the book do not look like the typical fodder offered to executives and managers. Too many business books steer clear of anything even slightly technical or complex. To put it bluntly, we find the "dumbed-down" books often written for executives to be both baffling and insulting. They are baffling because some of the most technically sophisticated and intelligent people we have ever worked with are executives, often with background training in highly technical fields such as engineering, finance, accounting, and the like. They are insulting because the writing assumes that executives are incapable or unwilling to bear down and work through a complicated set of thoughts. Our experience couldn't be more different—executives are more than capable of and willing to use a more technical approach, provided they believe it will pay off in the end, that the result will be worth the effort. Still, we have tried to minimize the use of technical material and held it to a minimum; we are not logicians ourselves and recognize that this approach likely opens us up to criticisms of oversimplifying things. We can live with that.

So, what are the payoffs for learning this system? A great strategy, for sure. Drilling down a bit, we would say the concrete payoffs also include:

1. an ability to *isolate the key factors driving a strategy* and a way to focus on the key decisions behind a strategy;
2. a facility for *identifying tacit assumptions behind a strategy's success* and a way to make explicit these assumptions for inspection and debate;

3. *enhanced engagement and contribution* of members of the strategy-making team;

4. identification of specific observable *factors to be monitored* to understand the strategy's ongoing performance; and

5. an organization capable of *high-performance execution* of the strategy.

In using the materials presented in this book to teach hundreds of executives and managers across many years, we have found that most of them figure out two things pretty quickly. First, while the materials (specifically the logic representations) look a bit different than things they might be accustomed to, after a small investment in developing fluency, it becomes clear that none of the activities offered here are really very technically challenging. Second, the payoffs to learning this system are real, and they start coming fast once implemented in a team or organization. Many executives come away thinking that these activities help them clarify and simplify matters rather than make them more complicated.

The materials presented in the book were developed over the course of our years teaching strategy and organizational design to executives, entrepreneurs, and MBA students. Especially important to our thinking in developing the book was a course we helped develop and taught at Stanford that was not on strategy per se, but on "critical analytical thinking" (CAT informally). This course was designed to teach students the fundamental principles of disciplined reasoning including logic, argumentation, and civil debate. What if, we wondered initially, we applied the tools of CAT to strategy and strategic management? Would it help structure thinking about strategy? Could the somewhat technical tools of CAT be learned and used effectively by business leaders to make great strategy?

Obviously, we eventually answered these questions affirmatively, but it took us years of experimentation, learning, and feedback from executives and students. In that regard, we are especially grateful for the opportunities to use and develop the system of activities in classes, and especially in extended executive programs that we designed, directed, and taught for Alfa, Caterpillar, Intel, and General Motors, as well as others.

The book would not exist but for the encouragement of our friends and colleagues. For insightful discussions on strategy, we especially appreciate the extended time we spent with executives Mike Ableson, Michael Arena, Ned Barnholt, Paul Branstad, Bill Meehan, Ed Rapp, David Rogier, and Tom

Wurster. For encouragement and helpful comments on earlier drafts, we appreciate the suggestions of Michael Arena, Bill Barnett, Jon Bendor, Paul Branstad, Patricia Chang, John-Paul Ferguson, John de Figueiredo, Frank Flynn, Mike Hannan, Özgecan Koçak, Bill Meehan, Melinda Merino, Giacomo Negro, Charles O'Reilly, David Pervin, Paul Pfleiderer, Laci Pólos, Garth Saloner, Tim Sullivan, Rob Urstein, Lihua Wang, and Tom Wurster, none of whom should be blamed for any remaining errors or misleading statements. Garth Saloner deserves special thanks for shaping our thinking about strategy and for being a champion of the CAT course at Stanford that set us down this path. Aaron Cash read a near-final version of the manuscript and helped identify problematic elements. We also appreciate the professional editorial advice of Marcus Ballenger, James Cook, Melinda Merino, David Pervin, and Tim Sullivan. Finally, we are grateful to the Stanford Graduate School of Business for creating such a productive environment in which to explore these issues, and for generous support, including the Robert A. and Elizabeth R. Jeffe Chair in Organizational Behavior and the Katherine & David deWilde Faculty Fellowship to Sørensen and the Adams Distinguished Chair in Management, Laurence W. Lane Chair of Organizations, and the Spence Faculty Fellowship to Carroll.

Most importantly, we thank our wives and children for their support and patience. Much too often over the past few years their questions and requests were answered with either blank stares or, worse, "What's your argument?" We don't pretend to think that the completion of the book makes their experiences worth it—but it does make it over. Thank you! We could not have done it without you and dedicate the book to you.

MAKING GREAT STRATEGY

PART I

Introduction

CHAPTER 1

||||||||||||||||||||||||||||||||||||||||||||||||||||||||||||||||||||||||||||||||||||||||||||||||||||||||||||||||||||||||||||||||
||||||||||
Arguing for Organizational Advantage

STRATEGY CHALLENGES EXECUTIVES FACE: THREE EXAMPLES

On an earnings call with Wall Street analysts in July 2016, a J.P. Morgan representative sharply challenged Southwest Airlines CEO Gary Kelly: "The impression that investors have is that your priorities at the moment might be somewhat out of order. The impression is that passengers come first, then labor unions, and then shareholders. And that's certainly fine when all is right with the world . . . but during a time of industry crisis . . . most companies would consider revisiting their sort of priority order, at least in the short run."[1]

Other analysts piled on in questioning Southwest's failure to implement a variety of revenue-producing and cost-saving schemes that competing airlines had implemented successfully. Full-service airlines such as American, Delta, and United had recently increased revenues and profitability by adding new fees or raising prices for checked baggage, schedule changes, and advance seat assignments. So too had low-cost carriers such as WestJet and JetBlue. Another group of analysts wanted Southwest to follow the other major U.S. carriers and cancel scheduled flights to better match capacity to demand. But to date, Kelly had refused.

The analysts complained, despite knowing Southwest's remarkable history of sustained success. At the time of the earnings call, Southwest Airlines had reported forty-three straight years of profits, the only U.S. airline to do so—in a relentlessly competitive industry known for its ups and downs, its waves of consolidation, entry, and bankruptcies. Since its founding in the early 1970s,

Southwest had grown steadily from a small, regional carrier based in Texas to become the largest domestic carrier in the United States. Southwest pioneered a unique, low-price business model that other low-price carriers around the world eventually copied. As a result, Southwest has been widely taught in the world's leading business schools as an exemplar of excellence in strategy and organization.

Past performance does not guarantee future success, however, as all executives know. Moreover, analysts on that 2016 earnings call pointed to recent declines in Southwest's revenues and profitability. The analysts used Southwest's failure to adopt new practices as evidence that the company's leadership was stuck in the past and not up to the new challenges presented by the marketplace.

Kelly faced a classic problem of a strategic leader. With both revenues and profit margins under pressure, what, if anything, should be done about the situation? Was the decline in performance a reflection of problems in Southwest's basic business strategy, as the analysts claimed? Or were the performance problems due to factors beyond Southwest's control, and the strategy fundamentally sound? In the latter case, making changes in the absence of real strategic problems could be enormously disruptive. For example, loyal Southwest passengers accustomed to showing up early at the gate to get in line for their preferred seat might resent finding that the best seats had been sold in advance.

* * *

An eighteen-year veteran of Anheuser-Busch (AB) InBev, Pedro Earp was surprised to receive a call from CEO Carlos Brito in late 2014. Even more startling, Brito asked him to move to New York from Brazil to take the reins of a newly formed independent business unit called the Disruptive Growth Organization.[2] Brito had created the unit after being taken to task by the AB InBev board of directors, which thought the company was too slow in adapting to emerging consumer trends.

Of particular concern to the board was the pronounced and persistent rise of craft beers in its key markets. "With the total beer market up only 0.5 percent in 2014, craft brewers are key in keeping the overall industry innovative and growing. This steady growth shows that craft brewing is part of a profound shift in American beer culture," noted Bart Watson, chief economist, Brewers

Association. He continued, "Small and independent brewers are deepening their connection to local beer lovers while continuing to create excitement and attract even more appreciators."[3] In 2014, craft beer represented almost 20 percent of industry revenue. Having focused on consolidating and improving the marketing and operations of mass production brewers worldwide, AB InBev had little presence in the craft-brewing segment.

Tasked with devising a strategic response, Earp and colleagues adopted an approach to craft brewing that relied heavily on acquisition—not unlike AB InBev's history of acquisitions of famous brands such as Budweiser, Stella Artois, Corona, and Beck's. Following Earp's lead, by mid-2017, AB InBev had bought total or controlling interest in, and kept operating, some of the most highly revered and fastest-growing brewing companies in American craft beer, including Goose Island, Elysian, Ballast Point, Devils Backbone, Blue Point, 10 Barrel, Meantime, 4 Pines, Pirate Life, Boxing Cat, and Wicked Weed Brewing. As Earp explained things: "We transformed AB InBev into a platform that could partner with craft breweries. We did transactions, but actually the original teams continued to lead the businesses, innovating and all. So instead of trying to innovate inside, we became an ecosystem for innovation in craft."[4]

Questions remained, the most important being whether AB InBev's platform-based craft beer strategy would succeed in the long run. Was it a great strategy? Would it move the dial on AB InBev's reputation and participation in the high-status, high-margin craft beer business? AB InBev's corporate identity had blocked prior success in craft. Was the platform model enough to overcome it? More pressing operational questions presented themselves as well, including how Earp should identify and choose future acquisition targets. He also needed to be able to assess the ongoing health of the strategy he had devised. What were the relevant key performance indicators? What data could tell Earp whether the strategy was on the right track? Finally, Earp had to wonder if and when the AB InBev corporate center staff would attempt to intervene, and if they did, what he could do about it.

* * *

Ellie Fields and her marketing team at Tableau faced an unusual challenge in 2009 when the company's executive team announced that the company would launch a free version of its primary software product.[5] Trained as an engineer at Rice University, Fields had built a successful career in marketing at Tableau, one focused on the company's paid versions of the software. She was now tasked with designing and implementing the new free version, to be called "Tableau Public." Fields and her team faced a classic problem for a product manager: How could she design and launch a new product that dovetailed properly with the company's overarching strategy?

Tableau, a data visualization software company in Seattle, was founded in 2003 by a team of Stanford alumni, based on ideas from founder Chris Stolte's doctoral research on visualization techniques for relational databases and data cubes. The company's software technology, known as VizQL, let users explore and analyze data by building drag-and-drop pictures of what they wanted to see. The company's products were user-friendly, allowing nontechnical users to develop and analyze patterns in data based on their natural intuitions and insights. Technical users had the ability to go much deeper into the software and write their own code for making calculations, managing metadata, and creating dashboards to display their data. As the company put it: "Tableau harnessed people's natural ability to spot visual patterns quickly, revealing everyday opportunities and Eureka moments alike." Industry analysts thought that Tableau's software had cracked the code of making visualization both comprehensive and interactive.

Tableau helped create the self-serve business intelligence software segment. For its first five years, the company offered two primary software product packages, Tableau Desktop and Tableau Server, with a personal version of Tableau Desktop starting at $999 for a perpetual license for a single user, with an annual maintenance fee. The company grew dramatically, with sales doubling year over year in the early years. Outside reviewers raved: in 2008, Tableau won a Codie Award for Best Business Intelligence Solution from the Software Information and Industry Association.

Tableau suffered a slowdown in 2009 in the wake of the 2008 financial crisis; sales growth dropped to 37 percent. Tableau's existing customers largely remained loyal, but management and staff began searching for new potential users in the market and creative new ways for them to answer questions with data. This was quite a challenge, as Fields explained: "We had traction, but we weren't one of these startups with a ton of cred that was hitting the front page of TechCrunch every day. . . . we were a total 'nobody.' "[6]

The outcome of this exploratory period was the decision to design and launch the free version, Tableau Public. Cofounder Christian Chabot was a primary advocate. As he saw it, Tableau Public would accelerate awareness of the company's enterprise product. Like Tableau Desktop, it would allow users to open data sets and use Tableau's drag-and-drop functionality to create visualizations, although the data sets were more limited in size. Critically, visualizations created in Tableau Public could only be saved by sharing them publicly on the internet through Tableau's public cloud service, where others could see them. Users could then share the visualizations more widely through social media or by embedding them in a web page if they wished. These features were included in Tableau Public to minimize the cannibalization of sales, as corporate customers would rarely want to make public visualizations based on their internal data.

Charged with turning concept into reality, Fields and her team had to design the user interface and features of Tableau Public and decide which customer segments to target. While it was clear to them that the aim of Tableau Public was to increase product awareness for Tableau, the specific implementation strategy was less clear. Should it be a stand-alone application that users could download and use to design visualizations to be published elsewhere on the web? Many software companies pursue similar "free sample" approaches, allowing potential customers to experiment with a restricted feature set in the hopes of converting them to buying the full-feature version. Or should Tableau invest in building a destination site where visualizations with Tableau Public would be shared? This required a more substantial commitment of resources to build and maintain a vibrant destination site. Because enterprise clients would find a destination site unappealing, this approach would require Tableau to engage with new audiences such as bloggers, data journalists, and knowledge workers. Would such an effort be worthwhile, given that Tableau's main revenue source was enterprise clients, and bloggers would likely never convert to being buyers of Tableau Desktop?

LOGICAL ARGUMENT UNDERPINS STRATEGIC SUCCESS

Obviously, the challenges faced by Gary Kelly, Pedro Earp, and Ellie Fields differed in many respects. The three leaders operated in different industries, experienced different demands, and carried different levels of responsibility. Like a general leading his troops, Kelly's situation at Southwest represents a canonical example of what people imagine when they think of strategic leadership: a CEO facing pressure, after a period of relatively poor performance, to change course and conform to what his competitors have done with some success. Kelly must make and justify a decision without alienating analysts entirely. By contrast, Earp at AB InBev was being asked to formulate a new approach to the craft-brewing segment. Critically, he must ensure that the platform strategy avoids the mistakes of the past, disappointing efforts by the company to make inroads in the segment. Earp needed a way to assess whether the new strategy was working, and what adjustments might need to be made, while still operating within the broader constraints of AB InBev's strategy. And Fields at Tableau needed to translate a somewhat unclear mandate from "on high" into a product that strengthened Tableau's revenue-generating products. She needed to make sense of her mandate and understand what kinds of customers should be targeted, and why, in order to drive Tableau's enterprise sales.

Despite these differences, the challenges faced by Kelly, Earp, and Fields share a crucial element: achieving strategic success requires relying on a *logical argument*, unless they want to depend on luck. By *argument*, we mean a chain of reasoning by which a conclusion is drawn from a set of assumptions or premises. By *logical argument*, we mean an argument that passes the test of logic. We define *logic* as reasoning conducted or assessed according to strict principles of validity.[7] As we illustrate later, *validity* in this usage means that the premises automatically imply the conclusion: the chain of reasoning makes sense and is logical. So, a logical argument is a valid argument in this usage (but it is not necessarily sound, another logic concept discussed later). To be sure, not all arguments offered in strategy discussions in organizations are logical arguments; indeed, that is an important reason to invest in logical argumentation. Sustained success has a logic to it, so logical argumentation will help ensure success.

Strategic success demands an ability among executives throughout an organization to step back, think critically, and see the big picture. The days have long passed when an executive could hope to be judged solely on his or her ability to execute a fixed strategy set by someone else. Given today's pace of market and technological change, there no longer exists (if there ever did) a clear division between strategy and execution. Effective strategies do not get set once a year in boardroom meetings; they get realized on a daily basis as multiple managers and leaders regularly make decisions about how to allocate resources in response to unanticipated changes. Strategy is what happens when executives act, ideally putting well-considered plans into action.

This reality puts pressure on executives at all levels. They must be able to make decisions that are clearly informed by an understanding of their organizations' expected logic of success. They must be able to adapt their strategies when prior assumptions are proven wrong but stick with their strategies through rough patches when the fundamentals still hold—and they must be able to tell the difference between the two.

When the pressure starts to build (as with Kelly, Earp, and Fields), leaders are tempted to respond to each challenge in the heat of the moment by following their gut or doing what has worked before. Doing so can easily lead to an ad hoc, almost random, pattern of decisions, unmoored from (and perhaps destructive to) the otherwise successful operation of the firm. To respond effectively under uncertainty, executives need strategic direction, some guideposts to making hard decisions but also to keep the firm from careening off the highway of success. They must be able to communicate their strategy clearly, both to external audiences and internal stakeholders. And they need to be able to think critically about how to assess the firm's strategic situation—to determine whether the current strategy remains on track and to make decisions about what might be done to improve it.

Faced with these strategic challenges, leaders look for help. Perhaps they turn back to their training in business school and try to apply the knowledge and skills learned there to the current situation. Frequently, they seek out and buy business best sellers, hoping that one out of the increasing profusion of strategy frameworks will help lead them to clarity about the right course of action. Or they bring in high-powered strategy consultants and facilitators to help them develop (and justify) their approach. Each of these sources of advice can be found easily and in abundant supply, yet none guarantee success.

With all the accumulated strategic wisdom and the multitude of advice available, you would think that contemporary executives would feel confident in their strategic decisions. Yet they do not. Strategy&, the strategic consulting arm of PricewaterhouseCoopers (pwc), surveyed more than six thousand corporate executives for a report released in 2019.[8] Only 37 percent of respondents said that their companies had well-defined strategies, and only 35 percent felt that the strategies would lead their firms to success. Only 20 percent of the surveyed executives felt that there was agreement in their companies about which capabilities were key to their firms' success.

This lack of confidence is nothing new. In a survey of more than two thousand executives by *McKinsey Quarterly* a decade earlier, only 28 percent characterized the quality of strategic decisions in their companies as good. Six in ten executives thought that the quality of strategic decisions was essentially a coin flip, with bad decisions happening as often as good ones, while 12 percent thought good decisions were rare.[9]

These statistics are stunning, to the point of being hard to believe when you first read them. Unfortunately, they strike us as true. We have witnessed senior leaders express (or betray) a lack of common understanding about even the fundamentals of their firms' strategies. Yes, they understand what their firms do, but they often do not comprehend fully why (or whether) those actions make sense. Even in situations where the fundamental strategy is solid, the lack of confidence among key executives is real and disconcerting. It is also often consequential; executives who do not display confidence in their firms' strategies produce lower commitment among employees, witness poorer execution of critical strategic tasks, and miss out on opportunities for strategic adaptation.

Despite all the strategy frameworks, case studies, and consulting advice, many executives and entrepreneurs struggle to see the systematic elements that unite a successful strategy. Problematic as this may be, it is also understandable. Modern executives have far too little time to step back and think deeply. Moreover, the ways in which strategy has been taught to them and discussed in meetings makes it difficult to see the proverbial forest for the trees.

As business school professors, we not only know this from experience, but have inadvertently contributed to it. We have spent years teaching cases about highly successful companies as diverse as Southwest Airlines, Walmart, Apple, *The Economist*, Facebook, Taobao, Airbnb, and Disney. These companies' strategy stories—and many others—are worth telling, not only because they are compelling narratives in their own right, but because they convey important lessons about how markets and organizations work.

Yet each strategy story is different; Apple did not succeed for the same reasons that Walmart did. The reasons for success are as diverse and numerous as the firms themselves, tied to the specifics of the firms' environments and reflective of different economic and sociological principles. Given this proliferation, no wonder the forest is lost from view: it is easy to conclude that no single path ties all of these stories together, that each story is purely idiosyncratic.

But one underlying theme does indeed unite all sustainably successful strategies, a common truth that is as simple as it is insufficiently recognized. The success of any consistently winning organization's strategy possesses a coherent logic, a logic that can be expressed as an argument, or what we call a *strategy argument*. While the specific reasons for success vary from firm to firm, each firm's accomplishments can be understood through a strategy argument that is logically coherent. Yet this more general dimension—the strategy argument—usually gets lost in the analysis of multiple cases with specific detailed pathways to success. As it gets lost, so too does an understanding of how to formulate and develop great strategy tailored for a new situation, a task that relies on using this general skill of logical argumentation. Accordingly, we made it the focus of this book.

In our depiction, a strategy argument represents an articulation of how the firm's resources and activities combine with external conditions to allow it to create and capture value. Generally speaking, an argument is a set of reasons offered with the aim of convincing others that an action or idea is right or wrong. Similarly, a strategy argument is the set of reasons someone—usually the executive in charge—offers to convince others that a particular combination of resources, activities, and external conditions allows the firm to create and capture value. It is the story the leaders (or someone else) tell about why the firm performs as it does.

Some strategy arguments are better than others. In part this is a question of empirical accuracy, whether the argument represents the facts of the situation correctly. But ultimately the quality of a strategy argument rests on its logical validity.

Unfortunately, the general skills needed to formulate and assess strategy arguments are rarely taught explicitly in business schools or popular strategy books, especially as applied to issues of strategy. Nor are they, in our experience, particularly celebrated or systematically implemented in most companies. No wonder many leaders find it difficult to think systematically about their strategies. Doing so requires abstracting away from the specifics of a decision—where the production facility will be located, who the marketing campaign's spokesperson should be—and instead examining the structure and quality of the reasoning. Unable to assess their strategies as arguments in this way, they instead act, following their instincts. As Cynthia Montgomery notes in *The Strategist*, many leaders possess a shallow understanding of their chosen courses of action:

> Many leaders haven't thought about their strategy in a very deep way. . . . They can't identify the specific needs their businesses fill, or the unique points that distinguish them from competitors on anything but a superficial level. . . . If leaders aren't clear about this, imagine the confusion in their businesses three or four levels lower.[10]

In short, in the absence of attention to the coherence of corporate strategic reasoning, execution—doing *something*—all too often substitutes for systematic thought.

Skill in constructing, debating, and assessing strategy arguments constitutes the pillar of the strategy-making process. A strategy without this pillar collapses into a jumble of customer empathy exercises, analytical insights, and market research. Without this pillar of disciplined deductive reasoning in place, executives find themselves in a position of really not understanding what their strategies are. Skill in strategy argumentation is not a substitute for other tools in the executive's arsenal, but it does constitute an essential complement, one all too often missing. The aim of this book is to give leaders, and their organizations, an advantage, by sharpening their skill base in disciplined strategic reasoning.

STRATEGY ARGUMENTS IN ACTION: THE EXECUTIVE EXAMPLES RECONSIDERED

Consider again the dilemma faced by Gary Kelly at Southwest. There could be no denying the facts: Southwest had suffered its first year-over-year decline in margins in more than three years, while other airlines saw margins improve following the introduction of (or increase in) various kinds of fees. Were Kelly and his executive team too convinced that the company's tried-and-true strategy would still work even though conditions might have changed? Analysts certainly thought so.

The challenge for Kelly was that performance—particularly short-run performance—is a poor indicator of strategic health. The number of factors that *might* explain a firm's past performance always exceeds the evidence available to reach a definitive conclusion. Did a company succeed in this particular quarter because it followed a great strategy? Or were market conditions particularly favorable to the company, and it just happened to be in the right place at the right time? If performance sags, as with Southwest, is that due to flaws in its strategy or factors beyond its control? The risk of overreacting and undermining a great strategy is real.

If recent performance cannot dictate the decision, then how can someone in Kelly's situation react with confidence? The answer lies in being able to understand and communicate the firm's logic of success, in having a clear representation of the firm's strategy argument. With a clear strategy argument in hand, a leader in Kelly's position can quickly and confidently diagnose the nature of the challenges facing the firm and assess whether proposed actions are likely to succeed or will instead undermine the firm's logic of success. As Gary Pisano notes, "Without a [well-articulated] strategy, every decision has to be debated."[11]

Having worked for the company for more than thirty years, during which time the firm's strategy changed largely incrementally, Gary Kelly knew the strategy of Southwest Airlines well, how it worked, and why it had produced sustained success. He had pondered the many details of the strategy, knew how and where they worked together, and understood how they drove customer appeal. This knowledge gave him the confidence that Southwest's performance declines did not reflect challenges to the critical assumptions of the airline's strategy argument. It also led him to conclude that adopting the practices of other airlines was more likely to undermine Southwest's logic of success than strengthen it.

Kelly and his team resisted the pressure to copy the pack of airlines putting new fees in place for just about everything. Based on their strong belief in the strategy argument, Kelly's team claimed that bag charges and change fees would alienate Southwest's customers by "nickel and diming" them; they also reasoned that reducing the number of flights in the short run would break customer confidence in the airline's availability and reliability. Indeed, Southwest went so far as to turn their refusal to make these changes into a point of differentiation from other airlines and to present them as an attraction to customers. Southwest's "Transfarency" ad campaign, for example, hilariously featured a passenger on a rival airline not having enough change to get into a pay toilet.

Afterward, some analysts harshly criticized Kelly and downgraded the company's stock. One analyst wrote, "For a company that is facing its first year-over-year margin decline in 13 quarters, we and the market were hoping for a more tangible response, [such as] capacity cuts."[12] But Kelly was ultimately vindicated: Southwest quickly resumed its record positive growth and earnings run. Thanks to a clear strategy argument, Kelly's communications about the strategy were clear and impactful to customers and analysts; his messages also deepened beliefs long revered in the organization's strong culture.

Without a clear well-defined strategy argument that he fully believed in, Kelly might have questioned the viability of the strategy. He might have gone back to his team and launched a soul-searching review and reanalysis that consumed time and led to changes that undermined the competitive advantage that Southwest still held. By contrast, with an articulated strategy argument in hand, Kelly could quickly and forcefully rebut his critics, explaining in detail the deleterious implications of the changes they proposed for the company's competitive advantage. Most importantly, he could point out how and why Southwest's customer base was different from that of other air carriers, especially their sensitivity to "hidden" added fees. Kelly also likely realized that standing still strengthened Southwest's competitive advantage, because doing so differentiated them even further from competitors.

* * *

Few people familiar with the brewing industry in general, and with Anheuser-Busch, AB InBev's corporate predecessor, in particular, would have envied Pedro Earp his assignment. When craft brewing first emerged in the United States in the 1980s, Anheuser-Busch had pursued a strategy not that dissimilar to the one Earp proposed. Like all major breweries at the time, AB had initially ignored the growth of craft brewing, considering it a hobbyists' curiosity. Eventually, AB responded and made its own versions of the same traditional malt beverages offered by craft brewers—ales, porters, stouts, wheat beers, and the like. Despite critical praise for quality, however, AB did not succeed in marketing these products in a commercially viable way. Studies suggested that a major reason for this failure was that consumer expectations for a craft producer precluded association with a mass producer like AB: consumers wanted craft beer to be made "by hand" in small-scale artisanal breweries.[13] Eventually, AB shifted course and took minority equity positions in several leading craft brewers such as Redhook Ale and Widmer Brothers, providing capital, distribution, and even production resources. But these ventures were modest successes at best and did little, if anything, to stem the growth of the craft-brewing segment or to strengthen AB's position within it.

Perhaps cognizant of this history, Earp's strategic approach to craft beer differed from AB InBev's previous forays into the segment. Where Redhook and Widmer had been integrated acquisitions, Earp likened the new approach to incubation instead, allowing the original leadership teams in the acquired breweries to continue operating their businesses. The idea was that an incubation model would give AB InBev the best of both worlds. The acquired craft breweries would have the levels of autonomy needed to engage effectively with their customers, while benefiting from the scale and clout of AB InBev in non–customer facing activities, especially distribution.

Pedro Earp's challenge was very different from Gary Kelly's, and not only because Earp reported to a very demanding boss. Where Kelly considered modifying an existing, well-proven strategy, Earp needed to chart a promising course for the future, through waters that AB InBev had failed to navigate before. He needed to develop a compelling strategy that the company's leaders could have confidence in; so much confidence, in fact, that they would approve large expenditures for acquisitions to enact an untested, unproven strategy. Moreover, the strategy had to be clear enough to allow Earp and others to identify the critical capabilities, resources, and environmental contingencies that would determine its success or failure.

This was a tall order, but one that could be made easier with a clearly articulated strategy argument. Why? Without a clear strategy argument, Earp and his team might be tempted to snatch up any promising-looking craft brewery without regard to its compatibility or fit with others in the portfolio and to let it continue to operate in idiosyncratic ways once acquired. By contrast, specifying the strategy argument would force Earp and his team to explain how and why a specific set of investments and activities would lead AB InBev as a whole to success in the craft-brewing segment. Once spelled out in this way, the argument can be assessed in terms of its logical validity: whether the presumed outcomes follow from what the team has assumed, or whether there are flaws in the team's reasoning. Such logical validity should be a minimal requirement for any decision to move forward with the strategy. Moreover, if the strategy argument were developed in a disciplined manner, critical assumptions would come to the surface, including requirements that might not be apparent at first glance. Earp should ask: What needs to be true—about consumers, about the company, about competitors, etc.—in order for the strategy to succeed?

What happens if those assumptions turn out to not be true? Without such an argument, each craft partner runs the danger of turning into a one-off venture managed by ad hoc and inconsistent criteria.

Our own inexpert ruminations suggest that the success of AB InBev's craft beer strategy appears to hinge on at least three assumptions: a first about the evolution of consumer tastes for beer (stable or continuing in the current direction), a second about the extent to which a brewer's identity figures into consumers' purchase decisions and enjoyment of beer (mass producers are still "tainted" to some craft drinkers), and a third about the AB InBev corporate organization and its policies and practices (concerning craft brewer autonomy, even when divergent from policy).

These assumptions are not philosophical issues but compelling practical matters that managers can act on:

- For the first assumption, consider that beer is a fashion product in some ways and tastes can change overnight, perhaps even more so in the craft beer segment where popular beer styles such as double IPA (India pale ale) and sour emerge from what seems like nowhere. Will AB InBev's approach allow it to track evolving tastes? Or will purchasing established brands mean that AB InBev is always behind the curve?
- With respect to the second assumption, note that within the taste-defining community of craft beer enthusiasts, the reaction to AB InBev's takeover of top independent craft brewers has been to reject them and threaten boycotts. Enthusiasts played a critical role in sealing the demise of AB's early efforts in craft brewing. Will history repeat itself, or has demand for craft beers become less influenced by enthusiasts as more casual drinkers have entered the market?
- When considering how AB InBev's broader policies might shape the success of its craft-brewing efforts, note that AB InBev already announced, in its 2017 annual report, that "specialized teams are dedicated to accelerating our growth rate [in beer markets including craft] versus historical past performance." Will these specialized teams diminish the autonomy of the teams in charge of the craft brands? Similarly, consider that in 2018 Budweiser started a television advertising campaign for Bud Light that explicitly mocked the "mouth feel" and "layered" aromas of craft beers before throwing the craft beer advocates in a medieval dungeon.

Having a clearly articulated strategy argument would give AB InBev executives several advantages. First, it would help them to determine which questions to ask, both before launching the strategy and as it evolves. For example, do beer drinkers accurately associate craft brands with corporate owners? If so, does association with a mass producer carry a stigma that reduces demand? Might trends about consumer interest in authenticity in products and services, broadly defined, presage the stability and future of craft beer demand?

Second, a clear statement of the strategy argument can help executives identify current or proposed policies or practices that might work (perhaps indirectly) at cross-purposes with the strategy and ask whether these can be modified before causing too much damage. For example, would AB InBev's corporate mandate for growth adversely affect product innovation and marketing in the craft brands? What effect would common uniform human resource practices exert, especially with respect to compensation?

Third, with a sharp strategy argument in hand, Earp and his colleagues would be better able to identify good acquisition targets and to persuade their owners that selling to AB InBev would make sense for them too. Less time and energy would be wasted in dealing with ill-suited potential acquisitions.

Finally, a well-developed articulation of the assumptions behind the strategy can also help executives identify a set of background indicators to be monitored to ensure that the future strategy is on course. These indicators in turn would lead naturally to a consistent set of performance indicators with which to evaluate and compare the portfolio companies, perhaps based on their stages of development.

No one should expect executives in Earp's position to get the strategy right in the first go-round. Strategy formulation is inherently forward-looking, and no one can perfectly forecast the future. Strategy making requires an iterative process of formulating an argument about what it is going to take to win and then refining it as initial assumptions prove to be wrong or as conditions change. Successful strategic learning through iteration rests on having a rigorously formulated strategy argument with explicitly articulated assumptions about what needs to be true for success. With experience, learning results in the assumptions getting tweaked and even sometimes radically altered.

* * *

The structural situation Ellie Fields found herself in may be endemic to product managers and many other midlevel executives. As the person responsible for a particular product, the executive wants to do things that enhance the product's quality and sales. However, what he or she does should also be consistent with the broader company's overarching strategy. Above all, it must not undermine what already works successfully in the company's markets. Ideally, the overarching strategy provides guidance about how to manage the product, but even in the best cases, many details are not spelled out. The product manager must regularly make scores of small but potentially impactful decisions and cannot simply run to senior executives with every question. Any manager in this situation yearns for a framework within which to think about and make these decisions.

For Fields, the core question was whether to develop Tableau Public as a stand-alone product or to invest in developing a destination site where users of the product would share their visualizations. The choice between these options was fraught, as either would likely achieve the stated goal of increasing public awareness for Tableau. Building a strategy argument to evaluate the options involves asking for each one: What conditions or assumptions need to be true to make it a viable course of action? In the context of Tableau Public, the critical assumption of the stand-alone approach holds that the main obstacle to greater sales rests on the inability of enterprise customers to experiment with visualizations before buying. In this view, customers know that they want to create visualizations, but they need "free samples" to help persuade them to invest at least $999 in Tableau Desktop. The argument for the destination site, by contrast, starts from the assumption that many potential customers do not understand what a visualization could be and that there is weak brand recognition for Tableau among the uninitiated. The public destination site solved both problems: it created a forum where potentially thousands of users could share a wide range of use cases for Tableau's visualization capabilities, convincing customers that they could productively use visualizations in their companies, and it established Tableau as the premier technology.

Evaluating future options by developing distinct strategy arguments carries a number of advantages. In some cases, systematically spelling out the logic of each option will immediately make clear which is preferable, because doing so reveals that some options can only succeed by invoking heroic and intolerable assumptions. In many other situations, such as the one faced by Fields, several approaches show merit.

How does working with strategy arguments help in this situation? First, as in Kelly's and Earp's situations, clearly articulated arguments will help clarify what assumptions need to be tested and what the best performance indicators for each option are. Second, and more importantly for Fields, well-formed strategy arguments facilitate the process of comparing alternative strategic scenarios that might otherwise seem impossible to reconcile. Without clear strategy arguments laying out the assumptions and expectations of each alternative, the choice might seem arbitrary or might be based on idiosyncratic personal experience. With rigorous strategy arguments in hand, Fields and her team can identify the most consequential assumptions for each option, those conditions or events most critical to the success of the strategy and about which great uncertainty exists. In doing so, Fields can clarify precisely the nature of the bet that she will be making. She could also see more clearly and monitor potential problems such as the failure to attract sufficient new traffic and ideas to the site or the creeping cannibalization of the primary for-sale product. Such an understanding not only increases the chances that the right decision will be made in the moment, but also improves the likelihood that the project will be executed successfully.

After careful deliberation, and research with potential consumers like tech bloggers, Fields chose to implement Tableau Public as a destination site. The outcome proved very positive: users posted many imaginative and novel uses of the product, including creative usages that surprised even the Tableau staff. Subsequently, Tableau grew 82 percent annually from 2008 to 2015, with sales in that year reaching $654 million. Tableau served more than 3900 customers, including such large organizations as Wells Fargo and Dow Chemical.

LEADING BY ARGUING LOGICALLY

In our view, the essence of successful strategic leadership involves developing and communicating a strategy argument that makes sense of the firm's successes and failures. A strategic proposal carries integrity only when the argument which supports it is robust, logical, and comprehensible. The argument must be able to explain both the facts of the current dilemma or opportunity and how to (re)gain a winning hand. It must persuade, but it must persuade because it is logically coherent. Without an argument, strategy is often vacuous, confused, or misdirected. In the worst case, strategy without an argument may involve cluelessly gambling the future of a company.

The scenarios facing Gary Kelly, Pedro Earp, and Ellie Fields highlight how an executive can benefit from having an explicit argument about strategy in hand, replete with background assumptions stating what needs to be true for the strategy to succeed. Both evaluating strategies as arguments for how the firm will succeed and seeing strategy formulation as a form of argumentation give the practicing executive a number of powerful advantages. The advantages of this approach include:

1. It allows executives to apply simple, universal principles for assessing the coherence of a given strategy. These are well-known activities, not rocket science algorithms, although they are too rarely used in business. As we will show, the key activity involves establishing the validity, or internal logical coherence, of the strategy argument. Not all uncertainty will be removed—far from it—because ultimately any argument consists of a set of assumptions. But focusing on validity gives leaders clear criteria for assessing the quality of their strategies, criteria that apply independent of the firm's performance record and can thus be applied before strategies are enacted.

2. Explicitly articulating a strategy argument allows executives to identify the critical capabilities, investments, and environmental uncertainties that will determine the success or failure of a given course of action. A leader with a clearly articulated, logically valid strategy argument can deliver on his or her twin responsibilities—driving execution and adapting to change—much more effectively than a leader solely in possession of a strategic vision. Resource allocation decisions become less contentious when everyone understands the strategy argument. The argument helps executives identify what has to be true for a strategy to succeed, such that they can monitor the performance of their strategy and change course if needed. Moreover, working to ensure the coherence of a particular strategy argument allows leaders to identify unstated or implicit assumptions in their strategies.

3. Recognizing that all strategies are arguments that can be evaluated according to objective criteria allows executive teams to adopt a more disciplined and less contentious approach to debating and making strategic decisions. When teams focus on first ensuring the logical

coherence of different strategic proposals, concerns and objections to a proposed course of action are channeled into recognizing what has to be true for it to succeed. This approach not only improves the quality of strategy arguments, but also allows different voices to be heard and helps the leadership team to take collective ownership of the firm's strategy.

4. Coherent strategy arguments equip executives to make the most compelling case for a proposed course of (in)action and respond thoughtfully to objections. A clear and coherent argument provides the template for effective strategic communication, both within the firm—leading to superior execution—and outside the firm—leading to superior stakeholder management. Executives can replace vague nostrums about growth and execution with clear and explicit accounts of how actions will lead to outcomes. Key performance metrics flow from the core tenets of the strategy argument, so assessing progress toward long-range goals becomes easier.

This book provides a flexible system of activities for formulating, assessing, and communicating strategy arguments. The system uses disciplined reasoning and applies it to analysis of the firm's core competitive opportunities and challenges. We think the system can help executives make better strategic decisions, feel more confident in the decisions they make, and identify the key indicators of the strategic health of their firms.

The book rests on two fundamental assumptions. First, we believe that any firm's long-run success possesses an underlying logic. While firms get lucky all the time, sustained success only happens for a set of logically interconnected reasons. Second, we think that a major aspect of any top leader's role consists of understanding, shaping, and communicating this logic of success. Contributing effectively to a firm's strategic success requires an executive to develop and evaluate logical arguments that make sense of the firm's successes and failures.

ACTIVITIES FOR ARGUING LOGICALLY

We believe that the sharpest strategy arguments rest on a formal representation of the firm's logic of success. Ideally, that representation is central to the firm's strategic debates and decision making. Accordingly, great leaders and great strategists create environments that embed the logic of success at the center, one in which people continually grapple with their understanding of the strategy argument, use that understanding to shape their strategic decisions, and engage in thoughtful and respectful dialogue that hones and advances the strategy.

When logical argument supports strategy like a pillar, the act of arguing itself becomes essential to strategic leadership. If this is so, then many may assume that expertise in formulating, assessing, and revising logical strategy arguments is widespread. Unfortunately, this is often not true. In fact, we would go so far as to say that in many firms, executives do not recognize or appreciate the importance of a disciplined process for developing, assessing, and communicating strategy arguments.

To the contrary, many executives we have talked to about this matter feel that arguments should be avoided at all costs. Perhaps this aversion arises from a wish to maintain organizational unity or control. But we think it also arises because strategy discussions in many firms often consist of people sharing their intuitions about the future, rather than exchanging well-reasoned arguments. When faced with a choice between two or more options, executives form an intuitive preference for one. This is fine, and a natural part of any decision-making process. The question is what comes next, when the options need to be debated and evaluated before a decision.

In our experience, the executives in the room will sometimes agree in their intuitions, but they often don't. Then the fireworks start. Volume levels rise and the various sides dig in and persist until they are blue in the face. When this happens, few people will likely be convinced by the other side, and the exchange resembles something of a sporting match in its atmosphere of rabid one-upmanship. Eventually, one side gives in, either because the other side yelled more loudly and showed more stubbornness—or because the winning side can count on more powerful allies in the company.

It should be obvious that this is not a good way to reach strategic decisions. Some people leave the meeting feeling defeated. More importantly, many participants leave unconvinced that the chosen course of action represents the best option. Confidence in the strategy declines, as people see decisions being driven by power and politics rather than by a fair and well-reasoned consideration of the alternatives. Ultimately, execution suffers too, because people do not buy into the decision and do not really understand the reasoning behind their marching orders.

Even when executives agree in their hunches and avoid a fight, trouble looms beneath the surface if the argument supporting that option has not been brought to the surface. For example, two colleagues might agree that outsourcing part of the product development process is preferable to doing the work in-house—but they may each believe that for very different reasons. That may not seem to matter at first—at least they agreed and avoided a fight! But when it comes to implementation and subsequent decision making, these unstated disagreements can be quite consequential. One person may favor outsourcing because he thinks it will be cheaper than internal development; the colleague may favor it because she thinks it will allow access to superior product development capabilities. At worst, the two will work at cross-purposes, for example, by alienating a high-quality developer through penny-pinching. At best, the fight simply got postponed.

Contemporary treatments of strategy unfortunately provide little concrete guidance to leaders (or aspiring leaders) on how to translate a market insight or strategic vision into a well-reasoned, actionable strategy. On the one hand, many popular business books celebrate the strategic creativity, vision, and drive of successful leaders, but pay little heed to the analysis and reasoning that separate genius from lunacy. On the other hand, a plethora of strategy books draw on insights from economics, sociology, and psychology and the success of leading companies to arm executives with an abundance of analytical tools and frameworks. These analytical skills are critically important for understanding the world as it actually is; if entry barriers to your market are low, your strategy must take heed of that fact. But a framework rarely provides a guide to action; the analytical approach to strategy provides little insight into how leaders should take the insights gained from strategic analysis and turn them into a strategy—a logically valid argument that links a series of investments and actions to a set of desired outcomes.

By contrast, this book provides a flexible system of activities for making strategy, and as a consequence, for improving the quality of strategic decision making throughout the firm. The system consists of three related but distinct activities.

1. *Visualization.* The first activity emphasizes the power of visualization as a means of formulating, articulating, and revising strategy arguments. We focus on the process of mapping or diagramming the various factors that contribute to the success or failure of a firm. Visualization is a

means not only of discovering connections between concepts, but also of working creatively and collaboratively to harness different points of view.

2. *Formalization.* The second activity involves translating the outline or sketch of an argument into a more formal logical representation. Formalization imposes discipline on one's thinking and helps to identify the key relationships between the factors generating the different outcomes. While formalization is perhaps the most challenging of the activities, it has an important payoff: coherence. Any successful strategy will cohere logically, and while formalization cannot guarantee that all of the strategy's assumptions will hold, it can ensure internal logical consistency.

3. *Constructive Argumentation.* The third activity focuses on the process of arguing with others. Visualization and formalization improve an individual leader's strategic reasoning skills, but arguing provides even greater power, especially when done in disciplined groups. The successful strategic leader thus wants productive debate within the organization and needs a way to not only communicate the strategy argument, but also to update it and modify it as circumstances warrant.

This flexible system of activities is a means of developing the skills and habits of mind needed for individual executives to develop strategy arguments. While we describe these activities in what seems like a natural order, we recognize that they will often be used nonsequentially, iteratively, or even simultaneously. That is not only to be expected, but to be encouraged. Most importantly, the system we offer here also provides a basis for creating an environment for focused and productive strategic debates.

Our approach is a novel way to make strategy, but it retains consistency with many widely used strategic theories of sustainable competitive advantage. That is, the system uses commonly known strategic-thinking and problem-solving techniques that most managers will find familiar, but which they often do not apply with adequate discipline.

The activities developed and illustrated in this book benefit leaders of all types of organizations, from entrepreneurial ventures just starting out to large, established firms, and from for-profit ventures to nonprofits and government agencies. Similarly, the activities are relevant to senior executives who must lead the strategy formulation and decision-making process, but are equally relevant to midlevel managers who want to ensure that their decisions reinforce the organization's strategic logic. The book should be particularly valuable to leadership teams, who often hunger for ways to engage productively with each other around strategy and seek ways to reconcile differing viewpoints and interests to develop a shared commitment to the best way forward. We strongly believe that great strategy comes about and maintains its quality only when elements of the system are widely known and fully embraced—indeed, practiced—throughout the organization, and most especially among the ranks of decision makers.

A great deal of this book explains in depth what we mean by a strategy argument—its component parts, its level of abstraction, and its evaluation. We also go beyond these scenarios to illustrate the many ways that a strategy argument can be used productively and can convey value to executives, leadership teams, and organizations. In pursuing both tasks, we rely on many examples and cases, including Southwest, Apple, Walmart, Intel, Twitter, Google, *The Economist*, Honda, and Disney, among others. Some of these we explore in depth, while others are presented in more anecdotal fashion.

Where should the strategy argument come from? How is it communicated? How is it maintained? We also address these important questions in the book. Because our basic view on these matters strikes many as counternormative, it is worthwhile stating it upfront: we believe that the development, communication, and maintenance of a strategy argument is best achieved through an open process of *actually arguing* within the organization, engaging in productive debate. Many people will find this surprising, believing that arguing is counterproductive. Indeed, as noted earlier, many companies openly discourage disagreement and conflict, and even punish it. As Gary Pisano observes, "In some companies . . . debate is tacitly discouraged for running counter to norms of 'teamwork' and 'cooperation.' "[14] Lots of other companies consider arguing wasted effort and lost time—rather than argue, better to get on with business.

We object sharply to these views. We recognize that arguments in organizations often become dysfunctional. But in our view, this happens when people do not have a clear idea about what the strategy is, and when they do not know how to argue productively about it. But when done correctly, strategy is ultimately *best* done when people in an organization—directors, leaders, and some employees—openly argue about it. An organization benefits enormously when some or all of the strategy-making process involves people openly arguing about the issues.

It is imperative to note that by *arguing*, we do not mean people flaming each other about their opinions, intuitions, and preferences, while ignoring those of others. Rather, as we will explain below, the essence of great strategy formulation and strategic management involves arguing constructively, in thoughtfully composed groups, and with clear and well-understood ground rules of interaction.

But what about the CEO and other top leaders of an organization—aren't strategy formulation and decision making mainly their jobs? In some ways, yes, they are—these leaders are certainly the people who will be held accountable when the strategy fails, and they are usually very well rewarded when the strategy succeeds. But accountability does not mean execution of all the details of a task or even total control over its accomplishment. Accountability simply means credit or blame for the outcome however it was achieved. Good strategists and executives who achieve long-term success typically encourage constructive arguments in decision-making groups and often larger discussion forums, whether they do so consciously or not. The arguing process makes the strategy and its rationale transparent to all, including especially those who may be dubious about it. The process also allows many members of the organizational to feel like they have been heard, that they had input on important issues, and that their views are valued by their leaders. Without constructive arguments among multiple stakeholders, strategy runs the risk of being disconnected from key parts of the organization and of being misunderstood. Strategy developed without the involvement and consultation of many parties can easily miss the mark and will prove difficult to execute.

OUR APPROACH

Our system of three interrelated activities and associated structures for strategic theorizing differ from most strategy texts, in two ways. First, we do not advance a particular theory of strategic success, and do not seek to be prescriptive about how a company should try to win in its market.[15] Rather, we offer a system of activities that sits comfortably alongside any number of different theories of strategic success, and indeed could be used to help decide which theory best applies in a given situation. Second, we explicitly emphasize the acts of formulating, developing, and revising strategies. We do so because we think these parts of strategic management often get lost in strategy discussions within firms. Accordingly, we offer pointers on, among other things, how to translate insights into arguments, how to use visualization activities to structure productive strategic debates, and how to use logic to surface unstated assumptions. We offer a way to formulate, develop, and manage strategy using argumentation, through the specific activities of visualization, logic, and debate.

Among other things, we aim to illustrate in this book how to use a sort of simple propositional logic with deduction, a way of thinking that will seem vaguely familiar to many (perhaps reaching back to early years in high school or college). Despite that sense of familiarity, we appreciate that thinking this way is not natural or easy (at least at first) for the modern business executive. We also recognize that this material may be seen as dense reading and that it may need to be absorbed slowly over time. Accordingly, we regard this book as something between a discursive essay, a workbook, and a textbook. We have tried to be comprehensive and to include as many details of the approach that we think will be useful. As a result, we imagine that many readers will not read the document cover to cover in one sitting, but will take it in piece by piece, perhaps in a different order than presented. No matter how it is read, we hope the book will be a guide to assist managers in attempting to develop formal arguments about their organizations' strategies and creating coherent organizational action based on it.

While we try to deemphasize the more technical aspects of the logical approach, some amount of technical detail simply cannot be avoided, especially concerning propositional logic. For those interested in going into greater technical detail, connections to other treatments of logic should be obvious. We do not think doing such a deep dive is needed or even recommended; we have tried to make the book self-contained and complete on this issue.

Of course, saying leaders should develop skills for developing logical argumentation and use them in planning and execution is far easier than doing it. There is a vast gap between the language of logic-based science and that of management, even if the problems they face are similar conceptually. That is why we wrote this book—to try to bridge that gap and to make the activities of theorists and scientists accessible and to adapt them as needed for the particular problems of strategic management.

HOW TO READ THIS BOOK

The book makes the case for the importance of formulating, debating, and assessing strategy arguments. It provides concrete, practical guidance to executives on how to use the three interrelated activities of visualization, logic, and debate. Accordingly, each of the subsequent chapters (excepting the final concluding chapter) contains three sections. The first section describes the benefits of adopting the proposed approach for the particular topic at hand in that chapter. The second section turns to more practical issues, with a detailed explanation of how to use the various activities. The final section closes with a summary of the chapter's key points, and offers key takeaways.

We have endeavored to make the book as a whole accessible to an audience of well-educated executives and management students, relying on vivid examples and nontechnical prose throughout. That said, we recognize that some of the materials relating to logic and formalization are more technically challenging. They can be heavy going at first, particularly for those readers not familiar with ideas from the discipline of logic. Our hope is that these more technically challenging materials do not prevent readers from absorbing and appreciating the insights that we think can be gained from thinking of strategy through the lens of logical arguments.

The chapters are designed to address this challenge, with the first section ("The Benefits of . . .") and third section ("Closing Thoughts") in each chapter providing a nontechnical discussion, while the second section ("The Practice of . . .") contains the technical material. One approach to reading the book would be to first read the first and third sections of each chapter in order to absorb the value of the three activities, and then return to the more technical second sections of each chapter as one turns to applying each activity. Similarly, leaders wishing to increase the logical rigor of strategic discussions in their organizations might ask their teams to read the first and third sections of the relevant chapters, and then use the second sections as a guide for themselves as they turn to leading debates.

KEY TAKEAWAYS

- The frustration and lack of confidence many executives feel about the strategy process stems from the difficulty they have seeing the systematic elements common to great strategies. In particular, transferring the inspiring lessons learned from leading companies to a leader's own organization can be very challenging. Overcoming this challenge requires recognizing that the success of *any* winning organization can best be understood through a strategy argument that is logically coherent.

- This book offers a practical and systematic way to formulate, develop, and manage strategy using argumentation. Specifically, we unveil and explain a system of three interrelated activities for developing great strategy: visualization, logic, and debate.

- Strategic leaders hold the central responsibility to develop and communicate a strategy argument that makes sense of a firm's successes and failures. Focusing on the logical coherence of strategy arguments provides executives with clear and objective criteria for assessing the quality of different strategic proposals. If these arguments are widely understood, executive teams can adopt a more disciplined and less contentious approach to making strategic decisions than what characterizes strategic debates in many organizations.

- A clearly articulated, logically valid strategy argument positions leaders to deliver on their core obligations—driving execution and adapting to change—much more effectively than leaders who rely solely on intuition and reason. A coherent strategy argument makes for a more compelling and persuasive case and allows leaders to anticipate and respond to objections.

PART II

Three Activities for Making Great Strategy

CHAPTER 2

||||||||||||||||||||||||||||||||||||||||||||||||||||||||||||||||||||||||||||||||||||||||||||||||||||||||||||||||||||||||||||||||||||||||||||||||||||||||||||
||||||||||
Mapping Strategy

THE BENEFITS OF MAPPING STRATEGY

A unicorn, that's what the rare billion-dollar startup gets called in 2020. Before 2000, these wildly successful entities were even rarer and had no popular nickname. But in the 1990s Jim Clark founded two of them, Silicon Graphics and Netscape.

Clark was known for thinking big. So, it was no surprise in 1995, when the Stanford engineering professor-cum-entrepreneur announced to various assembled Silicon Valley venture capitalists on legendary Sand Hill Road in Menlo Park that his next project would be his most ambitious yet. Clark boldly said he was going to fix the U.S. health-care system. His idea aimed to reduce waste in health care by eliminating the paperwork. By Clark's calculation, a third of the $1.5 trillion that Americans spent annually on health care represented pure waste. He imagined that:

> the Internet enabled all of the many parties of any health-care transaction to be present in the same room. The patient could walk into the office of a doctor he'd never met, supply the doctor with a password, and a few seconds later the doctor would have his medical record and insurance coverage. A few minutes after the patient left, the doctor would bill the insurer over the Internet, and be paid by the insurer over the Internet. If the patient needed drugs, those too could be ordered from the screen, right in the doctor's office. No forms, no papers, no hassle.[1]

Clark calculated that if he cut out the waste, he could keep half of the savings as profit, a stunning figure that would make his new company, which he
initially labeled Healthscape, bigger than Microsoft.

The idea was huge, grandiose, audacious, unthinkable really. Putting it into
place faced formidable technical, legal, and social obstacles. Yet Clark was able
to convince the leading venture capital firm with health-care expertise, New
Enterprise Associates (NEA), to invest in it up front; he also got leading venture capital firm Kleiner Perkins to take a stake. Moreover, to make Healthscape happen, Clark convinced almost a dozen of Silicon Valley's best engineers
to sign on to work as its first employees.

How did Clark do this? Certainly, his history and reputation mattered
a lot, people like to follow a proven winner. You might also think he had
a great business plan, filled with strategic answers to all the tough questions about how the company was going to overcome the complex, major
obstacles it faced. You would be wrong. Clark not only did not have a great
business plan, he did not have a business plan at all. What he did have—and
what was presented to numerous potential investors, partners, customers,
and employees in the coming years—was a visual model about what the
company was aiming to do, a simplified representation of the core idea.
Clark's visual model is shown in figure 2.1. It depicts a network of the main
actors in the health-care system; the idea was that the company, renamed
Healtheon, would sit in the middle of the network and take a small piece of
every transaction. Clark and his associates called this the "magic diamond."
It was eventually revised, first in an elaboration that included eleven actors
in the network, and finally in a simplification that included only three
actors (patients, doctors, and health-care institutions) and was called the
"golden triangle." Healtheon always sat in the middle. Using this simplified
visual model, the CEO of Healtheon pitched the company widely to potential investors in early 1999 before the company's IPO.

How effective was it? By the end of trading on its opening day, Healtheon's
market value rose to $2.2 billion; in the weeks following, it climbed to more
than $3 billion. And, just like that, Jim Clark had his third unicorn, the first
person ever to accomplish that feat.

The visual model depicted by the Golden Triangle dramatically simplified a very complex reality and showed in a nutshell what Healtheon hoped
to accomplish strategically. It organized the essential information behind
the business idea. It was also a powerful communication device that allowed

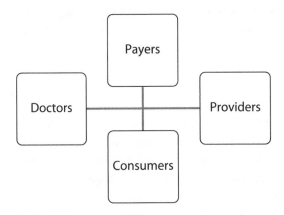

2.1 Jim Clark's magic diamond depiction of Healtheon

Adapted from Michael Lewis, *The New New Thing* (New York: Norton, 2000)

people to comprehend a complex problem and to think that the problem could be solved. Such a powerful visual model is a great way to start a company, to attract investors, and to recruit customers and employees.[2]

It's also a great way to start developing a more rigorous strategy argument for a company or other organization. Indeed, we advocate and use a special type of visual model we call a "strategy map" as the starting point for strategic analysis.[3] As a concept, a map usually refers to an image of areas of land or other physical entities, but at its core a map is about visualizing the arrangement of places or objects or actions relative to one another. A strategy map shows the arrangement of strategic concepts and resources relative to one another; it also shows the direction in which cause-like forces proceed to generate organizational outcomes. A strategy map can then be used as the basis for building the more formal logical argument needed for a rigorous assessment.[4] (To be clear, Jim Clark's Magic Diamond does not qualify as a strategy map.)

To construct a strategy map, we suggest starting simply, and then proceeding iteratively in small increments, that is, building first on what is easiest to recognize, writing it down, piecing things together, and then reflecting on it and revising it in incremental steps, producing in the end a strategy map. In short, sketch out the flow of the strategy argument in a strategy map, and do so in a flexible way that allows the structure of the argument to change as new and better ideas arise. The mapping process gets the main facts and concepts up on the board, and thinking through their arrangement relative to one another forces a consideration of how things relate to one another in a coherent whole.

This chapter describes a process for generating the strategy map. We demonstrate mainly through example. The process can be done individually, but our experience suggests that it is easier (and more fun) when done in small groups where at least some members are well informed about the organization under scrutiny. The social element of visualizing collectively generates energy and allows people to bounce ideas off one another and to iterate rapidly. At the same time, a group visualization exercise needs to have some discipline and a sense of urgency, and should be conducted in different ways at different stages of the conceptualization. Here we begin by focusing on the visualization process itself, and in later chapters we provide some suggestions on how to manage some common group-process issues.

The Value of a Strategy Map: Southwest Airlines

To illustrate, let's return briefly to the situation faced by Gary Kelly at Southwest Airlines described in chapter 1. We want to show how a simple visualization of a strategy argument can illuminate the potential consequences of a strategic choice like the one he faced.

Through most of its history, Southwest Air practiced "open seating," meaning that it did not assign passengers to seats at either the time of ticketing or check-in. Instead, when passengers checked in, their boarding pass showed a boarding group (A, B, or C) followed by a number. Shortly before boarding, passengers lined up according to the group and number on their boarding pass, and they subsequently boarded the plane in that sequence. As they boarded, passengers chose among the seats still open on a first-come, first-served basis.

Other airlines long allowed customers to choose their seats when issuing the ticket. Starting in the 2010s, some airlines began to view the ability to choose a preferred seat as a potential revenue source. Customers either paid higher fares for the right to choose their own seat or paid additional amounts to reserve a particular seat. Seeing the increased profits this practice generated for these airlines, analysts pressured Gary Kelly and Southwest to adopt similar policies. The analysts' point of view seemed clear: introducing seat assignments would not be technically difficult (almost all airlines do it!), and the direct costs of implementation were likely low. Failing to do it seemed like leaving money on the table.

Southwest's resistance to this idea suggested that things were not quite so simple; the airline's leadership felt that abandoning open seating might produce important follow-on complications. Why might this be? We draw on our experience in using Southwest in classroom case discussions to analyze the question of seat assignments.

In discussing Southwest's strategy, attention soon turns to the airline's remarkable ability to quickly "turn around" their planes—in other words, to deplane arriving passengers and board departing passengers in a short time. Early in Southwest's history, an operations manager declared that the only thing that would keep Southwest from continuing to lose money would be if they could do a "10-minute" turn, something unheard of in the industry.[5] Even as it grew, Southwest maintained gate turnaround times of fifteen minutes or under for many years, whereas other airlines often took half an hour or more.

When class discussants first raise this fact, the discussion turns to understanding why this was critical to Southwest's success. Insightful participants quickly realize that capacity utilization is critical to controlling costs in the airline business. Airplanes represent large, fixed-cost investments, and they only make money when they are carrying passengers through the air, not when they are sitting on the ground. The more segments a plane can fly each day, the better. For a long-haul carrier, turnaround times do not substantially affect capacity utilization; if the flying time is ten hours, it makes little difference whether the plane sits at the gate for fifteen minutes or thirty. But Southwest started as a regional carrier with flights between cities in Texas, and even today many of its flights are under two hours. With many more take-offs and landings every day, every minute of time saved at the gate improves capacity utilization appreciably.

Being able to execute rapid gate turnarounds reliably and repeatedly requires operational discipline and coordinated execution. Accordingly, discussion of the Southwest case turns to organizational design, specifically, the central role of teamwork among people in different jobs. When a plane arrives at a gate, everyone springs into action to prepare it for quick departure. Departing passengers are lined up and ready to go. Everyone at the gate and on the plane—flight attendants, pilots, baggage handlers, gate agents, etc.—helps out. Teamwork gives the airline flexibility to respond to unforeseen issues quickly, instead of waiting for someone whose official job it is to take care of the problem, as occurs at many other airlines. Teamwork also allows for better labor utilization; it was reported that in the mid-1990s, for example, "Southwest's gates are typically manned by a single agent and have a ground crew of six or fewer, rather than the three agents and twelve ground crew that are common at other airlines."[6] Decades later, Southwest still flies more available seat miles per worker than other major carriers, despite having shorter flight lengths than those carriers.[7]

In discussing these issues with a class, we will typically sketch a diagram on the whiteboard that lays out the different ideas and their relationships to one another. These diagrams reflect our attempts to capture the argument as it develops in the evolving discussion. Figure 2.2 shows an example of such a diagram; it attempts to capture the ideas described earlier about seating at Southwest.

The diagram in figure 2.2 illustrates what we mean by a strategy map. A strategy map consists of a "word and arrow" visualization of a strategy argument. The words reflect ideas, concepts, resources, or even actions; the arrows represent likely causality. So, an arrow from A to B implies that idea/concept/resource/action A likely causes (or leads to or produces) idea/concept/resource/action B.[8]

A strategy map may try to capture all aspects of a strategy argument or, more typically as in this case, a portion of the argument. In the map, resources, actions, and states are briefly described and linked to one another using directional arrows to show how inputs lead to outputs, or how causes lead to effects. In this way, a strategy map conveys the causal path believed to generate a particular outcome of interest, such as a firm's competitive advantage—in this case Southwest's low-cost advantage. We call it a map because it shows how different elements in the strategy argument are arranged and the pathways by which they are connected to one another.

Are strategy maps useful? If so, why? Consider again the pressure Gary Kelly faced with respect to introducing assigned seating. He was being asked to speculate what would happen if Southwest abandoned open seating: Would profits go up, as the analysts believed, or would the impact be minimal or negative? Such speculation invites counterfactual thinking: Kelly needed to imagine what Southwest's performance would look like in two different future scenarios, one in which open seating persisted, and one in which passengers

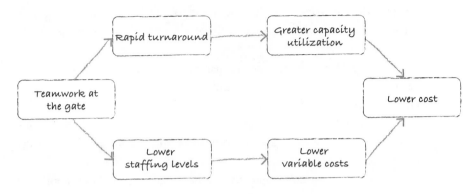

2.2 Strategy map for Southwest Airlines

chose seats in advance. Neither of these future states of the world yet existed, and only one could exist at a given time. How can a leader decide which is better?

Contemplating such alternative scenarios is easier with a model in hand, a simplified representation of reality that allows for ready identification of the relevant forces, and predicts what would happen if some conditions or variables were changed. Models can take many different forms, ranging from simple visual diagrams to complicated graphs of causal processes to complex mathematical formulations.[9] Among other things, a strategy map is a simple yet intuitive model of a strategy argument that makes it easier to picture how a change might reverberate through the system.

For example, the strategy map in figure 2.2 focuses on how teamwork among the workers at Southwest gates both improves capacity utilization and helps lower staffing levels. In this example, teamwork at the gate is a critical variable, because it has multiple influences on Southwest's cost structure; if the teamwork breaks down, Southwest's competitive position will deteriorate.

By using the strategy map, we can trace out the impact of introducing seat assignments. Moving away from open seating would seem to increase the workload of the gate agents. At a traditional airline, much of a gate agent's time is spent responding to questions about seat assignments, addressing seat-change requests, upgrades, etc. Southwest gate agents, by contrast, spend no time worrying about who sits where, and simply work to ensure that people line up correctly when it is time to board. As a consequence, the map suggests that introducing assigned seating could lead to a decline in teamwork, as gate agents dealing with seating issues will have less time to prepare the next flight for departure.

Switching from open to assigned seating would also likely affect passenger behavior. Frequent fliers are familiar with the seemingly interminable boarding process at traditional airlines, where passengers board in a jumbled sequence, search for their seat locations, and have to get up and stand in the aisle to let someone in. Boarding a Southwest flight is not painless, but the first-come, first-served process does speed things up considerably.

The gist of this reasoning suggests that the open-seating policy at Southwest exerts subtle but important indirect implications for the firm's competitive advantage. Accordingly, we revised the strategy map by putting the open-seating policy in it. Figure 2.3 suggests that open seating facilitates teamwork at the gate, and thus indirectly supports rapid turnarounds as well as lower staffing levels. Open seating also directly improves turnaround time by changing passenger behavior and getting people to board faster.

If this model of Southwest's strategy is correct, then it suggests that assigned seating would likely disrupt a number of organizational routines and undermine some of the reasons behind Southwest's lower-cost structure. At the briefing, Kelly also expressed concerns about "nickel-and-diming" passengers, suggesting that he was skeptical that advance seat assignments would increase revenues, given the expectations of Southwest's customer base. His comment suggests that assigned seating was unlikely to increase profits and might indeed backfire for the airline.

Our point here is not to claim that the strategy map in figure 2.3 reflects the consensus view of Southwest's leadership team, or that they rejected advance seat assignments solely for the reasons we have outlined. Indeed, Southwest's leadership team—or analysts, or readers—may disagree with our claims about the consequences of moving to assigned seating. Perhaps it can be implemented in a way that does not affect the workload of gate agents, or perhaps the impact is minimal. Maybe passengers board more quickly with assigned seats than under open seating. Indeed, perhaps even our understanding of the critical role of teamwork, as reflected in the strategy map in figure 2.2, is mistaken.

Such disagreements are reasonable—and even to be expected—when comparing different hypothetical scenarios. But we hold zero doubt that these debates will be more productive when the people involved are clear about

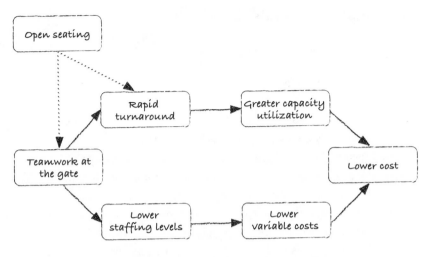

2.3 Revised strategy map for Southwest Airlines

what they disagree about and have a structured way of identifying the precise reason for their disagreement. By visualizing a plausible strategy argument, the strategy map in figure 2.3 creates opportunities for people to recognize and express clearly how their own strategy argument differs. If they assess a shift to assigned seating positively, then it allows them—indeed, virtually begs them—to articulate exactly why they disagree. And while such an exchange provides no guarantee that the group will ultimately land on the right decision, it increases the likelihood that they will get it right by enabling greater clarity about everyone's reasoning. Just as importantly, if things do go wrong, being clear about the reasoning behind a decision will help leaders to learn from their mistakes.

By emphasizing the main forces at play in a firm's logic of success, strategy maps make it easier to imagine what would happen after a specific strategic change, as in the Southwest case. They provide structure for strategic thinking. They serve as effective communication devices by clarifying often complex relationships between the elements of a firm's strategy. Finally, strategy maps can serve as focal points for strategic discussions in a leadership team. Team members can express their ideas and concerns within the context of the strategy map and more easily identify and resolve areas of disagreement about the firm's true logic of success.

THE PRACTICE OF MAPPING STRATEGY

Case Study: Walmart

We now illustrate further how to visualize with strategy maps. We do so using Walmart Inc. as the example. Focusing on a company with a record of sustained successful performance relative to its peers is advantageous, because we can confidently attribute its success to its strategy, as opposed to luck or external factors. We also think it is useful to focus on Walmart because the underlying analysis is relatively straightforward and uncontroversial; it is also a company personally familiar to many readers.

In the fiscal year ending January 31, 2020, Walmart reported over $524 billion in revenue, employed 2.2 million people (1.5 million in the United States), and reached almost 275 million customers on a weekly basis. Walmart operates various business segments, both in the United States and in 27 countries. It is best known for its discount retail operations, including its Supercenters, which combine general merchandise and grocery offerings; for Sam's Club, a membership-based warehouse-type store for retail customers; and for its e-commerce efforts at Walmart.com. For this analysis, we focus on Walmart's dominance in the traditional discount retailing business in the United States. Although Walmart has suffered occasional down periods and currently faces a formidable threat from Amazon.com, the challenges it faces are few compared with most companies. In other words, few would doubt the sustained strategic success of Walmart over the last forty years or more.

The history of Walmart is well known.[10] Founded in the early 1960s, Walmart began operations in small, rural towns in Arkansas, rather than the rapidly growing suburbs where its rivals such as Kmart, Target, and Venture focused their efforts. At a time when many Americans were moving (or had moved) from rural areas to cities and suburbs, Sam Walton's decision to locate in rural areas was counterintuitive to many (including most investors). Yet today many analysts point to this decision as crucial to Walmart's success, as it meant that Walmart faced early competition from small mom-and-pop retailers rather than other big discount retailers. Walmart subsequently expanded its rural footprint very deliberately, consciously locating new stores in towns close to established stores in other towns. Once a sufficient density had been reached in a region, Walmart would build a distribution center that served all of the stores within a defined radius and establish its own trucking division to service the stores. Walmart was a leader in the practice of "cross-docking," whereby goods would arrive at a distribution center from suppliers and immediately be placed on trucks destined for stores. Walmart also invested heavily in information technology, including early adoption of bar code scanning, and used its own satellite to transmit data between stores, distribution centers, and headquarters.

From the 1970s on, Walmart grew rapidly. In that decade, the store count increased more than tenfold to over 250 stores, primarily in the central United States. By 1990, the year Walmart became the largest retailer in the United States, it had approximately five times as many stores again, and it more than doubled again by the 2000s, during which time it converted a number of its stores to Supercenters by adding groceries. As a result, Walmart today accounts for a substantial share of retail sales in the United States.

From its inception, Walmart displayed a strong culture of frugality, emanating from Sam Walton himself. Store fixtures were bare-bones utilitarian, and Walmart for many years spent very little money on advertising. When traveling, employees shared hotel rooms—perhaps with Sam Walton himself. Walmart became famous for driving a hard bargain with suppliers. When they visited Walmart headquarters for negotiations, suppliers were shown into spartan conference rooms with uncomfortable chairs and tight time limits. Suppliers were required to accept collect calls from Walmart and were forbidden to send letters or contracts using express mail. Walmart introduced its own private-label product lines. At the same time, sophisticated suppliers benefited from Walmart's rich data on purchasing patterns, which allowed them to plan their own production more efficiently.

Walmart invested heavily in sharing best practices and information across its growing network of stores. Walmart's satellite was used to hold regular company meetings where store managers and staff were kept apprised of developments and new initiatives. Real-time data from stores allowed headquarters to track performance carefully and were coupled with a fair degree of autonomy for store managers. Instead of creating an elaborate organizational hierarchy to manage its far-flung operations, Walmart stipulated that its managers at headquarters would travel continually between stores and return weekly to Bentonville with a good idea that could be shared more widely.

Building Blocks for Walmart's Strategy Map

As described earlier, a strategy map is a diagram of a strategy argument. In the map, ideas, objects, resources, and actions are briefly described and linked to one another using directional arrows to show how inputs lead to outputs, or how causes lead to effects. In this way, a strategy map conveys the process believed to generate a particular outcome of interest, such as a firm's competitive advantage.

Any given mapping exercise will have its own dynamic, but we advocate a small set of guiding principles to keep the process focused and productive. These principles involve how to start, how to build out the argument, how to refine it, and how to evaluate it.

Start with the Conclusion

How to start building a strategy map? Our strong suggestion is to start by stating clearly what it is you are trying to explain, the destination at the end of the map. In other words, starting the map involves asking: What is the conclusion you are trying to reach about the strategy? What is the desired outcome of the strategy and hence this strategy argument? The answers will usually be based on the vision or mission of the organization, as well as its long-term goals. Particularly valuable in these situations are conclusions about the generic nature of a firm's competitive advantage, such as a value creation advantage due to low cost or perceived quality. Or a bargaining advantage, or a positioning advantage. (If these strategy concepts are unfamiliar, see appendix B for a brief primer.)

Starting from the conclusion and working backward may seem counterintuitive. When we encounter formal arguments, we usually read them in the opposite direction—from initial assumptions to the conclusion: think of the proofs of geometric theorems you encountered in high school textbooks. However, if you talk to leading mathematicians and scientists, you will find that usually they start with an insight or intuition that they want to prove. They then proceed with their work of building a proof by trying to uncover the conditions (assumptions or premises) that need to be true to make the conclusion hold.

Starting the strategy-mapping process with the conclusion carries similar advantages. The most fundamental advantage is that strategic intuition often manifests itself in the form of sudden insight about an attractive potential opportunity, and the fundamental strategic question is what it would take to make that opportunity a reality. In addition, because the conclusion in a strategy argument will often describe a desirable outcome, starting with the conclusion provides positive focus and energy at the outset of the mapping process.

Of course, a large number of possible conclusions may initially occur to you as possible starting points. Which one should you choose? In our experience, a strategy-mapping exercise can be particularly productive in two types of situations. The first situation arises when trying to make sense of an outcome, such as an organization's or initiative's success or failure. We saw this approach earlier, when we tried to make sense of the reasons for Southwest's success in the airline industry.

In addition, mapping can be highly effective in situations in which a specific decision or action is being contemplated that involves a new strategic initiative—for example, a proposal to enter a new geographic region. Implicit in considering such actions is a conclusion (by its advocates) that the new initiative will be beneficial in some way. A mapping exercise can help clarify the reasons why, provided that it starts with a clear specification of the hypothesized advantage—i.e., the conclusion.

A good mapping exercise may very well lead to questioning or even rejecting the conclusion the exercise started with. This process can seem frustrating and even lead some to question the point of the whole exercise, considering it a waste of time. Just as in a scientific experiment, it is important to appreciate the value of rejecting a conclusion. Doing so means abandoning a preconceived notion in the face of reason. It is almost always better to find out that a conclusion doesn't make sense after an hour working on a whiteboard than after spending months and tons of money trying to make it come true.

One Conclusion at a Time

When strategy mapping is done in a group setting, different views and preferences will likely emerge. Indeed, people may begin the mapping exercise with radically different preferred conclusions. Group disagreement creates an obvious potential source of tension that can lead the exercise astray. But even when performing a mapping exercise alone, it is not always easy to determine or choose which conclusion to focus on. The overall strategy argument for any given firm contains many moving parts, as a firm might have multiple different sources of advantage.

For example, in trying to make sense of Walmart's success, we might point to a number of sources of strategic advantage for Walmart. The company's history of locating in rural areas, away from other discount retailers, suggests that it has benefited from a positioning advantage. Walmart's current scale similarly suggests that it has a bargaining advantage over suppliers. And, of course, Walmart likely has a low-cost advantage for a number of different reasons. All of these factors likely contribute to its overall advantage. Should we start with the broader conclusion, or with the specific components of its advantage?[11]

There is no universally correct answer to this question. The right approach depends on the situation and the state of one's understanding. However, it is important to clarify from the outset which conclusion will be the focus of the mapping exercise. The trick is to do this without getting into an emotional and unpredictable dispute! In other words, you do not want to start hashing out the argument structure for each possible conclusion as a means of deciding which conclusion should be focused on; that path would take a lot of time and would likely produce an overwhelming amount of material. Instead, the process of choosing a conclusion to focus on has to be less formal, driven by the strategic priorities of the organization, the leader, or the participants. For example, the organization may already have established goals to be the revenue leader in its segment by holding the highest market share, or to be a top innovator that stays ahead of competitors, or to be a responsible community member that gives back in specific ways.

Many organizations proclaim multiple high-priority goals, meaning multiple conclusions. If there are multiple conclusions that might be developed, then perform the mapping exercise separately for each one, perhaps over the span of several sessions.

Sometimes the mapping process itself will suggest additional conclusions demanding elaboration. For example, someone wishing to make sense of Walmart's overall advantage might start there and then realize that the different reasons for Walmart's advantage—such as its value creation advantage or positioning advantage—are sufficiently complex that each requires a separate mapping exercise.

For illustrative purposes, the conclusion we will focus on here is the broad claim that Walmart has a low-cost advantage over its rivals, other retailers. We focus on this conclusion in part because it should not be very controversial—Walmart is known, if anything, for rock-bottom prices, and its ability to deliver those low prices consistently while simultaneously being more profitable than its rivals requires it to have a cost advantage. The conclusion of our strategy map thus states the following:

Walmart has lower costs than its competitors.

We like this conclusion, because it states Walmart's strategic advantage in unambiguous terms. It also makes clear that the advantage is a relative one, relative to its competitors. At the same time, this low-cost advantage likely has several sources, including a value creation advantage and a bargaining advantage, meaning that our illustration will not be trivially simple.

Finding Plausible Explanations

Once a (tentative) conclusion for the argument has been settled upon, the next step is to identify and write down the causes (or conditions, or assumptions, or premises) that might plausibly generate the conclusion. In other words, given what we know about the firm and its market environment, what are the important elements that likely generate the strategic advantage we are trying to explain? Because our goal is to construct an argument for why Walmart has a low-cost advantage, this stage involves identifying all of the different factors that might contribute significantly to the company's lower costs. At the moment, we won't worry about whether a cause is independent—works in isolation—or whether it is dependent on another cause to exert its effect. The important issue is to identify plausible explanations. This step represents the core of the strategic analysis.

Brainstorming

One of the major benefits of the mapping process is the potential to move beyond initial, superficial explanations. The goal of the exercise is to generate new insights, not simply to represent one's initial preconceptions. To do this, we strongly recommend adopting a brainstorming mindset when trying to identify the factors contributing to the conclusion. Brainstorming is about generating as many ideas as possible, including some (many) that are really "outside the box." There are many ways to do brainstorming effectively but usually they include the following components:

1. a tightly *fixed period of time* with a deadline announced in advance;
2. *active participation* of all members of the group;
3. *high levels of energy* among participants, often boosted by standing and snack consumption;
4. starting by having participants *generate ideas individually*, followed by sharing and posting them in a way that all can see;
5. *not allowing criticism* of any idea at this stage—enthusiasm for a proposed idea is encouraged;
6. encouraging ideas that *build on ideas* already proposed (a "yes, and" orientation); and
7. trying to get *as many ideas as possible* recorded (on the board or elsewhere) in a short period of time.

When brainstorming, it can be helpful to focus initially on quantity of ideas over quality: offer a large number of ideas without worrying initially about whether or how they explain the outcome. Similarly, do not worry at first about whether the different ideas are redundant or are different ways of getting at the same underlying idea. Commonalities can be identified later, and overlapping ideas can be a valuable indication of shared viewpoints when several people are working together.

This process—often known today as ideation—should be as unstructured as possible to allow unexpected insights to emerge. However, some minimal structure may be helpful, especially for people who do not know where to start with constructing a strategic explanation. One simple prompt that may be helpful is to ask people to focus on the distinction between what the organization *has* and what the organization *does*, or the firm's key assets and resources, on the one hand, and its distinctive activities and capabilities, on the other.[12]

A good example of a key asset or resource would be a firm that owns a patent to a critical piece of technology and this patent is effectively protected by law, such as when a pharmaceutical company owns a patent on a widely used drug such as Lipitor. Key resources can be both tangible and tradable assets, such as a store network or distribution centers, or intangible resources, such as a brand reputation or an installed base of users.

In addition to assets and resources, an organization may also have distinctive activities or capabilities. Distinctive activities are processes the firm undertakes that other organizations do not, while capabilities are processes and routines that the firm performs better than other firms. For many years, for example, Southwest's practice of boarding passengers by lining them up in order of check-in was a distinctive activity, as no other airlines adopted the practice, while their ability to do rapid gate turnarounds was a capability— Southwest simply did it better and faster than other airlines.

We should note that in many cases, the strategic conclusion you may be trying to establish is a relative one. In our Walmart argument, for instance, we are not trying to establish which factors influence Walmart's cost structure. Instead, we want to determine which factors cause Walmart to have lower costs than its competitors. A practical issue that arises in constructing such arguments concerns when in the process to introduce explicit comparisons to the firm's competitors. For example, should every idea suggested in the brainstorming phase be a relative statement?

Our suggestion is to leave the comparisons implicit rather than explicit early in the mapping process. Forcing explicit comparisons early on inhibits idea generation, because people spend too much time trying to assess whether or not their intuitions about differences between a firm and its competitors are really true.[13] Instead, a more productive approach is to allow people to follow their instincts about the key ways in which the firm differs from its rivals, and then return later to make these relative claims explicit.

In our experience, generating lots of ideas is easiest when each idea is jotted down briefly on a sticky note, such as a Post-it. (This is true even when working alone.) The format of a medium-sized sticky note (4 × 6 inches) encourages people to express ideas concisely. Quickly jot down an idea on a note, and then set it aside and move on to the next note. An additional advantage of using sticky notes is that they can easily be moved around and rearranged, which will be useful later in the mapping process.

Table 2.1 illustrates a possible outcome of an idea generation session for analysis of Walmart's low-cost advantage, based on our brief summary of the company, along with facts that are commonly known about Walmart. Underlined elements in the table are what might be considered Walmart's key resources and assets, while boldface elements are those that might be considered distinctive activities and capabilities. We highlight these items to demonstrate the kinds of ideas that might be generated by asking people

Table 2.1 List of ideas from brainstorming about Walmart's low-cost advantage

Rural locations	**Cross-docking**	Low-wage workers
Sharing of best practices	Distribution centers	Nonunionized workforce
Private-label product lines	IT investments	Own trucking operations
High volume purchasing	Economies of scale	Bare-bones store fixtures
Sophisticated logistics capability	Cheap real estate	**Culture of frugality**
Hub-and-spoke distribution system	Nationwide store network	**Tough negotiating style**
Bargaining power	**Data analytics skills**	Little competition in rural areas
	Reputation for low prices	Massive sales volume
	Limited advertising	
	Real-time performance data	

Key: <u>underline</u>, key resources and assets; **bold**, distinctive activities and capabilities.

to analyze the Walmart case in those terms. Note, however, that a number of ideas included in table 2.1 do not fit neatly into these categories—which is a good thing.

Many of the ideas in table 2.1 are expressed simply as factual statements. Some are very concrete ("rural locations," "bare-bones store fixtures"), while others are more abstract and conceptual ("bargaining power," "economies of scale"). This is a common outcome of the idea generation process. One might object that simple factual statements in particular are incomplete as explanations and that the relationship between any of the items in table 2.1 and Walmart's cost advantage is largely implicit. This is certainly the case! The absence of explicit explanatory connections is a feature, not a flaw, at this stage of the process, where we want as many and as diverse ideas as possible. If every idea's relevance has to be firmly established and explained before being written down on a sticky note, then creativity and insight will ultimately be diminished. In short, at this stage one should trust that if someone suggests that a particular fact might be relevant to what is being explained, there is some potential connection worthy of consideration.

Clustering and Refining

Once a rich and diverse set of ideas has been generated for the mapping process, attention turns to detecting patterns and similarities in the ideas. A really good brainstorming session will result in a welter of ideas, so much so that it may seem overwhelming. As the number of ideas increases and starts to seem unmanageable, it is helpful to cluster them into related themes and concepts. This is particularly easy to do if the initial ideas have been captured on sticky notes, as they can be moved around as similarities are detected and easily moved again as new patterns and insights are generated.

How should ideas be clustered? For example, for the ideas in table 2.1, it would be tempting and natural to cluster the ideas according to the distinction between key resources and assets, on the one hand, and distinctive activities and capabilities, on the other. Alternatively, members of an organization might find it natural to identify themes that correspond to functional responsibilities within the organization, such as marketing, sales, manufacturing, etc. In both of these cases, ideas would be considered similar to the extent that they belong to common "input" categories.

For a strategy-mapping exercise, we think that such approaches to identifying themes are unlikely to be very useful. Recall that the goal of the mapping exercise is to create a representation of a strategy argument. As a result, ideas should be clustered with the end in mind: What is the conclusion you are trying to justify? In the Walmart case, we are trying to explain why "Walmart has lower costs than its competitors." Ideas should therefore be considered related to the extent that they seem to tap into the same potential explanation for this conclusion. They should be linked through their common output, not common inputs.

To see what we mean, consider the ideas about Walmart in table 2.1. In our view, the following ideas could be usefully clustered together, at least initially: "private-label product lines," "high volume in purchasing," "bargaining power," "data analytics skills," "culture of frugality," and "tough negotiating style." Our intuition is that these ideas belong together because they all relate to how Walmart interacts with its suppliers. Similarly, we might cluster "sharing of best practices," "sophisticated logistics capability," "hub-and-spoke distribution system," "cross-docking," "data analytics skills," "own trucking operations," and "real-time performance data" together because they seem related to Walmart's ability to operate very efficiently, particularly in its distribution operations.[14] Other clusters are possible as well.

The process by which we arrived at these clusters may seem mysterious. Indeed, as in any creative process, it is somewhat unclear exactly how the mind arrives at these particular insights. Nonetheless, in our experience, executives armed with a good understanding of the business and a basic sense of key strategic issues—such as supplier power or cost-efficiency—have little difficulty seeing how the ideas are connected. This occurs mainly because the ideas were generated with an explanation in mind, even if the explanation was not made explicit on the sticky note. In other words, when someone suggests "high volume in purchasing" as being a possible explanation for Walmart's lower costs, it is highly likely that the (perhaps implicit) explanation connects to Walmart's relationships with its suppliers. For this reason, it is good practice to ask people to describe briefly why they think an idea is relevant as they share it with the wider group. In fact, as people do so, an initial clustering of ideas will often take place.

Once ideas have been assigned to different clusters, attention can be turned to arranging the ideas within the thematic clusters themselves. At its simplest, this involves reducing redundancy by removing sticky notes that refer to the same idea in different ways. However, there will often also be a hierarchy among the ideas within the clusters, whereby they differ in their levels of abstraction. Some statements—like "private-label product lines"—are very concrete, while others—like "bargaining power"—are more abstract. For example, the fact that Walmart has private-label products contributes to its bargaining power over suppliers, because it means Walmart can afford to walk away from a negotiation with a supplier and still have something in the product category to offer its customers.

Ideas with higher levels of abstraction are particularly useful when generating strategy maps, because they form the basis for more general explanations.

So, it is good practice to devote some effort to arranging the ideas within a cluster to reflect this hierarchy of abstraction. The more abstract concepts will generally arise naturally from the clustering process itself. If none of the ideas in a cluster is stated abstractly, then add new sticky notes that capture the more general idea represented by the cluster.

The end result of the clustering process is a set of themes and abstract ideas that will serve as the primary building blocks for the mapping process. Each of these abstract ideas—such as "bargaining power" or "economies of scale"—is a strong candidate to play a central role in the strategy argument. At the same time, the more concrete ideas will play a role as causes of, or evidence for, the more abstract ideas.

Constructing the Map

After generating and refining ideas about Walmart, we are left with a set of potential causes of Walmart's low-cost advantage over its competitors. It may be tempting to stop at this stage and consider the strategic analysis completed, much as when one has completed all of the cells in a conventional strategic SWOT (strengths, weaknesses, opportunities, threats) analysis. But for building a good strategy argument, this is merely an intermediate stage—a necessary and important input to the critical stage of showing *how* these different potential explanations relate to one another and to the conclusion we are trying to support.

After generating and refining ideas, we have the proverbial "laundry list." In saying so, we do not want to denigrate the value of writing down one's thoughts about strategy or to underestimate the value of engaging in a collective brainstorm and synthesize, which can be huge. But we do think there is much to be gained by pushing beyond the laundry list and actually washing items, in part to rule out things that are not relevant, but also to deepen our understanding.

In other words, it is time to construct the strategy map, to start doing the laundry. We suggest doing this by combining ideas in a sensible way to show how inputs lead to outputs, or how causes lead to effects. The basic structure of this map, once completed, represents the basic structure of the strategy argument.

How to do this? We suggest leaving the various clusters of ideas that have been generated on their own pieces of paper or whiteboard and starting the mapping process with a clean sheet. We begin by writing our intended conclusion on a piece of paper or on a new board. The conclusion should be placed in such a way that it allows for the development of the strategy argument supporting the conclusion. We recommend placing it at the right-hand edge of the paper or board, in order to leave plenty of room for the rest of the strategy map. We place it on the right-hand edge because we generally read completed maps from left to right, or from causes to effects. Others may prefer to represent the causal flow right to left or vertically (from top to bottom or bottom to top). The choice is immaterial as long as everyone understands the agreed-upon direction.

When mapping, the goal is to represent visually the sequences of ideas that generate the conclusion. In other words, the goal is to depict how different factors impact one another. A sequence is represented by a series of directional arrows between ideas, which we typically place in boxes or on sticky notes. Some of these sequences will be relatively short, while others are longer chains of causes and effects. In the Walmart case, a simple causal sequence would be:

Private-label product lines ⟶ Bargaining power over suppliers

This sequence should be understood to say something like the following: "The fact that Walmart has private-label product lines leads to it having bargaining power over its suppliers."

We can make this causal sequence slightly more complex by relating bargaining power to the final conclusion. This can be seen in figure 2.4, which should be understood to say: "The fact that Walmart has private-label product lines leads to it having bargaining power over its suppliers, which in turn results in Walmart having lower costs than its competitors."

2.4 Visualization of tentative cost argument for Walmart

Note that figure 2.4 is a strategy map! It is a very simple and tentative one, and surely only the beginnings of a fuller strategy map for Walmart. But it is an important starting point, one that can be built upon and revised to create a more complete representation of Walmart's strategy argument.

Before elaborating on the simple map in figure 2.4, we offer some general suggestions on how to move from a conclusion and a laundry list of ideas to a strategy map.

First, the construction of the map can proceed forward or backward. The list of ideas generated in the brainstorming phase contains many potential starting points for the strategy argument. Moving forward involves thinking about the implications of an idea as they relate to the ultimate conclusion one has in mind.

In other words, we move forward from "Walmart has private-label product lines" by considering what follows from this fact that is relevant to "Walmart has lower costs than its competitors." As it happens, in this case one of the implications of "Walmart has private-label product lines" was already found in our list of ideas from the brainstorming stage, namely that "Walmart has bargaining power over its suppliers."

Identifying such patterns of relationships between ideas from the initial brainstorming phase is an important part of clustering and refining the ideas and often comes quite naturally to people as they consider and make sense of the set of ideas in front of them. But the search for the implications of an idea need not be restricted to those ideas that have already been generated—new ideas may emerge in the mapping stage through a combination of synthesis and novel insight.

The challenge with moving forward from the list of ideas is that any given origin point can take you in many different directions—not all of which will get you to the intended conclusion. This danger is mitigated somewhat if people have the conclusion in mind when generating ideas, but even so, discussions can range far afield. This is why it is generally important and useful to work backward from the conclusion.

We move backward by asking what prerequisites or preconditions would lead to a conclusion being true. For example, in trying to support our conclusion that Walmart has lower costs than its competitors, we know that one possible way to have lower costs is to have a bargaining advantage over suppliers. As it happens, this is one of the more abstract ideas that was identified as a

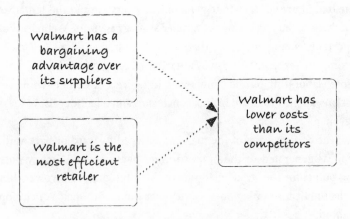

2.5 Revised visualization of cost argument for Walmart

possible explanation in table 2.1, although this insight could also be generated through a basic understanding of strategy and industry analysis. Similarly, we might recognize that a different basic way of achieving lower costs is to have the most efficient operations, in other words, to incur lower operating costs for distribution, etc., per transaction. We integrate these two ideas in our revised strategy map, as shown in figure 2.5.

One advantage of moving backward in constructing the strategy map is that one can decide how far back one needs to go, based on what needs further explanation. In other words, to what extent can the left-most statements in the strategy stand on their own? In figure 2.4, the statement "Private-label products" is a simple factual statement that is easily verified, and hence we do not need to move further back from there. On the other hand, in figure 2.5, the two left-hand statements do need further justification: Why do we believe that Walmart has a bargaining advantage or the most efficient operations?

With respect to bargaining advantage, part of the answer has already been provided by our examination of the implications of "Private-label product lines" in figure 2.4. But there are other ideas in table 2.1 that may seem relevant once we consider the tentative map offered in figure 2.5. We can, therefore, continue to work backward in a next iteration of the strategy map and construct figure 2.6. What we do here is treat the statement "Walmart has a bargaining advantage over its suppliers" as a statement that requires justification, and hence we treat it as a conclusion in its own right.

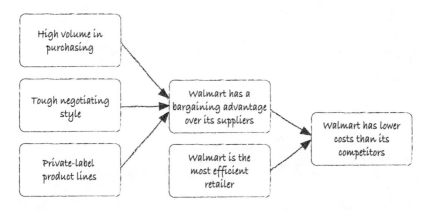

2.6 Elaborated visualization of cost argument for Walmart

Our strategy map is gradually getting more elaborate. We do not yet consider it complete. For example, there are further ideas in table 2.1 that might be seen as relevant to our idea that Walmart has a bargaining advantage. In addition, some of the ideas that we have included in table 2.1 may not, on further inspection, be relevant to Walmart's bargaining advantage: when dealing with sophisticated suppliers like Procter & Gamble, for example, does a tough negotiating style really help drive down prices? We do not want to resolve these questions here. Instead, we want to emphasize that debates over such matters can be very productive.

A careful reader will observe that in our construction of figure 2.6, we introduced a very broad idea that is absent from the list of ideas in table 2.1, namely, "Walmart is the most efficient retailer." We introduced this idea in figure 2.6 while working backward from our conclusion that Walmart has a cost advantage. It arose through a speculation process—by asking ourselves what the different reasons might be for a firm to have a cost advantage *in general*. In our view, this approach points to an advantage of working backward for at least part of the mapping process. Doing so loosens the grip, so to speak, of the many facts we might know about a particular case and forces us to think in more general theoretical terms. Having introduced such a concept into the map, it is of course incumbent upon us to see whether we can justify it using facts and ideas about Walmart. Incorporating some of the ideas from table 2.1 in a preliminary way leads to the version of the strategy map in figure 2.7.

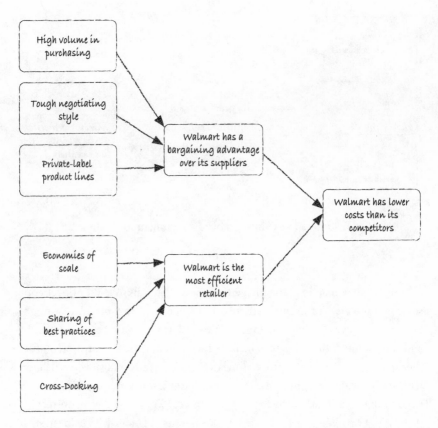

2.7 Expanded visualization of cost argument for Walmart

In particular, figure 2.7 adds three premises about the underlying reasons for Walmart's efficiency. Each premise represents a possible separate causal force contributing to overall efficiency. "Economies of scale" means that because of its size, Walmart is able to offer products at a lower per-unit cost. "Sharing of best practices" means that once a good lower-cost way of doing things is discovered somewhere in the company, other parts of the company learn about it and adopt it if useful (in many companies these practices fail to get communicated broadly and are even sometimes hidden from others). "Cross-docking" means that as supplies are received at Walmart's distribution centers, they are immediately and directly reloaded onto outbound vehicles for distribution to retail stores, spending no time in a warehouse. In adding these three premises to the map, and not adding possible others from table 2.1, we are exercising our best judgment to say essentially that these forces are the primary and most important factors producing efficiency at Walmart.

At this stage, these statements are just unfounded claims in the strategy argument, and their veracity and importance have yet to be demonstrated. That comes later. Of course, we are trying our best to get it right, to state things as we believe them to be true. Still, we are going a bit out on a limb. Making this kind of claim often causes discomfort among managers, not only because they could be wrong, but perhaps because it may cause disagreement and conflict with others. Living with this kind of ambiguity in the workplace, especially when you are in charge, takes some getting used to and some practice. That's part of what makes doing strategy so hard!

Even with the elaborated map in figure 2.7, much work remains. For example, the "Economies of scale" claim requires further justification. This might be accomplished by pointing to Walmart's enormous sales volume as well as its substantial fixed-costs investments in distribution centers, a trucking fleet, and information technology (IT). However, at this stage in the mapping process, we are going to make another judgment call and decide to leave the further elaboration of the map for later. In our view, we have succeeded in articulating a basic strategy map for Walmart's advantage over competing retailers; we think we have captured the more important factors involved in producing and sustaining this advantage. For those who think another aspect of the company or its behavior is equally or more important, we encourage you to keep working and build out the map further as an exercise. We will also return to this map in chapter 8, where we illustrate a deeper elaboration of the strategy argument.

In summing up strategic mapping, we offer a number of suggestions regarding the mechanics of the process:

1. Arrows in a strategy map represent cause-and-effect relationships between ideas. They lead *from* the cause *to* the effect, or *from* the input *to* the output. In other words, the tip of the arrow should always point at the effect or the output.

2. Ideas, concepts, resources, system states, and conclusions all go in boxes or on sticky notes.

3. Arrows should generally convey a sense of process. Before drawing an arrow between boxes A and B, ask, "What is the process through which A turns into B?" If no clear answer suggests itself, then do not draw an

arrow. Instead, think about the problem some more: maybe part of the argument is missing.

4. Mapping is an iterative process that requires patience and good humor. It is difficult for us to convey the iterative nature of a good mapping exercise in writing. Nonetheless, most good strategy maps are the product of a lot of false starts, attempts at clarification, a search for new ideas, and the emergence of new insights that require revisiting and revising the structure of the argument. This can seem frustrating at times, but in fact is very valuable.

We should also mention here a very important point that will not always be true. In this formalization of Walmart, we have assumed that each cause (premise) has an independent ability to generate the conclusion. That is, we see the premises as separate causes that act independently to produce the conclusion, meaning that any one of them could do so by itself. So, per the argument, Walmart could have lower costs *either* because it holds a bargaining advantage over its suppliers *or* because it is the most efficient retailer. Similarly, in the same argument, Walmart's supplier bargaining advantage might be the result of high-volume purchasing *or* tough negotiating *or* private-label product lines. As we explain in chapter 3, figure 2.7 is depicted precisely in a manner consistent with these causes as independent contributors. Of course, in some arguments, the various causes (premises) will not be considered independent. For example, one might believe that the bargaining advantage requires *both* high-volume purchasing *and* tough negotiating. We will discuss in chapter 3 how to map these co-dependent causes and write them out in an argument.

CLOSING THOUGHTS

As a visual representation, a strategy map is both a powerful means of developing one's strategy argument and an effective means of communication. Part of the power of mapping comes from the flexibility and creativity that it allows: it is easy and often intuitive to draw an arrow between two ideas on a whiteboard, and the fact that the concepts and relationships can quickly be rearranged allows for rapid iteration. Many people are visual thinkers, at least in part. Seeing a diagram of the relationship between concepts can quickly spark new ideas and new associations, and as a result the process of mapping can be enormously generative. Similarly, a good visual representation of the argument will make clear that some actions or assets are more critical to others, because these will have lots of relationships to other parts of the argument.

As a result, a good strategy map is a potent coordination device. Without a strategy map, people will often think differently about the connections between specific actions and outcomes. They may not agree that actions are related to one another, or they may conceive of the nature of the connections differently—and they may not even realize that they hold such different views! A good strategy map can surface such latent disagreements, allowing for discussion and deeper investigation using facts and data.

Despite these strengths, strategy maps are not perfect. In fact, strategy maps can be misleading if not developed carefully, just as a local person's map to a place scrawled on a napkin can lead you astray. Drawing an arrow between two concepts on a whiteboard is deceptively easy, and supposed connections may be merely unreflective or wishful thinking, rather than rigorous consideration. Unfortunately, mapping does not eliminate poor reasoning. Similarly, while maps can help identify and resolve areas of disagreement, their highly simplified nature can leave many disputes unresolved or ambiguous—people can look at the same connection in a causal map and interpret it differently. This is why the logical assessment tools we discuss in chapter 3 are a critical part of the process of developing and refining a strategy argument.

KEY TAKEAWAYS

- A strategy map visually represents a strategy argument, the causal path that leaders believe generates a particular strategic outcome. The map illustrates the hypothesized connections between organizational activities and resources, environmental conditions, and the outcomes of strategic interest, such as an organization's competitive advantage.
- Strategy maps facilitate the development of strategy arguments through iterative thinking and revision. Just as important, maps serve as potent coordination and communication devices. Maps allow people to discover how they think differently about strategic issues, and to resolve those differences to come to a common understanding. Subsequent reference to a

collectively developed strategy map can help ensure alignment and consistency in how executives approach strategic challenges.

- As simplified representations of a complex strategic reality, strategy maps serve as mental models. These models allow leaders to engage productively in counterfactual thinking. Faced with strategic decisions, a map that identifies the relevant forces makes it easier for leaders to imagine what would happen if some conditions or variables were changed.

- Productive strategy mapping requires a frank and forthright exchange of ideas. Boxes and arrows can easily be drawn on a whiteboard, but people need to see and interpret the map in the same way for it to provide a sound foundation for strategic decision making.

CHAPTER 3

‖‖‖
‖‖‖‖‖‖‖‖‖‖
Logic for Strategy

THE BENEFITS OF FORMALIZING ARGUMENTS

A well-known story among students of organizations describes a team of Hungarian soldiers operating in the mountains of Switzerland during World War I.[1] The team had been sent out by their lieutenant on a reconnaissance operation, but did not return as scheduled, and were still missing after several days. It had been snowing, so the lieutenant became worried that the unit was lost and in peril. Struggling with feelings of guilt, he began to question his judgment as well as the purpose of the entire war. Happily, on the third day the troops surprisingly returned to camp, to everyone's relief and joy. When asked what had happened and how they had survived and gotten out safely, the soldiers gave an unexpected answer. Although initially they had been distraught and feared that they would die, one of the men had found a map in his pocket. After making camp and waiting for the snow to ease up, they had used the map to find their way safely back to the base camp. After asking to see the map, the lieutenant discovered that it depicted the Pyrenees Mountains—and not the Alps, where the soldiers actually were. The troops had, in fact, followed the wrong map to reach home!

In the lore of strategy, the lesson drawn from this story is that when you are lost, "Any old map will do." The idea is that a map, even an incorrect one, is better than no map, because it provides hope, instills confidence, and inspires action. Applied to strategy, the lesson bespeaks the value of having a strategic plan in uncertain times, even an imperfect one.

We mention the story here to make a different but equally important point. It builds on the observation that the troops themselves did not realize that they had an incorrect map. Indeed, they thought that they possessed an accurate map of the mountain region they were in. How could this be? The answer, we suggest, lies in the ambiguity inherent in maps. A map is an abstraction from reality. By definition, that means it leaves many things out. Two people looking at the same map might see two different things, make varying interpretations of what they see, and fill in the missing parts in different ways. Good maps succeed by convention: we agree implicitly on what it is important to include in the map and how various things should be represented. But imagine if you were given a map without knowing or understanding its purpose or notation. You might think that you understood it, because it looks like many other maps, and so you would perhaps use it as a basis of action, interpreting it and filling things in the way you imagine it implies. But if later you found it was a depiction of, say, unpassable trails rather than paved roads, you could easily have acted in inadvisable and unsafe ways.

So, too, with the strategy maps of chapter 2. After working through the Walmart maps, we imagine many readers may ask whether strategy maps are enough to guide an organization. Our view is that they can be—provided they are done rigorously enough and their limitations are fully appreciated. Certainly, we believe that having agreement on the map being used will have the coordination and motivational benefits captured in the phrase "Any old map will do." But to maximize your chances of success, you do not want any old map—you want a good map. In our experience, a mapping exercise such as the one described in chapter 2 is rarely sufficient to ensure that the result is a good map. At the very least, stopping at the mapping stage misses the opportunity to deepen one's understanding of the strategy argument. More importantly, mapping can make it much too easy to wave one's hands to make it seem like the "argument" represented in the map is coherent—when in fact it is not.

What are the dangers? First, note that some of the ideas you have put up on the mapping board are likely to be insufficiently complete. In the Walmart example, "bargaining advantage" is not specific enough; we need to know something about how Walmart's bargaining advantage arose and the conditions under which it holds to truly understand the strategy. Identifying these conditions could require any of several possible additional premises, such as the ones we identified in chapter 2, like "high volume in purchasing" or "private-label product lines," or—more importantly—premises that we are missing. Identifying the key underlying ideas is central to analyzing the strategy and why it works; it also provides managers guidance from things they need to monitor to keep the strategy in line.

Second, it can be difficult to assess the validity of an argument diagrammed as a map. If you have sketched out the map reasonably well, then you will have sketched out the basic structure of the argument. But for the argument to hold, it must be *valid*: the outcome or conclusion you expect must follow from the other ideas you are invoking and often assuming. If not, you need to revise the structure, perhaps adding additional ideas and assumptions. As we explain in this chapter, assessing validity is a technical matter of logic—it is often easier to assess when arguments are stated in propositional form.

For these reasons, we think it is helpful—once you are reasonably satisfied with your strategy map—to formalize the argument. In fact, we believe that if the formalization of your map does not yield a logically valid argument, you most likely do not have a great strategy. You will also probably find that many people inside your organization don't know the strategy or are confused about it.

How can you start to learn to develop formal arguments and assemble the logic tool kit we advocate? Our experience is that learning first by reference to an example may be the easiest path. So, for most of our exposition, we return to the Walmart example and the mapping work initiated in chapter 2. Our goal in this chapter is to develop an analytical strategy argument based on the strategy maps developed in that chapter. So, we are still attempting to explain why and how Walmart's strategy generated its success. After developing an argument in this context, we will then assess the process of writing out the logic more generally.

The Value of Logical Rigor: The iPhone Launch

Strategic debates within firms rely heavily on relatively informal forms of argumentation. Executives express an idea about a rival firm, a change in government policy, or a new technology to some strategically relevant outcome or action. These claims are used as a means of persuasion; they are attempts to convince people to take a particular course of action by pointing to a reason (or multiple reasons) why it is the right thing to do. In short, these kinds of claims are arguments in support of a conclusion. But because such arguments are often presented and discussed in an informal, unstructured way, they are fraught with danger as a basis for strategic decision making.

As the Southwest Airlines seating assignment example of chapter 2 illustrates, a strategy map is a powerful way of moving from informal claims about strategic relationships to a more systematic understanding of how different factors connect. The power and utility of strategy maps come with some risks, however, because the maps represent informal arguments. The danger of these arguments emanates from the ease of drawing arrows between boxes: one can assert a connection between actions or ideas without fully thinking through the relationship. For this reason, we advocate complementing the visualized arguments in strategy maps with formal strategy arguments in propositional form. While formal arguments are less fluid and flexible than a visualized map, the time and discipline required to build one can prevent muddled or wishful thinking. A formal argument facilitates a focus on the logical structure of the claims one is making. A formal argument also crystallizes the key issues at stake, provides insight into the most critical assumptions, and facilitates more productive debates.

To illustrate the value of formalization, consider how cell phone manufacturers reacted to the introduction of the Apple iPhone in 2007. When the first iPhone was released, executives at market leader Nokia did not act concerned; if anything, they claimed to welcome Apple's entry as something that would help grow the market. Why? Among other things, Nokia's engineers had determined that the iPhone was not a very good mobile phone in terms of reliability and quality of calls. It only operated on 2G networks, while Nokia had a strong capability in developing phones for the new, superior 3G standard.[2] Nokia's phones also had long battery lives, were rugged, and fit neatly in your pocket. Nokia's chief strategist concluded that the iPhone would be a niche product, much like the Apple Macintosh was in the PC market. Other makers of smartphones were similarly unconcerned. Ed Colligan, the CEO of Palm, maker of devices like the Palm Treo, said, "We've learned and struggled for a few years here figuring out how to make a decent phone . . . they are not going to just figure this out. They're not going to just walk in."[3]

For the purposes of illustration, let's imagine how discussions about the launch of the iPhone might have played out in rival firms. (To be clear, we have no inside knowledge into the debates within established mobile phone firms, we rely here on public sources.) The sentiments described by the leaders at Nokia and Palm might be summarized in the following informal claim: "Because the iPhone does not have good cellular phone technology, it will not win in the cellular phone market."

Upon hearing this claim expressed, many executives would naturally respond with an opinion about whether or not they agree that the iPhone will not win. In other words, they express their gut feelings about the conclusion and perhaps provide a simple reason or two. For example, they may respond by saying, "Apple has an amazing design sensibility, so they will dominate the cell phone market." The proponent of the original claim may respond, "Come on! It's a lousy phone, there is no way they can win." And so on.

This kind of exchange is rarely productive, with people arguing until they are blue in the face. But it is a common trap, one that can ultimately lead to bad strategic decisions and a lack of commitment to the ultimate course of action. From our point of view, the problem starts with the initial informal claim ("Because the iPhone does not have good cellular phone technology, it will not win in the cellular phone market"). Like many informal claims, this one is an incomplete argument and thus logically invalid. The argument is invalid because the conclusion ("it will not win in the cellular phone market") does not follow from the stated premise or assumption on which it is based ("Because the iPhone does not have good cellular phone technology"). To be valid, these types of arguments require one to use an additional implied but unstated premise.[4]

Incomplete arguments can carry a lot of weight in strategic debates. That's because they appeal to implicit premises in the minds of the listener. Our minds, when presented with an incomplete argument, usually fill in the gap, subconsciously using as a premise an unstated idea lurking around in the backs of our heads. This automatic gap filling makes for easy conversation and lively debate, as people quickly exchange ideas and converge through a sort of shorthand wherein not every single assumption needs to be stated.

But it is also potentially very problematic. The process of filling in implicit premises typically occurs instantly and subconsciously. We may nod in agreement after filling in the missing premise in a colleague's claim, without making ourselves fully clear about what we are implicitly assuming. Moreover, leaving premises implicit increases the chances of subsequent confusion and disagreement, as two people may not recognize that they supplied *different* implicit premises.

The flaw in the original claim is easier to see by restating the argument as two statements:

> *Statement 1.* The iPhone does not have good cellular phone technology.
> *Statement 2.* The iPhone will not win in the cellular phone market.

The first of these is a premise, an empirical assumption about the iPhone that may or may not be true, and the second is the conclusion. The argument is usually thought of in the following way: IF (statement 1 is true) THEN (statement 2 is true), where the antecedent premise is implicitly preceded by IF and the conclusion is implicitly preceded by THEN. The logical problem with this particular argument is that the conclusion (statement 2) does not necessarily follow from the premise (statement 1).

It is easy to see why with the benefit of hindsight. Consider the following puzzle. The first iPhone was widely considered not to be a very good phone *as a phone*, compared to the other cheaper cellular phones on the market.[5] Yet we know today that Palm and Nokia were ultimately victims of Apple's success and retreated from the market. Apple won decisively in the cellular phone market. So, in retrospect, we can see that even though the premise of the argument is true, the conclusion is false—meaning that there must have been something missing from the argument, something that would allow the original premise to be true but the conclusion false.

More generally (and without the benefit of hindsight) we can identify incomplete arguments by recognizing that we lack a defined way to connect our two statements. How does the second statement follow from the first? Intuitively, we have a sense that they are connected, but we cannot be confident that everyone shares the same intuitions. Instead, we should be specific and precise about how the first statement is connected to the second.

Making this connection can be more difficult than it seems at first. Consider the following attempt:

IF
> *Statement A:* The iPhone does not have good cellular phone technology.
AND IF
> *Statement B:* If a product has good cellular phone technology, then it will win in the cellular phone market.

THEN
> *Statement C:* The iPhone will not win in the cellular phone market.

This expanded argument here does several things. First, we have added a new premise (statement B). Second, this new premise is different in several respects: (1) it is more abstract or general and is not tied to a specific empirical claim; and (2) it is more complex, in that it contains two premises themselves embedded in an "If-Then" clause. Still, the argument remains simple and readily comprehensible.

The expanded argument is a step forward in understanding, as we are now more explicit about what we believe and how our ideas are connected. With the addition of the new statement B, we have a way to connect the first premise (statement A) to the conclusion (statement C). Moreover, the general claim in statement B makes intuitive sense.

Unfortunately, while this argument is complete (there are no missing premises), it is logically invalid. It is an example of the logical fallacy that logicians call "denying the antecedent."[6] If we stop to think about it, it is easy to see why the conclusion does not necessarily follow. We can think of many examples in which the technically most superior product does not win in the market. Alternatively, it could be that none of the products in a market have good cellular phone technologies, yet there can still be a winner.

Nonetheless, a complete but invalid argument is still better than an incomplete argument, because we can reformulate the argument to make it valid. A logically valid argument would be something like the following:

IF
> *Statement A:* The iPhone does not have good cellular phone technology.

AND IF
> *Statement B*:* If a product does not have good cellular phone technology, then it cannot win in the cellular phone market.

THEN
> *Statement C:* The iPhone will not win in the cellular phone market.

Statement B* may, at a superficial level, not seem all that different from our original premise statement B. Yet the distinction between the two makes a huge difference. Statement B* is more precise, because it makes clear that good cellular phone technology is a *necessary* requirement for winning in the cellular phone market. It is not a "nice to have," as in the original premise, but a "must have." Without this more precise premise (statement B*), the original claim (statement A) does not hold water; the conclusion (statement C) does not necessarily follow, because someone who accepts the premises does not have to accept the conclusion. By contrast, with our revised argument, someone who does not believe either of the premises (statements A or B) will have to concede that if they *are* true, then the conclusion (statement C) will be true.

This is important, because it clarifies exactly what one has to believe—what must be true—in order to accept the original claim. What you have to believe is not that good cellular phone technologies are associated with winning, which seems reasonable enough, but that they are *required* for winning. Articulating the valid, complete strategy argument forces executives to wrestle with and justify the claim that good cellular phone technologies are a necessary condition for success in the industry. For example, is this the only (or the most important) criterion by which consumers choose a phone? Or are there other things that customers might be looking for?

Identifying this premise also helps to clarify what it is that executives at Apple must have believed, at least in part. Because they were willing to release a phone with inferior phone service, executives at Apple probably did not accept the premise that preventing dropped calls was necessary for success. At the time of the iPhone's introduction, it was not obvious that they were right. It would not have been unreasonable for executives at Nokia and Palm to believe that good cellular phone technology was a necessary prerequisite for success. The quality of phone connectivity had, after all, been a key dimension of competition to that point. But executives at Nokia, Palm, and other established cellular phone manufacturers would have been well served by trying to consider why Apple's beliefs on this matter differed, and what specifically the Apple executives were assuming would drive them to success instead.

These differing views on whether good cellular phone technology was a necessary prerequisite for success foreshadow an important distinction we make later between validity and soundness. *Validity* is purely a matter of the logical structure of the argument, of whether the conclusion follows from the premises as stated. *Soundness*, by contrast, is a question of whether the premises are true. If all of the premises are true, and the argument is valid, then the conclusion will be true; if one or more of the premises is false, then the argument implies the conclusion is false. If all this sounds abstruse, don't worry at this stage, we will return to this distinction several times and elaborate it with examples.

In 2007, Apple and Nokia executives (or executives within the companies) could disagree about the soundness of the argument, because they could honestly differ in their beliefs about statement B*. Was it really true? None of them could have been certain about what would happen at the time. But they could not disagree about the validity of the argument. The argument is valid whether they accepted the premises as true (statements A and B*) or not.

With the benefit of hindsight, we can recognize that at least one of the premises in the argument turned out to be false. The argument was valid, but not sound. The initial success of the iPhone despite its inferior cellular technology suggests that statement B* was false: good cellular technology was not a necessary requirement to win. In addition, when Apple later incorporated 3G technology into the iPhone, it may have rendered the first premise (statement A) false, although the iPhone 4 "Antennagate" fiasco suggests that perceived phone performance was an issue for several years.[7] However, we only know these things in retrospect.

Surfacing implicit assumptions and ensuring validity shifts the terms of debate in productive ways. Rather than simply articulating gut feelings about whether the iPhone will succeed, articulating a complete, valid argument allows the critical issues to come into focus. People shift from fighting about whether they believe the conclusion to recognizing what they have to believe for the conclusion to be true.

As a result, executive decision makers are forced to concentrate on whether and why they accept the premises as true. Ideally this focus leads to further productive discussion. For example, if you want someone to believe that good cellular technologies are not a necessary prerequisite for success, you will be pushed to make an argument supporting that claim. And doing so will likely surface additional implicit assumptions and differing points of view. Some executives, for example, might believe this claim because they think that great marketing can overcome any technological deficiency, while others believe that the superior design and functionality (beyond its ability to make calls) of the iPhone will make it win.

As noted at the outset, informal claims with implicit premises are ubiquitous in business discourse, both within firms and in the media. They are unavoidable; after all, who wants to speak in the stilted language of a formal argument? And in many cases, incomplete arguments are harmless. A good rule of thumb is that implicit premises are acceptable if they are obvious (i.e., everyone will immediately know what the implicit premise is) and uncontroversial (i.e., everyone would agree with the implicit premise). For day-to-day matters and routine business, both of these conditions are likely to hold. But when the stakes are high and the decisions are of strategic importance, it is dangerous to assume that these conditions will hold. For strategic decisions, the implicit premises will often be nonobvious and controversial, and the consequences of relying on faulty, unstated assumptions are high. Artificial as it may seem at first, the iPhone example illustrates the value of formalizing critical strategic claims and the importance of ensuring the validity of one's strategy arguments.

THE PRACTICE OF FORMALIZING ARGUMENTS

Revisiting the Walmart Strategy Map

In chapter 2, we walked through a brainstorming process that generated a strategy map of the factors behind Walmart's low-cost competitive advantage. Recall that we came up with a variety of different ideas and concepts that potentially could explain why Walmart has lower costs than its competitors, and began the process of arranging those ideas into a coherent strategy map.

Imagine that we have completed the mapping process to our satisfaction, and we have run out of new ideas to explain Walmart's advantage. At this point in our analysis, even though we seem to have come to a halt, we might worry whether our list is comprehensive, or even whether all of the elements on this list are correct. We could choose to ignore those concerns and plow ahead with making decisions based on our current strategy map. However, we think we will be better off if we push beyond our initial (perhaps augmented) laundry list. In part this will allow us to rule out things that are not relevant. But the most important reason to forge ahead beyond brainstorming is to deepen our understanding, both by better understanding how our ideas fit together and by identifying gaps in our reasoning that need to be filled.

The mapping process outlined in chapter 2 was the first step in this deepening of our understanding. In particular, mapping is a powerful means of visualizing and shaping the structure of our argument. Certainly figure 2.6 (reproduced and relabeled here as figure 3.1) from the last chapter gives us a

3.1 Strategy map for Walmart cost advantage

better sense of how different aspects of Walmart's operations relate to its cost advantage.

Strategy maps are an intuitive and powerful way in which we generate arguments and try to explain things. But a lot can be obscured, lost, or even miscommunicated by a simple arrow on a whiteboard.

Using the Map to Build an Argument

Diagrams lack the discipline of a formal argument. Our experience is that discipline matters—it keeps us from sliding into ambiguity, making loose arguments that don't really hold together, and hand-waving through difficult-to-see connections between ideas. We need a different framework to force us to be rigorous.

Fortunately, we think that the use of fairly simple propositional logic with deduction provides both the framework and the necessary discipline. While it is unlikely that you make arguments in propositional logic in the course of your daily life, the underlying basic form is familiar and widely used, if only implicitly. For example, a typical, simple argument takes the following form:

Boss: If my employees listen carefully to my instructions, then they will understand what to do.

Employee: We listen carefully to your instructions.

Boss: You know what to do.

To turn this exchange into propositional logic, start by making it a bit more abstract and rigorous. The first step is to depersonalize it by removing the source of each statement and then simply regard each as a dispassionate claim. Second, notice that some parts of the exchange are *premises* (or assumptions) and another part is the *conclusion*. Specifically, the first two claims are premises (we prefer the word "premise" to "assumption," because it more clearly signifies to us that we are formalizing the argument). The third claim is a conclusion—it is intended to follow automatically from the premises. It is a conclusion deduced from the premises, making this a deductive argument. In properly formulated deductive arguments, you *must* accept the conclusion if you accept the premises as true. Finally, represent the different ideas in the exchange symbolically, letting the letter *A* represent the claim "my employees listen to my instructions" and letting *B* be "they will understand what to do."

Putting all this together shows that the exchange has the form of the following simple logical argument, called a *syllogism*. We have given each a letter (S) or letter-number combination (S1) as a way of keeping track of them and making them easy to reference. The numbering or ordering plays no calculative role; it is simply an accounting system.

IF
> *Premise S1:* IF A is true, THEN B will be true.

AND IF
> *Premise S2:* A is true.

THEN
> *Conclusion S:* B is true.

Beyond the terms *premise* and *conclusion*, we want to note again one more conceptual distinction in the argument above. As with statement B, premise S1 contains two parts, the first starting with "If . . ." and the second starting with "Then . . ." (We capitalize IF and THEN in the formalization to highlight them.)

We refer to the first part as the *antecedent* and the second as the *consequent*. In developing arguments with premises such as this, we usually need a premise like premise S2, which logicians call "affirming the antecedent" or asserting that it is factually true. And we need to know how the premises are connected in the argument—do we need both of them to generate the conclusion, or will either do it? When they are both needed, as here, we connect the premises with an AND *connector*; when either can be used by itself, we use an OR connector. In chapter 2 we used only OR connectors, because we saw the premises as separate causes acting independently to produce the conclusion, meaning that any of them could do so by itself. When one or more premises or causes are needed together to produce the conclusion, then the AND connector would be appropriate. Despite what might look like increased complexity at first blush, decomposing things like this makes the argument more precise and often makes it easier to understand and evaluate.

The argument should be understood as follows: IF premise S1 holds (meaning it is true) AND IF premise S2 holds (true), THEN conclusion S follows. The argument is a simple exercise in deduction. It says that the conclusion will always occur if the two premises occur (are true).

Returning to our Walmart example in figure 3.1 and the case of bargaining advantage, what we have so far are (1) a description of the idea we will call "A" (Walmart has a bargaining advantage) and (2) a description of the idea we will call "B" (Walmart has lower costs than its competitors). What is missing is a connection between the two. In the diagram, the arrow between them captures our intuition that the two are connected. But how do we represent this connection in our formalization?

In a formalization, an If-Then statement that links these two claims captures the same understanding. To create a formalization of the arrow drawn from A to B, we introduce a premise of the form "If A, then B"—as in our earlier example. For instance, to represent the impact of Walmart's bargaining advantage effect on its costs, we say the following (switching to numbered premises and conclusions and the letter W to remind us that these are premises in the Walmart argument):

IF
> *Premise W1:* IF a firm has a bargaining advantage over its suppliers,
> THEN it will have lower costs than its competitors.

AND IF
> *Premise W2:* Walmart has a bargaining advantage over its suppliers.

THEN
> *Conclusion W1:* Walmart has lower costs than its competitors.[8]

Again, notice that premise W1 has a different character from premise W2 and conclusion W1. Why?

First, it is a more complex and abstract If-Then statement, while the other two are simple empirical claims (and premise W2 affirms the antecedent of premise W1). What's critical to recognize here is that premise W1 expresses a socioeconomic theory or believed conjecture about how the world works. If-Then statements form critical components of strategy arguments. These statements operate as the engines of explanation: they specify causal theories of how inputs are related to outputs, of how actions turn into outcomes.

Second, note that premise W1 makes no reference to Walmart. Instead, it is a *general* claim about firms. This is fitting, given that it is intended as a general causal explanation. We want to understand the success of Walmart as a specific case of some more general process, such that we can see where else that process might play out.

An advantage of the formalization should be apparent at this point: it has forced us to take our intuition and articulate a theory or principle about how the world operates. Currently, premise W1 represents the core theoretical claim. Relative to mapping, the formalization forced us to be specific about what we believe. While people can look at arrows on a whiteboard and mentally fill in what they imagine the arrow to mean, here we have put it into specific ideas and words—and might even find ourselves debating the ideas and words.

There is an additional advantage to formalization. Given the way this claim is stated, the argument suggests that we believe this theoretical claim holds generally. In our view, we are much more likely to realize this when looking at the words than when looking at the arrow on the whiteboard. Realizing this, we should ask whether we actually believe that it holds generally. Can we think of exceptions?

Surely there are. While premise W1 expresses something that feels true, it is not difficult to imagine cases in which it does not hold as a general rule. The simplest objection is to note that there is more to a firm's cost structure than its input costs. One can imagine, for example, that a firm might have the lowest per-unit input costs but much higher operating or labor costs. One way to address this problem is to revise W1 and add a kind of "other things being equal" clause:

IF

> *Premise W1**: IF a firm has a bargaining advantage over its suppliers AND at least comparable other costs, THEN it will have lower costs than its competitors.

AND IF

  Premise W2: Walmart has a bargaining advantage over its suppliers.
AND IF

  Premise W3: Walmart has at least comparable other costs.
THEN

  Conclusion W1: Walmart has lower costs than its competitors.

On the one hand, this change of adding "AND at least comparable other costs" gets the job done. It does not add much additional insight beyond the original argument, but at least it forces an acknowledgment of what is being assumed (in the form of the clause added to premise 1 and the insertion of the new premise W3). Nonetheless, if presented with an argument of this form, we would suggest trying to go further. There is nothing wrong per se with making the "other things being equal" assumption, but it often flags an opportunity to generate more insight by articulating things further.

One symptom of the missed opportunity here is in the ad hoc nature of the If-Then clause in premise W1*, which combines a statement about bargaining advantage with one about costs without clarifying their relationship. We can address this by being more specific about how bargaining advantages reduce costs and being explicit about what needs to be true about other costs. We can do this by building an argument that states a conclusion about lower per-unit costs:

IF

  Premise W4: IF a firm has a bargaining advantage over its suppliers,
     THEN it will have lower per-unit input costs.
AND IF

  Premise W2: Walmart has a bargaining advantage over its suppliers.
THEN

  Conclusion W2: Walmart has lower per-unit input costs.

Now we can put this newly elaborated argument together with what we had before to yield a more complex argument. In doing so, we put the per-unit costs argument first and make its conclusion an *intermediate conclusion* that functions as a premise in the argument about overall costs. See the accompanying box for the formal argument. It now has two If-Then statements embedded in premises, or two causal claims (premises W4 and W1*). We still rely on a blanket assumption (premise W3) that Walmart has comparable other costs, but we have made progress on specifying why we think a bargaining advantage over suppliers matters (premise W4). We have also structured the argument into two self-contained subarguments—in the first subargument (part I), the first two premises (W4 and W2) generate the intermediate conclusion W2; then in the second subargument (part II), the intermediate conclusion is thought of as a premise, and along with premises W1* and W3, it generates conclusion W1.

Argument About Walmart's Cost Advantage

PART I:

IF

Premise W4: IF a firm has a bargaining advantage over its suppliers, THEN it will have lower per-unit input costs.

AND IF

Premise W2: Walmart has a bargaining advantage over its suppliers.

THEN

Intermediate Conclusion W2: Walmart has lower per-unit input costs.

PART II:

IF

Intermediate Conclusion W2: Walmart has lower per-unit input costs.

AND IF

Premise W1*: IF a firm has lower per-unit input costs AND at least comparable other costs, *THEN* it will have lower costs than its competitors.

AND IF

Premise W3: Walmart has at least comparable other costs.

THEN

Conclusion W1: Walmart has lower costs than its competitors.

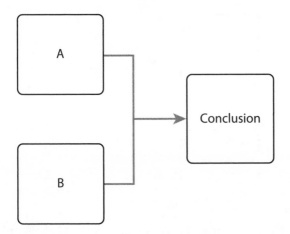

3.2 Strategy map showing premises with AND connector

Refining the Map

In the box, premise W_1^* contains an AND statement that conjoins two statements in the antecedent of the premise. The need for this AND statement arose because the process of formalizing our original strategy map made us realize that the map was implicitly assuming that all other costs were comparable. This insight should cause us to revise our original map to ensure the importance of the assumption is not obscured. But we need a way to diagram the difference between AND and OR connectors in the structure of an argument, something that we did not consider in chapter 2, because we were thinking about all of the statements as being linked by OR connectors.

We proceed as follows: in the strategy map shown in figure 3.2, the square bracket in the diagram indicates an AND relationship, meaning that both premises connected by the square bracket need to be true for the conclusion to hold.

By contrast, if the premises both imply the conclusion, but do so independently of each other, they are joined by an OR connector. We represent this with separate arrows leading directly to the conclusion (figure 3.3).

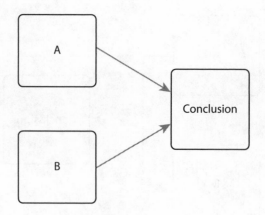

3.3 Strategy map showing premises with OR connector

When we formalize a strategy map, the arrows in the map are turned into theoretical premises or If-Then statements. You may, in the process of generating a strategy map, recognize the need for AND statements, and therefore include square brackets, as in figure 3.2. When formalizing such an argument, the theoretical premise representing the arrow needs to be one that includes an explicit AND condition. Thus the appropriate If-Then statement for figure 3.2 is "IF A AND B, THEN conclusion"—i.e., the same structure as premise W_1^*.

By contrast, when formalizing a strategy map without square connectors (such as figure 3.3), recognize that the map is implicitly using OR connectors. This gives you some leeway in how you approach the formalization. Figure 3.3, for example, could be formalized with a theoretical premise of the form "IF A OR B THEN conclusion." Similarly, part of figure 3.1 could be formalized as "IF Walmart has a bargaining advantage over its suppliers OR Walmart is the most efficient retailer THEN Walmart has lower costs than its competitors." In many cases, however, formalization is easier if one takes the independent branches of the map (i.e., those joined by OR statements) and works on them separately. However, in this case it is important to remember the implicit OR statements and examine critically whether they are correct.

Using the refined mapping tools, the logical structure of the Walmart argument is shown in figure 3.4. Here you can see how the subarguments fit together: notice how the intermediate conclusion W_2 acts as both a

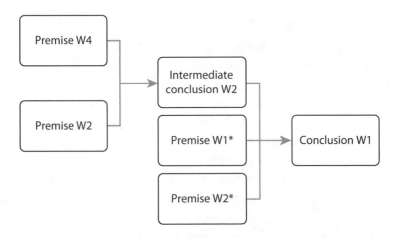

3.4 Logical structure of Walmart cost argument

conclusion in the first subargument (part I) and a premise in the second subargument (part II). Notice also that premises are tied to the conclusion via a common connecting arrow, indicating that they are related through the AND connector. If each individual premise had its own arrow pointing independently to the conclusion, then that would indicate an OR relationship among the premises (as with figure 3.1).[9] One possible misconception of going back to a map like this at this stage—after developing the formalization—is that the more complex premises, those with embedded If-Then structures, get glossed over and look like simpler premises. One could use a convention like coding those more complex premises in a different color, but the value of that depends on the context. For now, just keep in mind that not all premises are similar in structure.

In fact, we think that unless better information is available, it is usually safer to assume that premises in an argument are connected with the AND operator (this is a more conservative option). So, we will drop our explicit usage of the premise connector AND for many arguments in the book. That is, *for the rest of the book, we will present arguments in which the AND connector is implied among premises, and we will only make explicit the connector when OR is being used in some way.*[10] *For clarity of presentation, we will also remove from arguments the IF and AND IF and THEN connectors between premises, because they should be obvious based on the way the arguments are made.*

Elaborating the Argument

In thinking more about the Walmart argument shown in the text box, we should ask ourselves again whether we believe it holds generally. Most people, we think, would feel more comfortable with premise W4 as stated, although there is still room for greater clarification. For example, one might explore whether *all* suppliers reduce their prices when faced with a powerful buyer. What if the supplier operates in a commodity market, for example, and is already pricing at opportunity cost to all of its buyers?

While such concerns are legitimate, in our view a better use of intellectual energy at this point would be to elaborate the argument in two different directions. One direction involves turning premise W3 from an empirical claim into an intermediate conclusion. This would mean constructing an argument that supports the conclusion that Walmart has at least comparable costs. We return to this issue in greater depth in chapter 8 but note now that the other elements of our laundry list and the strategy map in chapter 2 are surely relevant to this subargument.

Another option is to continue moving backward in the strategy map in figure 3.1 and provide support for the empirical claim (premise W2) that Walmart has a bargaining advantage over its suppliers. This effort would involve turning premise W2 into an intermediate conclusion. For example, the subargument might look like this:

> *Premise W5:* IF a firm has high purchasing volumes, THEN it will have a bargaining advantage over its suppliers.
> *Premise W6:* Walmart has high purchasing volumes.
> *Intermediate Conclusion W3:* Walmart has a bargaining advantage over its suppliers.

It is fully legitimate, from a logical or substantive perspective, to decide not to elaborate the argument in this way. In the less-developed argument, premise W2 is a simple empirical claim. Provided that there are data to support this claim, it might suffice. However, the claim that Walmart has a bargaining advantage over its suppliers is a rather abstract assertion—it is something we might believe to be true, but any evidence we might cite could be contested. In general, when an argument relies on a more abstract or conceptual claim, it can be helpful to be explicit about the argument supporting that claim.

More generally, a lot can be learned by trying to flesh out the reasoning in support of specific claims, especially in terms of identifying potential weaknesses in our initial strategy maps. For example, consider the claim in the strategy map that there is a relationship between a tough negotiating style and Walmart's bargaining advantage (another argument possibly generating intermediate conclusion W3). We start the formalization as follows:

> *Premise W7:* IF a firm has a tough negotiating style, THEN it will have a bargaining advantage over its suppliers.
> *Premise W8:* Walmart has a tough negotiating style.
> *Intermediate Conclusion W3:* Walmart has a bargaining advantage over its suppliers.

The key theoretical claim in premise W7 should be met with substantial skepticism, as there seem to be many exceptions to this theory as a general rule. We can certainly think of lots of situations when treating your suppliers poorly during a negotiation might be a bad idea and backfire (if only in the long run), and perhaps more situations when it doesn't make any difference in the price that is ultimately paid.

Faced with this skepticism, one can react in either of two ways. One option would be to try, as we did for the first argument, to elaborate further the claim by clearly expressing the conditions under which we expect it to be true. For example, perhaps we can invoke insights about the social context or psychology of negotiation to support our case. A second option is to decide that maybe we have been imprecise in our mapping exercise. Perhaps having a tough negotiating style does not create a bargaining advantage. Indeed, the opposite may be the case—perhaps having a bargaining advantage (due to purchasing volume, for example) may allow a firm to treat its suppliers poorly, simply because they do not have to treat them well. Of course, often the realization that our initial claim was a mistake comes about after we have tried to construct the argument to justify it, when doing so forces us to make claims that we find untenable.

One might ask, at this point, whether formalization is really moving us in the right direction. After all, it seems that through formalization we might actually remove a branch from our strategy map. Simplification—this represents progress! Eliminating factors that do not matter for the firm's success is just as important as identifying factors that do. In this case, formalization moves us closer to the truth.

The Value of Abstraction

Our goal in this extended exercise has been to illustrate both the process and the virtues of formalizing strategy arguments. Working with what seems at first like a straightforward, intuitive argument, we have seen how the process of trying to formalize our argument requires us to be more precise, thereby allowing us to discover implicit assumptions or gaps in our reasoning. In our view, there is nothing particularly magical or mysterious about this process, although it does require patience. More importantly, progress requires a willingness to think abstractly, a willingness to move from the concrete empirical facts about Walmart to statements about general strategic processes and mechanisms. In other words, the key is to be able to formulate If-Then statements—theories—in general terms, such that Walmart's outcomes are only specific instances of more general processes.

This process of abstraction has two virtues. First, it is easier to recognize missing assumptions or gaps in logic when working with general, abstract statements. People are more likely to accept the specific statement "Walmart has lower costs than its rivals because it has a tough negotiating style" than the more general statement in premise W7. We suspect that this is because they have already accepted the conclusion that Walmart has lower costs than its competitors, making them prone to accept claims that seem consistent with this belief. Unmoor the mechanism from the specific case, and people (including you) are better positioned to identify possible exceptions, thereby strengthening the argument.

Second, abstraction facilitates generalization. Most people who study and think about the reasons for Walmart's success do not work for Walmart. Instead their goal is to understand whether any general lessons from Walmart apply to their situations. This can only be accomplished if one moves away from idiosyncratic details. Otherwise you end up simply trying to create a carbon copy of what Walmart did—after it has already been done. Furthermore, even when you apply the tools to your own company, abstraction is essential to generating insights that allow your organization to respond to unexpected situations and identify new opportunities.

Validity and Soundness

We have focused to this point on assessing individual premises. In particular, we have concentrated on trying to identify likely exceptions to the general If-Then claims that are so critical to our arguments. In so doing, we have focused on the external consistency of the claims: we have tried to see whether claims such as premise W2 are generally true as statements about the world. When we feel that we can identify exceptions to our statements, we call the external consistency into question and seek to revise our claims to make them believable. An important benefit of formalization, however, is that it allows us to identify flaws in the *internal consistency* of our arguments: situations in which the conclusion does not follow from the premises, even when the premises are true. When logical flaws in an argument exist, the conclusion does not necessarily follow, even when all of the premises are true. To put it differently, external consistency is no guarantee that you have a good argument: all of your premises may be true statements about the world, but the conclusion may still not follow.

Logicians refer to an argument that is internally consistent, or without logical flaws, as a *valid argument*. When an argument is valid, it is impossible for the conclusion to be false if all of the premises are true. To put it differently, if you accept the premises as being true in a valid argument, then you must accept the conclusion as true. Validity or internal consistency is desirable in its own right, of course. But more importantly, we want to assess the validity of an argument in order to avoid the kinds of common logical flaws that happen frequently in everyday conversation, particularly in fast-moving environments where we may feel pressure to reach a decision quickly.

Just as an argument's premises can be externally consistent without the argument being internally consistent, it is possible for an argument to be valid even if not all of the premises are true statements about the world. In our view, this is an incredibly important benefit of assessing the validity of strategy arguments, particularly when one is trying to formulate strategies for imagined new opportunities where it may be difficult or expensive to assess whether or not all of the premises are true (as we discuss in chapters 5 and 6). If the argument is not valid, it does not matter whether the premises are true or not, because the conclusion will not necessarily be true anyway.

These distinctions may seem confusing. To get our heads around them, consider the following "toy" argument:

> *Premise GM1:* IF an organization has blue in its logo, THEN it has exceptionally intelligent employees.
> *Premise GM2:* General Motors has blue in its logo.
> *Conclusion GM:* General Motors has exceptionally intelligent employees.

This argument demonstrates that an argument can be internally consistent without being externally consistent. As a matter of logic, the conclusion follows from the premises—the reason we might feel uncomfortable with it is that the first premise seems overly fanciful as a causal statement about the world. We can certainly imagine exceptions to this premise. In this case we may not be able to rescue the external consistency of the premise. Note, however, that we should not simply reject the conclusion that General Motors has exceptionally intelligent employees—in our experience, it does! Instead, what this tells us is that we need a different argument to support this conclusion.

Now consider the following, seemingly similar argument:

> *Premise GM1:* IF an organization has blue in its logo, THEN it has exceptionally intelligent employees.
> *Premise S1:* Stanford does not have blue in its logo.
> *Conclusion S*:* Stanford does not have exceptionally intelligent employees.

This argument is beset with problems. We certainly do not accept the conclusion as a true statement about the world! And, as with the prior argument, the external consistency of the first premise is questionable.

But the more important flaw in this argument is that it is logically invalid, because the conclusion is not a necessary implication of the premises. This is an example of an invalid argument that logicians term "denying the antecedent." There are lots of reasons why an organization might have intelligent employees, with none of those reasons having anything to do with the branding scheme. Even if we accept the absurd premise that the color of the logo causes some organizations to have intelligent employees, the fact that Stanford does not have blue in its logo does not cancel out those other reasons.

This example may seem fanciful because the flaw is so obvious. We suggest that the obviousness of the flaw is because most people believe (we hope) that Stanford has intelligent employees, given that it is a leading research university. Because that feels true, people disagree with the conclusion S* and will be on the lookout for flaws in the argument.

More difficult are the logically flawed arguments used to support conclusions that you are predisposed to accept. For example, the following argument has the exact same logical structure:

> *Premise IC1:* IF a company has talented experts in internal
>   combustion engines, THEN it will hold a perceived quality
>   competitive advantage in the car market.
> *Premise IC2:* Apple does not have any experts in internal
>   combustion engines.
> *Conclusion IC1:* Apple does not hold a perceived quality competitive
>   advantage in the car market.

Here the external consistency of the conclusion seems correct (at least as of right now), but the logic is still invalid. If we wish to establish logically that Apple does not hold a perceived quality advantage in the car market, we would need to formulate a different argument. Yet because we know, as an empirical matter, that Apple does not hold a perceived quality advantage in the car market (because they do not make cars), we are susceptible to accepting the argument as stated.

Another common form of invalid argument is termed "affirming the consequent." As an example, consider the following invalid argument:

> *Premise QS1:* IF a salesperson has a poor understanding of his
>   customers, THEN he will not meet his quarterly sales target.
> *Premise QS2:* Mike did not meet his quarterly sales target.
> *Conclusion QS1:* Mike has a poor understanding of his customers.

There might, of course, be lots of reasons why Mike missed his quarterly sales target: perhaps a hurricane disrupted operations for his customers or a competitor unexpectedly introduced a new product. Consider another similar argument:

> *Premise QS3:* IF a salesperson has a great sales strategy, THEN she will exceed her quarterly sales target.
> *Premise QS4:* Susan exceeded her quarterly sales target.
> *Conclusion QS2:* Susan has a great sales strategy.

Both of these arguments, and the problems with them, are intimately familiar to anyone who has managed a team and had to do performance evaluations. In both cases, the conclusion may be true as an empirical matter. But the arguments as stated do not support the conclusion. If the conclusion is important, then it is time to go back to the drawing board.

Table 3.1 provides an illustration of the most common forms of valid and invalid arguments; there are multiple forms of each beyond those in table 3.1 that we will not review here.[11]

Table 3.1 Common valid and invalid arguments

Valid Arguments	Invalid Arguments
Premise: If A, then B	*Premise*: If A, then B
Premise: A	*Premise*: Not A
Conclusion: Therefore, B	*Conclusion*: Therefore, not B
Premise: If A, then B	*Premise*: If A, then B
Premise: Not B	*Premise*: B
Conclusion: Therefore, not A	*Conclusion*: Therefore, A

Focusing on validity is useful for two reasons. First, validity assessments are a useful disciplining device, especially when we are formulating our own arguments. A common challenge in constructing arguments stems from the fact that we have a point of view: we believe (or want) certain things (conclusions) to be true. In our eagerness to justify our conclusion, we are prone to taking logical shortcuts. This is particularly the case when we present our arguments informally, or when we try to illustrate them in strategy maps, when it is so easy to draw arrows between boxes. Combining formalization with a focus on validity helps protect us against drawing the wrong conclusion, or at least forces us to be explicit about the assumptions needed to justify our conclusion.

A second benefit of focusing on validity lies in the quality of the strategic debates that result. One of the challenges of doing strategy is that people are—for a variety of reasons—often passionately committed to their points of view (their desired conclusions). This passion can lead to logical shortcuts and flawed reasoning that validity assessments can uncover. More importantly, passion can lead to vehement disagreements and fights. These fights are typically about the truth (external consistency) of the assumptions made by the different factions. Unfortunately, it can be hard to settle these matters empirically, especially in the moment. Focusing on validity can defuse the situation. Assessing internal consistency starts by granting the truth of an argument's premises—for the sake of determining validity. Doing so allows different points of view to be heard, an important component of productive strategic conversations. Moreover, in our experience, people will more readily admit to faulty logic (lack of validity) than to inaccurate premises.

In assessing arguments, of course, we are not merely interested in their validity. We are also interested in the truth of the premises! As noted earlier, when an argument is valid *and* each of the premises is true, it is said to be *sound*. If one or more premises are not true, then the argument is not sound. It is possible that an argument can be valid but not sound—the logic makes sense and generates the conclusion if we grant the premises as true. For instance, the argument concerning General Motors is valid but not sound. But if one or more of the premises is not true, then the argument is only valid. The argument will be sound only if it is valid *and* all the premises are true.[12]

The importance of soundness as a criterion for assessing arguments depends on the purpose of the strategy argument one is formulating. When trying to identify and analyze an existing strategy (whether successful or not), it is important to complement a focus on constructing valid arguments with an assessment of their soundness, i.e., whether the assumptions are true. For example, the earlier argument about Walmart's negotiating style is valid:

> *Premise W7:* IF a firm has a tough negotiating style, THEN it will have a bargaining advantage over its suppliers.
> *Premise W8:* Walmart has a tough negotiating style.
> *Conclusion W3:* Walmart has a bargaining advantage over its suppliers.

However, we find it difficult to believe that premise W7 is true as a general mechanism, so while the argument is valid, it is not sound. (It is not really clear what "tough" means in this context.) As a result, we do not think the argument as formulated is a satisfactory explanation for Walmart's success. (We return to the potential role of Walmart's negotiating style in chapter 8.)

While assessing soundness is important when trying to explain a known outcome, it is difficult to do when assessing a forward-looking strategic plan. That is why we think the place to start in learning to build a strategy argument is by analyzing a known case of sustained strategic success. In such an analysis, deficiencies of validity and soundness are easier to see and correct. One is better able to identify and specify the mechanism(s) that produced the outcome, as well as the conditions that allowed or facilitated its occurrence. If you cannot do this, then you have not identified the strategy behind the success.

By contrast, as we shall see in chapters 5 and 6, when formulating a potential future strategy, one is required to specify in advance the future conditions (premises) that need to be true for the strategy to succeed. These conditions need not be true at the current moment, but the strategy assumes they will become true at a future point. This conditional, forward-looking view makes the process of building and understanding the strategy argument exceedingly more complex. Hence, for learning the system of activities we advance here, we suggest starting with the simpler problem of figuring out what actually happened with a firm in order to understand its prior success, as opposed to conjecturing what needs to happen with a firm in order for it to experience future success.

CLOSING THOUGHTS

Let's review what we have covered up to this point about visualization and logical formalization:

- *Start by specifying the conclusion.*
  People often think that the construction of an argument starts from first principles, perhaps because proofs and textbooks are often written as though that were the case. A natural type of conclusion to emphasize in beginning a strategic analysis is the generic nature of the firm's competitive advantage, low cost or perceived quality.

■ *Generate and refine ideas that will serve as premises for your argument.*

The brainstorming and clustering techniques we discussed in chapter 2 are valuable at this stage. In addition, familiar strategic frameworks or tools (such as industry analysis) can be a good starting point. The goal here is to generate a large number of diverse ideas and then identify common themes and patterns in the ideas that emerge.

■ *Map the structure of the argument.*

Visualize the structure of the argument by moving forward from ideas (identifying potential implications) as well as backward from the desired conclusion (and any intermediate conclusions). Remember that it is surprisingly easy to draw arrows or connections between ideas or boxes on a whiteboard or to generate an outline of ideas. This is an important source of creativity and insight, as it is easy to quickly represent potential connections and rearrange the structure of the argument as new insights are generated. However, some discipline is beneficial at this stage, in order to make the formalization stage easier. Every time an arrow goes up or another point is added to an outline, ask whether you can articulate the nature of the connection between these two concepts or facts.

■ *Formalize and assess the validity of the argument.*

Determine whether the premises—if they are assumed to be true—are enough to force acceptance of the conclusion. If so, then the argument is valid. If not, then something is wrong or missing. Perhaps an important premise is not included—what is it? Or perhaps the premises need to be reconceptualized or elaborated. True insight is not possible without a valid argument.

■ *Once validity is established, assess the soundness of the argument.*

Ensuring validity typically involves making a number of assumptions without assessing their external consistency, or whether they are true statements about the world. Now is the time to go back and decide whether or not those assumptions are believable—or at least whether they are believable enough to make a bet. If ensuring a valid argument requires making outlandish assumptions, then something may be wrong, either with your understanding of why a firm has been successful or with your belief that your new strategy is worth pursuing.

Finally, let us stress emphatically that while we have tried to lay out the critical steps and tools in the process of constructing and assessing strategy arguments, ultimately it is a craft more than a science. As such, it is best learned through example and repeated application. Accordingly, we have tried in our expositions here and elsewhere in the book to develop arguments in steps, showing how one's thinking may develop and change as an argument is being articulated and scrutinized, with the approach being occasionally tentative and incorporating plenty of rethinking and revision.

Yet we worry that the necessities of good exposition in book writing require us to present arguments in rational and orderly ways, when in fact we sometimes struggle quite a bit to come up with an argument we like and find presentable. All the messiness of developing the argument gets swept under the rug so to speak, as do the many, many iterations that we often cycle through to get to the presentable argument. The problem is that, as when math textbooks present proofs in rational orderly fashion that took years to develop, we may mistakenly give the impression that arguments are easy to develop and you should be able to just write a good one down quickly. Then, when you can't do it so easily, you decide that you are no good at this and can't do it or that there is something wrong with the method. Both conclusions are wrong!

We apologize for any misimpressions. We are happy to confess that when we work on these formalizations, we typically iterate many, many times in many different ways, often over long periods to time. Developing a good argument is hard and messy work. As golfers say, you need to grind and then grind and then grind some more—never stop grinding.

KEY TAKEAWAYS

- Managerial discourse relies too heavily on the use of informal claims with implicit, unstated assumptions. Arguments relying on such assumptions are incomplete and logically invalid, meaning the conclusion does not necessarily follow from the stated assumptions. In many cases, this situation also leads to incorrect conclusions. Moreover, incomplete arguments generate unproductive conflict and increase the likelihood of confusion, because people do not realize that they are invoking different implicit assumptions.

- Developing formal arguments based on propositions requires concerted effort. Less fluid and flexible than either informal claims or strategy maps, formal arguments impose a discipline that prevents executives from sliding into ambiguity and giving way to wishful or muddled thinking. Formalizing an argument forces teams to face their assumptions head-on and test their beliefs about why specific actions or investments are related to desired outcomes. It also crystallizes the key issues at stake and reveals the most critical assumptions underpinning the strategy.

- Focusing on the internal coherence (logical validity) of a strategy argument forces executives to be explicit with themselves about the assumptions required to justify a particular conclusion. It generates more productive debates, because people will usually admit to faulty logic more readily than to inaccurate beliefs. A focus on validity shifts the conversation from fighting over the conclusion to identifying and recognizing what people have to believe in order for the conclusion to be true.

- The best strategy arguments use general and abstract concepts with clear causal theories that explain how inputs are related to outputs, or how actions turn into consequences. General claims not only force executives to identify the necessary assumptions, but also open up the possibility of identifying new markets where the strategy could also work.

CHAPTER 4

||||||||||||||||||||||||||||||||||||||||||||||||||||||||||||||||||||||||||||||||||||||||||||||||||||||||||||||||||||||||||||||||||||||||||||||||
|||||||||

Arguing in Organizations

THE BENEFITS OF CONSTRUCTIVE ARGUMENTS

In September 2017, Twitter announced that it was experimenting with a change in its platform: increasing the number of characters allowed per tweet from 140 to 280. As news spread, it ignited a classic firestorm of controversy on the service. People immediately took sides and engaged in heated debates.

Those opposed argued that the change was a desperate move to improve the company's sagging fortunes and would backfire. It would "irritate many users daily. . . . A good tweet boils information down into what's essential. You get the headline, and a little more detail. That's it. That's why whenever news breaks, Twitter is the place to go."[1] Others saw it as an ill-conceived attempt to compete more directly with Facebook, which had no limits on the length of a post. Longer tweets, opponents predicted, would be more complex, harder to skim quickly, and more poorly written. Twitter simply "won't be as much fun."[2]

Not so, claimed proponents of the move. Where opponents thought that the prior limit inspired creativity, supporters thought that "the extra word count will keep inspiring writers while enabling a better use of language."[3] Twitter itself thought the higher limit would make the service more approachable to new users, driving up engagement on the site: "Trying to cram your thoughts into a Tweet—we've all been there, and it's a pain."[4] Proponents noted that some users were already working around the 140-character limit by creating "tweetstorms" consisting of multiple consecutive tweets or attaching screenshots of text. One commentator asked, "Why do we think the text-message character limits of the early '00s somehow magically stumbled onto the platonic ideal of message length for a social network?"[5]

Much of this debate raged, of course, on Twitter itself, with the corresponding levels of sarcasm, humor, and combativeness that people have come to associate with the platform. What we find fascinating about the debate is that so many people, most of them with little knowledge of Twitter's strategy or inner workings, had such strong points of view. Like many if not most debates on Twitter, people had immediate reactions to the announcement and started debating right away. Few were likely convinced by the other side. Instead, the event resembled a longtime sporting rivalry in its atmosphere of rabid one-upmanship.

We do not know what the debate *within* Twitter was like. But we would not be surprised if it largely mimicked the public debate, because this is how many executives describe strategic debates within their companies—even when the stakes are much higher. (Twitter eventually decided to implement the change for all users, and the impact seemed minimal at best for the firm's overall performance.) An initiative is proposed, and people immediately take sides. At first there may be a respectful exchange of points of view, but frustration levels quickly escalate, volume levels rise, and the different sides dig in. Ultimately a decision may be made, and the losing side is rarely happy about it.

We call this phenomenon "arguing blue," because it reminds us of the common expression about arguing until you are blue in the face. The unfortunate fact about how strategy happens in many firms is that it all too often takes the form of arguing blue. Being on the losing side of such fights is not good for one's career. People try to avoid engaging with proposals they disagree with— better to let sleeping dogs lie. As a consequence, not only do strategic issues rarely get debated, but arguing about strategy itself gets devalued. Rarely is arguing about strategy regarded as a serious or productive use of time. And in many corporations today, from very large global companies to tiny entrepreneurial start-ups, there is a strong sense that the thing to avoid—at all costs—is having an argument, especially about strategic decisions, where real resources are at stake.

We disagree very strongly with this view. In fact, we think that reasoning about strategy is *best* done by arguing, and specifically by arguing in groups. While the activities we have discussed in chapters 2 and 3 can be used individually—and there can be real benefit to doing so—ultimately, we believe that an organization will benefit the most when some or all of the process is performed by carefully constructed groups. The essence of great strategy formulation and strategic management involves arguing constructively—when the strategy is being developed and as it is being implemented. Good strategists and executives who achieve long-term success encourage constructive arguments in decision-making groups, whether they do so consciously or not. Without constructive arguments among multiple stakeholders, strategy is often vacuous, and in the worst case may involve gambling the future of a company without even realizing it. As Gary Pisano warns: "For any proposed program of reasonable complexity, lack of debate is actually a worrisome sign."[6]

Vigorous argument should be encouraged and celebrated, provided that people are arguing constructively, not arguing blue. Arguing blue is about using every trick in the book to advance your point of view, deploying whatever powers of intimidation and persuasion you have at your disposal. By contrast, arguing constructively involves laying out key facts, stating core concepts, and articulating clearly why they are believed to be true. Arguing blue is passionate and heated; developing an argument constructively is dispassionate and cold. Arguing blue is about prevailing in your views no matter the cost; arguing constructively is about making your best case without resorting to tricks of persuasion or manipulation. Arguing blue is personal and ad hominem; arguing constructively is impersonal. Arguing blue is ruthless; arguing constructively is also ruthless. Arguing blue is about winning by force or deception; arguing constructively is about winning by reasoning.

The hitch in our claim is that you cannot develop an argument constructively without actually doing some real arguing. And, as we all know, arguing can sometimes go off the rails. Executives shy away from arguments, because they know disputes can generate problems, and even permanent damage and dysfunction, in organizations and among individuals. Arguing needs to be done constructively, in a way that generates positive results rather than damage.

In this chapter, we discuss ways to keep the arguing process constructive and productive. These ideas are drawn from observations at some companies as well as social science theory and research. They range from macroscopic matters like the design and functioning of an organization's culture to microscopic matters like how to set up and run a meeting. We don't think there is a single way to do this effectively, and we suspect that what works well in one organization may not work well in another. Executives should pick and choose from the ideas presented, experiment with them to gauge their effectiveness in any given context, and try to develop some new things on their own. In the process, the overarching goal should be to keep the conversations rational, civil, and dispassionate. Above all, you need to avoid shouting matches, appeals to emotion, displays of loyalty, backbiting, and personalized sparring. Don't argue blue.

Why Arguing Matters

Arguing can be messy and chaotic, even when the arguments are constructive, and even within cultures that promote healthy arguments. Arguing also does not always seem worthwhile: there must be more productive ways for people to spend their time, you might be thinking. Moreover, creating an environment for constructive arguments takes forethought and investment. And there is always a risk that things will deteriorate into people arguing blue. As a result, it makes sense to ask whether the ends justify the means. Is arguing worth the effort?

Consider Netflix, a highly successful company that has managed to navigate and lead across several fundamental transformations in its product market, from take-home movie DVDs, to online movie streaming of others' material, and now to original television and film content production. According to early chief talent officer Patty McCord, "The main reason the company could continually reinvent itself and thrive, despite so many truly daunting challenges coming at us so fast and furiously, was that we taught people to ask, 'How do you know that's true?' or my favorite variant, 'Can you help me understand what leads you to believe that's true?' " She goes on to explain how these kinds of questions spawned vigorous internal debates at Netflix that "helped cultivate curiosity and respect and led to invaluable learning both within the team and among functions."[7]

We think there are three compelling reasons for investing the time and energy required to argue in a group. The first is that having a well-chosen group argue in a constructive manner leads to *better arguments* and, ultimately, to better strategic decisions. The second is that arguing constructively helps generate *buy-in* from the people involved and hence helps address the political tensions that accompany any strategic change. Third, arguing constructively—unlike arguing blue—can *change how people think* and help people arrive at a common construal of the situation. This ultimately helps when it comes time to put a plan into action. We discuss each of these in turn.

Better Arguments

The most important reason to argue about strategy in groups lies in the quality of the decision itself. One reason is that the quality of information that is used to inform the decision-making process affects the outcomes, and groups with a diverse range of members can have access to more information than any one individual. Arguing in groups produces better-quality decisions when the process brings in people with varied information and beliefs and these contrasting views are pitted against each other. People working in different parts of the organization will, due to their differing responsibilities, hold different insights. Each possesses a partial view of the firm's situation, its challenges and opportunities. A process that surfaces and respects these differing perspectives is less likely to make avoidable mistakes, as each argument's assumptions—the argument's external consistency—is challenged from a variety of different viewpoints.

A more fundamental benefit of arguing collectively lies in the quality of the arguments themselves, particularly their internal consistency or validity. While it is important to have the right facts, in principle one could gather this information from different sources without involving those people in the decision-making process. But the quality of the reasoning is likely to be higher if the argument is constructed by a well-chosen group. The reason lies in the fallibility of humans—we are not good at reasoning consistently according to the rules of deductive logic, a fact well documented in psychological research over the past forty years. While groups have their weaknesses as deliberative bodies, this is one area in which they are superior to individuals working alone.

Perhaps the most compelling reason to argue about strategy in groups, rather than develop arguments in isolation, arises from the well-established individual tendency toward confirmation bias. This bias is the widespread tendency of people to look for and interpret evidence in a way that confirms their preexisting beliefs or hypotheses. In a strategic context, managers often have an intuitive reason for preferring a certain course of action, often rooted in their experience in certain roles, as well as (perhaps subconsciously) their vested interests. So, for example, a marketing executive may believe that the best way to increase revenue is to invest in a new marketing campaign, while the head of product development thinks the best answer is greater investments in R&D. With a desired conclusion in mind, each searches for facts and arguments to support his or her case and tends to dismiss or simply ignore evidence to the contrary. The marketing executive points to how much sales increased the last time a new campaign was introduced, while the head of product development points out that most sales come from a product her team developed.

For an individual decision maker, there are good reasons to be concerned about confirmation bias. As Hugo Mercier and Dan Sperber have argued, however, the tendency toward confirmation bias can actually be beneficial in a group setting. Specifically, confirmation bias:

> contributes to an efficient form of *division of cognitive labor* . . . When a group has to solve a problem, it is much more efficient if each individual looks mostly for arguments supporting a given solution. They can then present these arguments to the group, to be tested by the other members. This method will work as long as people can be swayed by good arguments.[8]

To see the potential of collaborative reasoning, consider a classic experiment called the Wason selection task. Individuals are presented with four face-down cards and are told that each has a number on one side and a letter on the other. The first card has an *E*, the second a *K*, the third a 4, and the last card a 7. The individuals are then given the following information: "If a card has a vowel on one side, then it has an even number on the other side." They are then asked to assess the claim by selecting the card(s) they would need to turn over to demonstrate conclusively whether the claim was true or false.

When working individually, very few people get this right—less than 10 percent, in fact. Over 80 percent will say that you should turn over the E and the 4. The correct answer is that you should turn over the E and the 7. Why? Notice that the claim is of the form "If p, then q" where "p" is "vowel" and "q" is "even." By turning over the E, you focus on a card where p is true and can determine whether q is also true, i.e., there is an even number on the other side. A card with an even number showing, like the 4, is one where q is true. But notice that q could be true for reasons other than p—the original claim does not rule this out. On the other hand, if you turn over a card where q is false (i.e., the 7), the claim can be falsified if the p is true, because then there will be a case where the letter is a vowel but the number is odd.

How does improving the success rate from less than 10 percent to over 70 percent sound? That is how much performance on the Wason selection task changes when people work on the problem in small groups, according to research by David Moshman and Molly Geil.[9] This increase occurs even when the group discussion happens after people have worked on it individually and gotten it wrong. It is not simply because the small number of people who got the answer right are able to convince their groups. In fact, Moshman and Geil found that groups where no one had originally gotten the answer right were able to arrive at the correct conclusion through a collaborative reasoning process. The reason is likely that while people suffer from confirmation bias when *producing* arguments, they are better able to *evaluate* arguments, especially the arguments of others. Groups can succeed where individuals fail because they can filter through a variety of arguments:

> Individuals thinking on their own without benefitting from the input of others can assess only their own hypotheses, but in doing so they are both judge and party, or rather judge and advocate, and this is not an optimal stance for pursuing the truth.[10]

The surviving ideas in a group process are battle-tested, so to speak. An argument honed through such a process has had its weak spots identified and shored up. It has been compared with alternatives and come out on top. Its assumptions have been explored and are well understood. If done properly, the arguing process has made the argument as good as it can be given the team's current state of knowledge. Moreover, the argument's weaknesses and critical assumptions—what needs to be true—are more likely to be recognized.

How can we be sure? At one level, it is obvious that you will get a more well-rounded picture of a situation if you have all of the facts. But arguing constructively is more critically about the nature of the dialogue that happens when people with divergent perspectives are brought together. Accordingly, Massimo Garbuio, Dan Lovallo, and Oliver Sibony[11] were curious to understand whether the nature of strategic debates shaped the quality of strategic decisions. They were particularly interested in what they call "disinterested dialogue," which they define as discussions that meet the following conditions:

- "Fact-based, open and based on transparent criteria."
- "Decision makers' participation should be based on their relevant skills or experience."
- Decision makers "should be able to voice conflicting opinions" and "discuss the assumptions underlying predictions about future states of the world."

- Recognizing that "each person sees the world from his or her own biased perspective."
- "Using logic and reason to understand the world, rather than on an authority through force or tradition."

To illustrate the concept, these authors quote an interview with Honeywell CEO David Cote, who says, "What I need are people who want to come to their own conclusions and are willing to think independently, and can argue with me in the right ways so that I will internalize it and keep it objective as opposed to emotional."[12] In short, disinterested dialogue corresponds to arguing constructively.

Garbuio and his coauthors studied more than six hundred strategic decisions spanning a wide range of industries and regions with the goal of isolating the effects of robust analysis—in other words, making sure that you have your facts straight—from the effects of disinterested dialogue on the effectiveness of the strategic decision that was made. What they found is stunning: strategic decisions were substantially better when careful analysis was combined with disinterested dialogue. In fact, what we call arguing constructively was more important than just having the right facts: the effect "of disinterested dialogue is substantially larger than . . . [that] of robust analysis . . . we found that disinterested dialogue explains significantly more variance than a robust analysis."[13]

Of course, we cannot guarantee that a group will arrive at a better argument and strategic decision. Groups have myriad complicated social dynamics of their own that possibly generate a variety of peculiar pathologies. At the same time, many of the most common challenges of decision making in groups are well understood and can be managed by thoughtfully deciding on group membership and adopting a well-conceived deliberative process.

Buy-In

Strategic decisions involve allocating resources toward some activities and not others; in many cases, they involve reallocating effort from old initiatives to new ones that seem more promising or urgent. Sometimes these changes can be material and substantial. Say, for example, the marketing budget has to be cut by 15 percent to fund an investment in new equipment for manufacturing. In other cases—like Twitter's change to 280 characters—the changes may not cause any meaningful changes in budgets or headcounts. But they may be more symbolic, challenging a manager's taken-for-granted beliefs about what the company is trying to do and whether it will succeed. As a result, any strategic decision that matters can lead the managers in the organization to see themselves as potential winners or potential losers. This explains in part why people argue blue, of course: they fight hard to protect what they think is theirs, and what they think is right.

Arguing blue carries danger, as the success of many strategic initiatives will depend on the energy and engagement of managers throughout the firm—including the marketing executive who just absorbed a 15 percent budget cut. If managers walk away from a strategic decision feeling like losers, their commitment to the initiative will suffer. This is particularly true if they feel they lost unfairly. And a "technically correct" decision that has limited buy-in is unlikely to succeed. As Fran Ackermann and Colin Eden note: "It matters that managers in an organization have a driving energy and wish to manage and control their and their organization's future. Indeed, this commitment may matter more than an analytically 'correct' future they envisage."[14]

In this respect, the benefits of arguing constructively with a diverse group of stakeholders should be easy to see. The process gets people to participate and express themselves; participation leads them to feel that they had an opportunity to provide input and shape the decision, predisposing them to agree with the decision or "buy-in." Most managers understand that they do not get to call all the shots and that organizational decision making is a process of compromise. They will "take one for the team" and act against their narrow self-interest if needed. But they also think that they know something and that their perspectives are important and valuable. Doubt and opposition do not come from self-interest alone; they also arise from genuine concern about what is best. Being heard and having your ideas taken seriously and engaged with lead to higher levels of commitment, both to specific strategic decisions and to the organization as a whole. Knowing you can and will have input on important decisions enhances motivation and drive; employees feel empowered. It makes them feel that they matter and that their work is important.

Changing How People Think

Perhaps the most powerful benefit of arguing constructively comes from changing how people think. As we have noted, managers from different parts of the organization approach any given strategic decision from their own vantage point, rooted in their roles and their prior experiences. John M. Bryson, Fran Ackermann, and Colin Eden find that "People construe the same event or situation differently. Even if they literally see the same thing, they will construe different things in what ostensibly is the same situation, and construct at least partially different concept systems to account for it and to make predictions about the future."[15] A valuable function of a constructive argument is to help participants in the dialogue to see how others in the group see the situation. By respectfully engaging with one another's ideas and arguments, participants begin to see alternatives to their own way of thinking—or indeed recognize that apparent differences are only superficial—and arrive at a common way of thinking.

If people at the start of a decision-making process have different opinions and points of view, then arriving at a common understanding requires at least some of them to change their minds. Arguing constructively, and in particular focusing on elaborating causal arguments, is more likely to cause such changes than a simple exchange of viewpoints. In fact, simply providing reasons for one's viewpoint is likely to harden people's points of view and lead to a stalemate.

Consider the following psychological study. Phillip Fernbach and his colleagues asked participants in an experiment to provide their opinions on a set of controversial issues—for example, whether they were for or against imposing unilateral sanctions on Iran for its nuclear weapons program. One group was then asked to list a set of reasons why they held this view. Another group was instead instructed to provide a causal argument supporting their position:

> Your explanation should state precisely how each step causes the next step in one continuous chain from start to finish. In other words, try to tell as complete a story as you can, with no gaps.[16]

When people were asked to provide a causal argument and were then asked again about their positions, they adopted more moderate views than they had originally. Remarkably, those who were simply asked to list their reasons stuck to their views. Fernbach and colleagues attribute this to what they call an "illusion of explanatory depth," wherein we think we know more than we do, but our certainty diminishes when we are forced to spell out the causal argument.

Arriving at a common understanding or construal of the strategic issues at stake is enormously important, particularly when the task changes from decision making to execution. How people think shapes how they act. When managers arrive, through disinterested dialogue, at a common understanding of the situation and an agreed-upon argument to justify their decision, they are more likely to act coherently—i.e., in line with beliefs that motivated the group's original decision. In the absence of a common construal, on the other hand, the strategic decision will be more difficult to implement and less likely to succeed:

> If strategic management does not change the way organizational members think, and so act, strategy can only have any real impact through coercion. Without changing ways of thinking, organizational members continue to see the same problems as they always did, and they continue to solve these problems using the same beliefs as before.[17]

The (Unattractive) Alternative

Still skeptical? Consider the alternative to arguing. Although many variants are possible, the alternatives all involve some specialized or dedicated group making strategic decisions themselves in relative isolation. In large corporations, this often takes the form of a strategic planning unit or committee. Typically, the group works out the strategy and then announces it to the rest of the company. In fact, we were once astounded to hear an official in one of these units announce to a set of highly placed executives at a company: "We make the strategy and then you folks execute it. No arguments, please, just go do it."

Obviously, this message did not sit well with the executives in the room. Clearly, they thought that they knew better what was going on, what was important, and what to do about it. As a result, as so often happens, these executives effectively ignored the announced official strategy from the planning unit and tended to regard it as nonsensical rhetoric to be tolerated quietly. They didn't understand it and they didn't even bother to try to figure it out. They were not motivated and did not feel empowered by the process that produced it. Although a dedicated strategy unit does not need to be like this, we fear that all too often this is how it is. In our view, arguing constructively with a broad group of executives is preferable.

THE PRACTICE OF ARGUING CONSTRUCTIVELY

Orchestrating Constructive Debates

Arguing blue is most likely to happen when there is a lot at stake. Consider the following example of a proposed acquisition by one bank (which we will call Bank A) of another (Bank B). The (disguised) example comes from Alaric Bourgoin and his colleagues, who worked with the CEO of Bank A and witnessed the discussion within the executive team after the CEO proposed that Bank A acquire Bank B. According to Bourgoin and his colleagues, the discussion quickly turned into a fight:

> Tony, the CFO, dived straight into talking about figures, pushing forward a 30-page report he had prepared. If his calculations were correct, the merger would reap +10 points in net banking income and boost their stock price. The head of transformation, though, refused to even look at the document. With his change management experience, he knew that the merger would jeopardize the digital banking program he had to deliver by the end of the year. "How would the merger impact our program?" he demanded. "What are the concrete steps and the timeline?" Then Cynthia, the chief HR officer, threw in her two cents. She was distraught that she had not been consulted earlier on this critical issue. "I would have told you this is a big mistake," she admonished. "Bank B's corporate values are a world away from ours!" Within minutes, the conversation descended into acrimony as the three VPs went head to head. Around the table, other directors slumped resignedly in their seats. Venturing an opinion would only create more friction.[18]

As this anecdote suggests, the benefits of collaborative reasoning are often not realized. Instead, people start arguing blue. This is perhaps more common than not; it is certainly the experience of many executives we meet. Bourgoin and his coauthors agree: "Senior executives expend considerable energy in unproductive conversations that change nothing at best or cause conflict at worst."[19]

The exchange among the three executives is something of a fight, akin in some respects to the kinds we all have had with our kids or partners. Why do such fights occur? Mainly, we think, because the reasons for Tony's and Cynthia's positions are not well articulated or sufficiently self-evident to the other party. This may not be due to a lack of effort—Tony, after all, has written a 30+ page report. Both Cynthia and the head of transformation may be at fault, perhaps, for not allowing Tony to spell out his argument. On the other hand, perhaps Tony did not share the report in advance (it's 30+ pages!) or incorporate their points of view in writing it. Whatever the dynamics that led to this moment, it is clear that much is left unsaid, making each person's preferred conclusion primarily an assertion of opinion. And because much is unsaid, ironically, people feel that they are not being heard. Emotions escalate, people jump to conclusions about what the others "really mean," and suddenly the decision about whether to acquire Bank B seems to be about much more than just an acquisition.

A constructive debate is one in which all parties craft arguments that conform to the same set of ground rules. As explained in earlier chapters, we think those ground rules should be based in propositional logic. But that set of rules is more about the form of the argument than the process of arguing, which requires its own set of ground rules, however subtle and tacit they may be. How do we go about ensuring constructive debates about strategic issues?

The problem requires attention at three levels. First, at the individual level, constructive debate requires a particular set of skills and a particular mindset. Second, at the group level, constructive debate requires careful attention to the design of those formal occasions where strategic issues are discussed, with a consideration both of who should be in the room and how the meeting should proceed. Finally, ensuring healthy dialogue on a consistent basis requires attention to the culture and organizational design of the firm, such that the behaviors conducive to productive strategy arguments are celebrated and rewarded.

Before turning to questions of meeting design and organizational concerns, we briefly consider what is required at the individual level. What makes someone a good contributor to a strategy argument? The core generic skills are those emphasized in chapters 2 and 3: the ability to think creatively but in a disciplined, well-reasoned way about the challenges facing the firm. A comfort with the principles of deductive reasoning is a must, as is an understanding of the distinction between the internal (validity) and external (soundness) consistency of an argument. The required mindset involves a commitment to getting to the best possible answer, given one's current state of knowledge, and an openness to the perspectives and insights of others. The best attitude mixes the confidence in one's knowledge and ability with appropriate humility and a willingness to revisit one's own beliefs.

Designing and Running the Meeting(s)

Bourgoin and coauthors wisely advise that "strategic dialogue is a structured debate among a small group of experts, who reach a shared understanding of the situation by debating and challenging well-supported ideas."[20] The rub is that structured debates rarely occur naturally. They usually must be designed. Intentional design may be especially needed when a leader is first trying to introduce constructive arguments into the strategy process.

What to do? In our view, the following issues need to be thought about carefully before initiating a substantial strategic conversation:

- Why is the dialogue needed? What is the purpose? Why are we doing this?
- Who should participate? Who's invited? Who's involved?
- What should people's roles be? Who does what?
- Where should the exchanges take place? Where to hold the discussions?
- How should the meeting be run?

We offer some brief suggestions on each of these topics.

Purpose: Why Are We Doing This?

A strategy argument is much more likely to be constructive if the purpose of the dialogue is clear to all of the participants. In some cases, a conversation is needed because a substantial decision needs to be made—for example, whether to enter a new market—or because there is a debate between different strategic options within the firm. In other cases, strategic dialogue is required because executives within the firm need to make sense of the company's current performance, whether good or bad. Or, perhaps the potential impact of an external event, such as a sudden economic downturn in core markets, needs to be analyzed to understand what the strategic implications are, if any. Still other meetings simply consider long-run strategic opportunities.

Whatever the focus of the proposed strategic dialogue, it should be clear to participants *before* the start of the meeting. Participants should be told in advance of any background work or pre-work they need to undertake before the meeting. This means devoting time and attention in advance, including perhaps consulting with others, to specifying the desired outcome of the meeting. Clarity about the scope of the problem being addressed helps participants prepare effectively. It also reduces the degree of uncertainty about what topics or issues are appropriate to raise during the discussion and what their roles in the discussion may be.

One particularly important factor to pay attention to is the "scale" of the discussion and the potential decision to be made. Amazon CEO Jeff Bezos advocates distinguishing explicitly between major and minor decisions in the organization. Major decisions he labels as "type 1" decisions and are essentially irreversible. Major decisions about strategy fall into this category. By contrast, "type 2" decisions are not as significant and can be reversed if views change later. Bezos notes that type 1 decisions require more time and deliberation—he says that they demand a "heavy-weight" process. Type 2 decisions can be made more quickly and with less deliberation and information.

In Bezos's view, the problem in many organizations is that people confuse the two types of decisions and use the wrong process. He worries that as Amazon grows, they will get bogged down by a tendency to use the heavy-weight type 1 decision-making process for type 2 decisions. As he explains: "The end result of this is slowness, unthoughtful risk aversion, failure to experiment sufficiently, and consequently diminished invention. We'll have to figure out how to fight that tendency."[21]

In light of this insight, we think there are two possible reasons that the discussion that occurred at Bank A went off the rails so quickly. One possibility is that the topic had not been introduced in advance. As a result, the participants were caught flat-footed and unprepared for a substantive discussion. Moreover, their initial response was likely an intuitive and emotional one focused on all of the things that could go wrong. Accordingly, their responses were emotional and their arguments consisted of rationalizations of their opposition, rather than calm, rational analyses.

More fundamentally, a proposed acquisition is clearly a type 1 decision—it needs to be weighed carefully. Even if the issue had been proposed in advance, it still seems that another problem at Bank A was that the acquisition proposal needed to be considered in the context of a number of other strategic priorities. The CFO's 30+ page analysis was likely narrowly focused on whether Bank B was a good acquisition target, *given that an acquisition should be made*. Part of the reason for the conflict likely arose from the failure to conduct a discussion—or to complete the discussion—about whether the company should acquire another bank at all. Is it the right priority given the other challenges faced by the firm? The lesson from this anecdote is that designing a constructive strategic dialogue often requires thinking in advance about the appropriate *sequence* of discussions. In other words, first decide whether acquisition is an attractive course of action, and then discuss the merits of a particular acquisition target.

Who's Involved?

A critical part of preparing for an effective strategic dialogue involves determining who should participate in the discussion. Without the right people in the room, all the necessary information will not likely be surfaced, and execution may suffer due to mistaken assumptions or a lack of buy-in and engagement. As a general rule, one should include people with the relevant information and expertise as well as those responsible for the execution of the strategy. This rule means identifying people with the power to make things happen (or not) and with an interest or stake in the outcome of the discussion. In some cases these stakeholders may be outside the organization itself—for example, critical suppliers.

In deciding who should be included in the discussion, Bezos's distinction between type 1 and type 2 decisions is particularly important. Each organization should have a core strategy team charged with making and monitoring strategy. Given the stakes involved, all type 1 decisions belong to this team. Members of this team are specifically responsible for the strategy and should spend a significant amount of their time on strategic questions. At the same time, this does not mean that they should occupy staff roles: ongoing responsibility for functional areas is key to generating the insights and perspectives needed for constructive arguments. While the core strategy team's membership should be stable, teams for type 2 decisions can be assembled on a more ad hoc basis.

Teams should be constructed to include people with the right mindset and a positive orientation toward constructive argument—i.e., a willingness to focus on the internal consistency of arguments even when they disagree with some of the assumptions made by their colleagues. To the extent that individual team members lack this mindset, coaching and training should be devoted to changing their orientation.

As noted earlier, while confirmation bias makes executives prone to produce flawed arguments in support of their own perspectives, in some ways it also makes them better able to evaluate the arguments of others. Self-interest is a major advantage of ensuring participation from managers with different functional backgrounds and expertise. At the same time, this benefit will only accrue to the group if the participants are not blinded by their own expertise. One way in which this can happen entails shooting down or ridiculing the assumptions that others make about issues within one's own area of expertise. Because people with different functional backgrounds are usually not experts in your area, it is natural that they will think about your area of expertise differently than you do.

Sociological research on groups suggests that the most effective groups are those that balance cohesion and trust among members of the group with diverse knowledge. Trust can be difficult to accomplish, as people's social networks are typically most densely connected within their own functional area; cohesion and trust are highest within functions. Pay careful attention to selecting people with strong relationships and to building cohesion among group members.

Individual personalities should also be considered. Avoid, to the extent possible, chronic cynics and people who already have their minds made up about the issue at hand. Someone unwilling to engage in a productive exchange and who is not open to changing their mind, should not be included, if it can be helped. That much is obvious. Less obvious may be the crucial importance of including idea generators and connectors—people who think creatively in response to unexpected stimuli—as well as people who can build bridges between different points of view.

In general, the size of the group should reflect a balance between the need for different interests and perspectives and the practicalities of conducting a productive discussion. Tension arises, particularly for substantial decisions, because seeking representativeness can quickly lead to unwieldy groups in which the discussion becomes difficult to manage. With too many people in the room, most participants become de facto silent observers and feel disengaged from the process—thereby undermining the purpose of including them. We recommend trying to limit the size of the group to approximately six members, ideally, and do not recommend a group larger than ten.

Who Does What?

In general, constructive arguments occur when people leave their different job titles and ranks in the organizations outside the room before the start of the meeting. As at the charity music festival Live Aid, participants should know to "Check your ego at the door." Of course, this atmosphere is not entirely possible, but it is absolutely critical to strive for a situation in which people feel comfortable expressing contrarian opinions without fear of reprisal. Assembling groups of people close to each other in rank and influence makes this easier.

In our view, there should only be two formal roles in a formal strategic dialogue: the facilitator and the devil's advocate. Thought should be put into choosing the facilitator ahead of time. For large, highly consequential discussions, it may be advisable to bring in an external facilitator to run the meeting. In that case, the person initiating the discussion should invest in familiarizing the facilitator with both the issues at stake and the people involved in the discussion, their roles, and their personalities.

In most cases, the facilitator will come from among the group and will be a participant in the strategic discussion. In selecting a person for this role, pay attention to both ability and appearances. By ability we refer to the facilitator's skill at building and assessing internally consistent arguments, as well as his or her ability to manage a discussion with rigor and impartiality. Appearances matter too: the participants in the dialogue must view the facilitator as capable and impartial.

In addition to a facilitator, someone should serve as a devil's advocate—a role charged with developing and articulating the best case opposing the majority or consensus view. All participants should understand that this is a role and not a personal view. If a group meets repeatedly, the role should rotate regularly among members of the group. If the same person opposes the group all the time, then he or she will quickly be ignored by the larger group. Research shows that including a devil's advocate does produce better decisions: it induces diverse opinions into the process.

Where to Hold the Discussion?

The physical setting for a meeting plays a surprisingly influential role in shaping the dynamics of a meeting, particularly when the topics may be contentious. When contemplating big decisions or the identification of long-range opportunities, it can be very helpful to break out of the daily routine and move the discussion from the usual conference room to a new setting. Being in a new physical space helps people break out of their normal roles and habitual behaviors and can add energy to the discussion. Off-site meetings are particularly beneficial in this respect, although finding an unusual meeting space within the organization can also have a powerful impact.

The space for a strategic dialogue should have a flexible setup. A conference room where everyone sits around a big table with little room to move around does little to encourage new ways of thinking. It should be possible to move chairs around, and people should have freedom of movement. There should be lots of whiteboards or flipcharts in the room for sharing ideas. It should be possible to arrange chairs or seating in such a way that people can sit in a semicircle facing the whiteboard or flipchart. This arrangement allows everyone to see the emerging strategy map, and the fact that people are not facing each other directly "allows participants to have time to 'mentally pause' rather than feeling pressured to respond emotionally to face-to-face and verbal communication."[22]

How to Run the Meeting

The leader and facilitator of the discussion should agree on a "starter question" in advance that will kick off the meeting. Choosing a good starter question requires trying to imagine the different ways a conversation could go and how the question could be interpreted by people coming to the question with different experiences. Avoid yes or no questions, as they can quickly polarize the discussion and will not lead to a productive consideration of the underlying issues and processes. Formulate the question in such a way that everyone in the room can understand it—avoid using specialized jargon.

If materials have been distributed to be read in advance of the meeting, then it may be helpful to review briefly those materials at the start. This process checks for comprehension and any questions concerning facts that people might have, but ensures that participants in the discussion work from a common set of facts. At Amazon, the first half hour or so of each major meeting is conducted in silence as members are expected to read any relevant documents then; Amazon officials have learned that it is too easy for people to "bluff" their way through meetings without doing the pre-reading. Also, any rules or expectations—formal or informal—for discussion, exchange, and sharing should be laid out.

Once the starter question is articulated, we recommend deploying what social psychologists call the "nominal group" technique for generating ideas and answers to the question. Research shows that groups are more creative and generate more useful ideas if group members first generate ideas individually, and then subsequently share and discuss them. This process involves having participants work quietly and individually on their answers to the question, for perhaps ten to twenty minutes. People should be encouraged to generate as many ideas or answers as possible and to do as much as they can to flesh out the ideas. Only after this period of individual work does the group discussion begin.

One of the key benefits of the nominal group technique is that it surfaces heterogeneity; it allows people to generate ideas without being influenced by the ideas or opinions of others in the room. This outcome is particularly important when the participants differ in their formal and informal authority, whether due to their rank in the organization, their gender or race, or their functional background (e.g., a marketing manager in a room full of engineers).

A complementary way of surfacing heterogeneity in the room involves systematic turn-taking, particularly during the phase when everyone's ideas are being collected. Here the facilitator plays an essential role in ensuring that everyone gets heard. Pay attention to the nonverbal cues of those not speaking—postures and gestures and poses contain hints about sentiments and predispositions. Even when the discussion shifts to more of a back-and-forth debate between different parties, the facilitator should attend to those who are not participating and ask for their perspectives.

Depending on the size of the group and the diversity of ideas, it may be helpful to create temporary parallel discussion streams. This technique involves the systematic generation of alternative views and approaches to a problem or decision. The idea is to set up separate but parallel dialogues within the group, with the intent of generating viable options. Groups should be charged with working independently, perhaps on designated unique goals. At some pre-specified point, each group should be asked to report and defend its decision. A process to choose among the alternatives should be outlined.

Shaping the Organizational Context

To this point, we have suggested a number of ways to approach a specific strategic dialogue in order to ensure that a constructive argument takes place. Ideally, however, you want constructive arguments to be the default in your organization. In addition, after a productive argument, you want the organization to turn to action, so the people in the organization need to be able to move on, even if the decision made was not the one they would have preferred. Once people walk out of the room, will the plan be put into action, or will the discussion drag on? These goals require attention to broader issues of organizational design, in particular the organization's dominant values and norms—i.e., its culture.

Intel has historically exemplified this ability, particularly under its previous CEO and chairman Andy Grove. A central norm within Intel has long been that people should "Disagree and Commit." Both parts of the phrase are important. "Disagree" refers to an internal process whereby Intel executives and managers are encouraged—indeed, even expected or obliged—to weigh in vigorously on upcoming major decisions planned by the company. They are especially expected to weigh in when they disagree with what seems to be the emerging consensus about the decision. Why? Intel executives believe that any major decision should be able to withstand the most searing criticism that could be leveled against it—and they want to hear those criticisms before the decision is made rather than after the fact. Accordingly, employees are encouraged to disagree and to make sure that their voices are heard before the decision is made. Intel's strong engineering-oriented culture, with its commitment to facts and reason, helps ensure that these are constructive arguments that do not devolve (too often) into arguing blue.

That's the Disagree part. The second part, "Commit," signifies that while you could and should argue vociferously up to the point the decision is made, the arguing should stop once the decision is made. After the decision is made, Intel employees are expected to get on board with the decision, to commit themselves to making it work—no matter what their earlier positions had been in the argument leading up to the decision. So, in essence, Disagree and Commit is a set of ground rules about the process of arguing around major decisions, including expectations about appropriate behavior before and after the decision, and the timing of those behaviors. Other companies said to have adopted similar processes include, most notably, Amazon.[23]

Why does Disagree and Commit work? One of the main reasons it works at Intel is because the process is well known and accepted. A long history within the company teaches Intel employees that while the process can be tough and at times is filled with biting criticism, it is also a good process for making hard decisions, for arriving at "the truth." The belief seems to resonate well with the hard science background training of many Intel engineers, scientists, and other employees, where debate or conflict is typically subordinated to pursuit of objective answers. It also likely stems in part from the legacy of Andy Grove, who was well known for blunt talk and impatience with social niceties. Maybe it would never work at some companies; some people see it as too adversarial and conflict oriented.

But the main reason it works now (long after Grove's departure) is that Disagree and Commit is a core part of Intel's organizational culture. What makes it cultural is that it is widely shared inside Intel as an appropriate and effective way of making decisions; it is typically not questioned or evaluated but instead implemented when needed. What makes it work is its consistency—indeed reinforcement—with other norms within Intel, such as not behaving primarily on the basis of self-interest, not attempting to have previous decisions overturned, and not holding grudges against those who argued the other side in the run-up to the decision. For it to work, people at Intel must recognize that risky decisions do not always work out and that the persons supporting them should not be penalized unduly if they acted in good faith.

In other words, you need to take the company's interests to heart and to be straightforward and sincere in working with others to try collectively to make the best decisions possible. Consider the culture at Netflix. Patty McCord reports that "while our debates at Netflix often got heated, they generally didn't become mean-spirited or counterproductive, because we set a standard that they all essentially be about serving the business and our customers."[24]

Any organizational culture will need some unique and idiosyncratic features to encourage productive arguing, just to allow it to mesh smoothly with the existing culture. However, it is also clear that a culture of constructive arguing will usually need a few explicit norms, or expectations about behavior. In our minds, these include:

1. clear specification of decision rights, as well as who has the right (or obligation) to give input;
2. freedom to express your mind (especially voice different opinions) without fear of repercussion; and
3. an expectation that there will be serious and civil exchange among participants.

As with any culture, there needs to be widespread agreement and understanding of the value of these norms, as well as endorsement and support from top executives. At McKinsey, a core principle of the culture, which every new recruit learns early on, is that they have an "obligation to dissent," meaning that every employee should speak up about things they disagree with.

The leader's job is to design and maintain a culture where debate and argument occurs regularly and constructively. To that end, the norms listed here provide a good start, but they need to be adapted to any specific organization. Norms about arguing also need to be examined in conjunction with other organizational norms, to ensure that they do not stand in contradiction to each other.

Perhaps the most important thing a leader can do is to explain why debate and argument is a good rather than a bad thing. Inevitably, this explanation involves recasting debate and argument as productive rather than harmful processes, ones that lead to better decisions or an underlying truth. Along these lines, Steve Jobs purportedly would tell a story from his childhood about his neighbor asking him to collect some rocks from his yard and give them to him. Jobs did this, but then—to Jobs's great annoyance—the neighbor put the rocks in a tumbler and turned it on, creating a loud racket for hours. Eventually, the neighbor called Jobs over and showed him the rocks. When the neighbor pulled the rocks out of the tumbler, Jobs was amazed by how smooth, polished, and beautiful they were. Jobs thought of this as a

> metaphor for a team that is working really hard on something they're passionate about . . . [a] group of incredibly talented people bumping up against each other, having arguments, having fights sometimes, making some noise, and working together as they polish each other and they polish the ideas, and what comes out are these beautiful stones.[25]

Leaders need to symbolize the culture in their actions and behaviors. Members of the organization typically interpret these behaviors as more meaningful than any official proclamations about the culture. Toward that end, there may be nothing a leader can do that is more important to dispassionate arguing than to show that his or her opinion is not ego-driven. This demonstration could involve stating what he or she actually prefers or would benefit most from, and then taking a different position. It could also be openly admitting to being convinced by someone else's argument, and admitting that your prior belief was wrong. Nothing could likely do more to show people that arguing is valuable, and mistakes are not unusual, and although they should be avoided when possible, they do happen and will not be punished.

The leader should try not to dominate and should encourage the team to be actively participatory—to argue before making decisions. He or she may find it helpful to think of his or her role as the "facilitator in chief." The leader may find it useful to lay out some bold strokes or general directions for a strategic decision, but should be careful to let others know that these views may not withstand the scrutiny of the team, and that is fine. His or her directions may be about identifying a tangible target for discussion rather than setting the direction itself.

Alan Mullaly, who was the CEO at Ford during its turnaround in the early 2000s, used a participatory process that he called "business process review." The team involved all his top executives, and its charge was operational as much as strategic. But Mullaly set up a process that assembled the right people to make major decisions and generate the needed information, however bad and uncomfortable it was. He required his team to report in at a specified time every week, ideally in person. A key part of the meeting required each team member to provide information about his or her area of responsibility according to a standardized template. In this way, the team could monitor how well the company was doing in each of its markets and functions.

Mullaly inherited an organization in which people often did not speak frankly and accurately, and it took a while to get his team members to have enough trust in him and others on the team to provide accurate assessments. Initially his team members did not want to share negative information. But once they did, it became the foundation for Ford's turnaround under Mullaly's leadership: all of a sudden, he could see the problems at Ford and start to develop a strategic plan for how to fix them.[26]

Michael Arena, the ex–chief talent officer at General Motors and current vice president of talent at Amazon Web Services (AWS), advocates the creation of what he calls adaptive space. He explains: "Adaptive space can be thought of as the relational, emotional and sometimes physical space necessary for people to freely explore, exchange and debate ideas. It involves opening up connections for people. Ideas, information and resources to come together and interact."[27]

We think the creation and maintenance of adaptive space is important for strategy making and debate. That is, in addition to the formal strategy decision-making process, which might allow ample room for debate, there also needs to be casual, less formal places where people can try ideas out, push back against each other, and think and say the unthinkable. Adaptive space is a figurative term, but it can be supported by physical space like a common lunch area, the coffee room, the patio outside, etc. Wherever it is, this kind of adaptive space is critical for the strategy team to function properly, but it is also useful for others in the organization.

Adaptive space allows people to speculate, react, and absorb information central to productive strategy making. Why is this necessary? Arena explains: "Organizations are driven by the operational system that drives formality, standardization, and business performance. They are also represented by many local groups."[28] In other words, in our attempts to make organizations efficient and to protect our interests, we have eliminated the opportunities and motivation to carry on casual conversations about important organizational matters. The legendary organizational theorist James G. March referred to this as "organizational slack."[29] Theory and research show that while this kind of behavior might be regarded by some as inefficient and counterproductive in the short term, it leads to better decisions and better implementation in the long term.

CLOSING THOUGHTS

In an infamous story about arguing, Uber founder and CEO Travis Kalanick was caught on tape arguing with an Uber driver about the strategy and pricing for its black cars. The Uber black car service required drivers to invest in nice quality vehicles in return for charging a premium price. The driver was upset because he bought a good car only to see the Uber pricing for black car pricing drop dramatically. The driver explained to Kalanick, whom he recognized, that he lost $97,000 in the prior year because his costs were high but demand was low. Kalanick at first replied that the company was in the process of reducing the number of black cars. The driver agreed that was a good thing but then complained that the company was also lowering prices charged to customers. As reported by Bloomberg,[30] the conversation developed as follows:

> **Kalanick: We're not dropping the prices on Black.**
> **Driver:** But in general.

Kalanick: In general, but we have competitors. Otherwise we'd be out of business.

Driver: Competitors? You had the business model in your hands, you could have the prices you want but you choose to buy everybody a ride.

Kalanick: No, no no. You misunderstand me. We started high-end. We didn't go low-end because we wanted to. We went low-end because we had to because we'd be out of business. . . .

Driver: But people are not trusting you anymore. Do you think people will buy cars anymore? . . . I lost $97,000 because of you. I'm bankrupt because of you. You keep changing every day. You keep changing every day.

Kalanick: Hold on a second. What have I changed about Black?

Driver: You changed the whole business! You dropped the prices.

Kalanick: On Black? Bullshit.

Driver: We started with $20.

Kalanick: You know what, some people don't like to take responsibility for their own shit. They blame everything in their life on somebody else. Good luck!

The tape was made public and outrage ensued; Kalanick subsequently apologized and admitted that he needed to improve as a leader.

The Kalanick incident is worth contemplating, because it was clear that he was trying to explain the company's strategy to the driver, and it exposes a number of common missteps leaders make, if less visible and dramatic. What exactly went wrong in this argument about Uber strategy?

We point to a number of issues to reinforce points made in this chapter. First, this argument was inadvisable, because the driver was not really an appropriate person for Kalanick to be debating strategy with. Sure, Kalanick and other Uber officials should get the input and suggestions of drivers, the core of the company. But this should be done in a more systematic way, not dependent on a chance encounter with a random single driver. Kalanick was cornered, you may say, and he had to respond. Yes, he did. But a better response would have been to seek details on the driver's situation, express empathy, and let him know that he had been heard and that his input and information were valuable. Kalanick might also even have offered to have someone follow up with him later.

Second, this chance encounter was not the best time and place for a strategy argument, even if you think he should have engaged the driver. No one knew the argument was going to happen, and given their seats, the two parties could not even look each other in the eye, plus the ride was coming to an end whether the discussion was complete or not.

Third, and perhaps most importantly, Kalanick lost his patience with the driver and resorted to a personal insult at the end. He refused to accept the validity of the driver's opinion and essentially asserted that he was right and the driver was wrong, ignorant, and unwilling to accept personal responsibility. Few in Uber were likely to want to debate with Kalanick after hearing this conversation.

After reading this chapter, we hope that executives will realize the lesson to learn from Kalanick's mistake is not that arguing is perilous and to be avoided. Indeed, the goal of this chapter was to change attitudes about the value of arguing about strategy in an organization and to provide some ideas about how to develop and institutionalize an environment and process of arguing constructively. We think it is imperative that managers keep this goal in mind and adapt the specific suggestions to fit their own organizations. We recognize that not all these suggestions are ideal for every organization. We do think, however, that arguing constructively about strategy will always lead to better strategies and easier implementation, especially when coupled with the visual and logic tools we have presented in other chapters. The activities should all be used together to the greatest extent possible.

KEY TAKEAWAYS

- Executives often avoid debating their organizations' strategies, because they fear tense exchanges that quickly become personal and do not change anyone's way of thinking. Yet the absence of constructive arguments about strategy undermines a firm's performance. Avoiding arguments results in either a vacuous compromise between contradictory viewpoints or a risky gamble on the most dominant person's flawed ideas.
- Arguing constructively about strategic issues benefits executives in three ways. First, leaders make better strategic decisions: debate forces consideration of alternative points of view, and discipline drives strategy arguments

to internal coherency. Second, arguing actively increases buy-in through-out the firm, because people get to offer input and learn why decisions are made. Finally, constructive arguments change how people think about the challenges and opportunities the organization faces, and thereby improve the execution of the strategy.

- Productive argumentation requires that individuals possess the skills and mindset required to construct and assess logical arguments. It also demands careful attention to the design of meetings and other occasions where strategic issues are debated, with attention to who should be included and how the meeting is structured and run. Arguments are more likely to be viewed constructively if the organization celebrates and rewards the respectful exchange of ideas.

- The most important thing a leader can do in encouraging constructive arguments involves explaining why debate and argument enhance the organization's culture. Allowing the leader's ideas and claims to be challenged and in some cases rejected without negative consequences shows members of the organization that dissent is welcome.

PART III

Applying Strategy Arguments

CHAPTER 5

‖‖
‖‖‖‖‖‖‖‖

Arguing About
an Uncertain Future

THE BENEFITS OF ARGUING ABOUT
AN UNCERTAIN FUTURE

No business domain is riper for disruptive change in the 2020 decade than the automotive sector. Established automobile manufacturers face at least three major threats: the design shift to electric drivetrains; the growth of ride-hailing and ride-sharing services; and the anticipated emergence of autonomous vehicles.

As technology progresses and costs drop, electric vehicles (EVs) increasingly drive down a road to becoming viable mainstream consumer products. Brands like Tesla and cars like GM's Bolt EV have caught the public's imagination thanks to the performance of electric drivetrains, increased driving range, and sustainability benefits. Subsidies and regulatory requirements from governments across the globe have spurred increased EV development and suggest that progress will continue. The rapidly rising Chinese automobile market, already the bulk of sales for conventional internal combustion engine cars for companies like Daimler, BMW, and GM, figures to be the major market for EVs due to government decrees mandating EV production and sales quotas.

The emergence and explosive growth of ride-hailing services like Uber, Lyft, Cabify, and DiDi have attracted huge loyal followings. Rather than paying tens of thousands of dollars for a car that spends most of its time parked and not in use, many consumers—particularly young buyers in urban areas—rely on their smartphones to summon rides on demand. As a result, auto manufacturers face a potentially large drop in demand for personally owned cars, with the possibility that many consumers may never actually own a car in their lifetimes.

Dramatic as all these recent developments are, they pale in comparison to the sci-fi–like promise of autonomous vehicles (AVs), which have seen remarkable advances in recent years due to increased computer processing power and storage, newly developing sensor technologies, and rapidly advancing machine learning techniques. Breakthroughs in AV technology could radically change mobility, promising a futuristic world in which no individual consumer owns a car, but instead calls for a ride from a self-driving car when needed. By their nature, AVs demand a set of skills and capabilities in artificial intelligence, data processing, and semiconductor design that traditional auto companies for the most part lack. As a result, AVs have led to interest and investment from major IT companies like Google, Apple, Intel, and Nvidia as well as a host of new well-capitalized startups like Nio.

Given this background, you have to wonder whether GM CEO Mary Barra actually understated things when she proclaimed in 2016 that, for the automobile industry, "We are in the midst of seeing more change in the next five years than we've seen in the last 50 years."[1]

These developments present huge new strategic challenges for automakers. What should they do to prepare themselves for disruption? Former Ford CEO Mark Fields was dismissed in 2017, apparently in large part because the board felt that he was not adequately building the company's capabilities in future technologies and services; he was replaced by James Hackett, who was something of an automobile outsider but had a background in technology.

For the leaders of established automakers, these trends pose two kinds of uncertainty. First, it is very unclear how far and how fast each trend will develop. How quickly will the technology and charging infrastructure for electric vehicles develop? How many consumers will be happy relying solely on ride-hailing services like Lyft? When will fully autonomous vehicles be a reality?

Second, it is unclear whether and how these firms can adapt to these developments—a calculation that is made more difficult by the uncertainty about the pace and trajectory of change. How quickly can companies with heavy investments in internal combustion engine technologies make the shift to electric drivetrains and battery engineering? Which technologies and markets should they invest in? Ride-hailing? Car-sharing? EVs? AVs? How should they position themselves? Will AVs initially be viable only as EVs in ride-hailing services, as many analysts now think, or can they be sold to individual consumers? Should auto companies build or buy the new technologies and services they want?

Of course, opinions about these matters cover a wide range of options, and we have heard many a heated and passionate debate about what's viable for this or that company, and what makes the most sense. These opinions are sometimes well-reasoned and sometimes not. Obviously, to be credible, any proposed strategy in this domain needs to be based on a set of assumptions about what is likely to happen with the various technologies, how consumer preferences are going to sort out, how governments at all levels are going to respond, who the competitors are going to be, and what their strengths and weaknesses are. The uncertainty inherent in these assumptions is colossal, and there is clearly room for legitimate differences of opinion about most of them. And, of course, the implications for what might be a viable strategy for the future for an automobile company are also colossal.

Looming, potentially disruptive challenges—such as those faced by automobile companies—are the perfect occasion for the use of logical arguments in strategic decision making. To this point, we have illustrated the ways logical reasoning can be used to uncover the logic of success that accounts for a firm's performance record—to understand why the organization has (or has not) been successful. As the Southwest Airlines example suggests, such analyses can be critical to decision making, as a way of preventing decisions that inadvertently undermine the firm's logic of success. This use of logical argument is valuable, in other words, for assessing incremental changes to a firm's strategy.

But as our discussion of Pedro Earp's situation at AB InBev in chapter 1 suggested, logical reasoning skills have an additional, perhaps even more powerful potential: to help leaders chart a path through an uncertain future and tackle initiatives that might require a wholly new logic of success. This is true whether that uncertainty is brought about by the behavior of competitors—for example, when new firms, like craft brewers, enter an incumbent's market—or by fundamental shifts in technology, the regulatory environment, or the like, as in the case of automobile manufacturers. Similarly, leaders can benefit from the use of logical reasoning skills when faced with devising the best strategy for a new company initiative, as in the case of Ellie Fields and the launch of Tableau Public. In short, logical reasoning skills can benefit strategy formulation challenges as much as they do strategy identification challenges.

The primary advantage of approaching strategy formulation through the lens of argumentation is that doing so forces executives to surface and state their assumptions. Some might say that the biggest threat to effective strategy formulation is wishful thinking—wanting something to be true. We disagree. The greatest threat, in our view, is *muddled* thinking, especially when combined with wishful thinking. There is nothing wrong with wanting something to be true—in fact, that is inherent to the process of imagining new possibilities. The danger arises when we let our hopes for the future crowd out dispassionate reasoning and fail to conduct a cold, sober analysis of what has to be true for our hopes to be realized: what are we assuming will be true about the external world (the state of technology, the nature of demand, etc.)? What are we assuming that our organization will be able to do? What do we think the new entrant's strategy is?

In our view, strategy formulation should be primarily about the process of formulating a logical argument for how the firm will accomplish a desired goal. This process requires clearly articulating the goal and then spelling out a theory of how that goal will be reached. It requires moving from a gut instinct about what we *want* to be true to a rational argument that clarifies what is *required* to make it true—what needs to happen to make it true, either through developments in the external world or actions taken by the firm.

Approaching strategy formulation in this way does not guarantee that we will not be misled by our hopes and fantasies, but by surfacing the necessary conditions, it gives executives a fighting chance and a way to track progress. As the strategy unfolds, leaders equipped with a clear argument will know which developments in markets, technologies, and governments to monitor. They will know which internal capabilities need to be developed, and what changes might be needed in the organization. And, most importantly, they will be in a stronger position to know when to recalibrate or reconsider the strategy as initial assumptions turn out to be incorrect.

In this chapter and chapter 6, we describe how to use logical argumentation to consider and evaluate strategies designed to produce success in the future. We rely heavily on the ideas presented in earlier chapters but emphasize several key differences in doing this while when considering a future strategy instead of analyzing an existing strategy with an observable record of past performance. We make this conceptual move in increments. In this chapter, we mainly consider how a successful incumbent firm might analyze and react to a new competitor entering its market. Success breeds imitation, and it is imperative for the incumbent to develop an understanding of the new entrant's strategy in order to respond appropriately. We use Apple's acquisition of Beats, and its subsequent transformation into the Apple Music streaming music service, to illustrate the approach. In chapter 6 we consider how a focal firm might use an argument to formulate, develop, and implement its own new strategy, and how constructive arguments can improve the strategy formulation process.

Validity Today, Soundness Tomorrow

The contemporary automobile context is notable because it looks like a veritable perfect storm—so many major things may change in the near future, disrupting and undermining existing strategies and market positions. But similar—albeit less dramatic—developments and threats face most organizations almost continuously. The future is almost always uncertain. And for most executives and managers, strategy is mainly about the future, not the past. They want to devise a strategy to guide their firms and organizations to sustained success.

In our view, the activities we developed in this book are essential to assessing strategies proposed for an uncertain future. In fact, the basics of forward-looking strategy assessment and strategy formulation are not that different from what we have done in prior chapters. You will be glad to learn that shifting the focus to the future does not involve learning or using any additional logic, and it does not necessarily involve making the analysis any more complex.

What is different, then, about assessing and formulating a logical strategy for the future, as opposed to analyzing a prior strategy? The answer is obvious, of course: the future hasn't happened yet. Formulating a strategy for the future therefore requires more speculation, and less reliance on established facts. This act demands a specific focus on articulating in advance the conditions (premises or assumptions) *that need to be true* for the strategy to succeed. These conditions may not be true at the current moment; in fact, they often are not. Some of the conditions may come about because of intentional actions by the firm, but many of them will not; rather, they are external developments that need to occur. The value of formulating logical strategy arguments comes from surfacing the requirements for success, in being able to identify what needs to happen.

Generally speaking, our confidence in our forward-looking assumptions will vary. Consider again the disruptions faced by automakers. For some assumptions, such as the size of the driving-age population in 2035, executives in these firms can be reasonably confident that their assumptions will prove true. For others, such as how long it will take to create a cost-effective, fully autonomous vehicle, executives are likely much less certain and may disagree much more vehemently. Some might even say that it will never fully come to fruition. The important thing in formulating a strategy, however, is to not let such differences in certainty stand in the way of articulating a coherent argument.

This is where the power of making assumptions "for the sake of argument" comes in. When formulating a strategy for the future, we think it is particularly important to attend to the difference between *valid* arguments and *sound* arguments, discussed in chapter 3. Recall that a valid argument is one that is internally consistent, or without logical flaws, while a sound argument is one that is valid *and* externally consistent, i.e., each of the premises is true. If one or more premises are not true, then the argument is not sound. It is possible that an argument can be valid but not sound—the logic makes sense and generates the conclusion if we grant the premises as true.

We appreciate that, when valid and sound arguments were introduced in chapter 3, the distinction between them may have seemed abstruse or overly academic. When analyzing a prior strategy, it seems obvious that one would want a sound argument—one that is not only logically valid, but also does not rely on false assumptions. In fact, when analyzing an established performance record, we often quickly rule out unreasonable premises, because we have a pretty good grip on the true facts. In formulating new strategy, however, the distinction between validity and soundness really comes to life and plays a big role.

When setting a strategy for an organization, what we want—ultimately— is one that is based on a sound argument: the logic of success must in the end turn out to be internally and externally consistent. But when assessing a strategy for the future, we have difficulty determining whether or not all of our assumptions are true. We cannot know whether the strategy argument is sound until the future has happened. Imagine an automaker deciding to wait until cost-effective autonomous vehicles have been developed before committing to a strategy for winning in the market. By that point, it is likely too late!

If we insist on trying to establish the soundness of our argument at the outset, then we run two risks. First, we may waste countless hours debating things that ultimately can only be known in the future, until either someone gives up or collective delusion sets in. The best computer scientists in the world disagree about when artificial intelligence will be sufficiently developed to allow fully autonomous vehicles. How can the leaders of an automaker know? More importantly, why waste countless resources trying to answer the question with certainty?

A second risk is that—faced with this uncertainty—we may seek comfort in the known. But in doing so, we may end up so conservative in our assumptions that we miss out on the ability to formulate bold and creative strategies. Firms facing disruption certainly cannot afford to restrict themselves to assumptions that they are highly certain will hold in the future. Nor can entrepreneurs. Herb Kelleher's success with Southwest Airlines did not come about because he assumed that all air passengers were like those of the full-service airlines.

We recommend a simple, useful mantra in formulating and assessing strategies for the future: *validity today, soundness tomorrow.* In other words, when formulating a strategy, concentrate on the internal coherence or validity of the argument: do the conclusions follow from the premises as stated? Avoid fights about whether or not the premises are accurate predictions, and instead concentrate on whether the premises necessarily imply the conclusion. The soundness of any given strategy argument can only be discovered as you enact the strategy and monitor its progress. Because validity is a precondition for soundness and therefore success, the work put into formulating valid strategy arguments pays off in the execution stage, both by eliminating strategies that have no chance of success (because they are invalid) and by making clear what the critical assumptions are and what the consequences might be if they turn out not to be true.

If, by articulating a valid strategy, we can specify in exact terms the premises or conditions that need to be true for the strategy to succeed, then we have laid out a set of things (patterns, trends, beliefs, breakthroughs) that can be watched, monitored, and evaluated as the strategy is put in place. This monitoring involves continuously assessing the soundness of the strategy argument. If some of the assumptions begin to look as though they will turn out to be false, then we know that our strategy may be in trouble. Eventually the strategy argument needs to be both valid and sound to yield sustained strategic success.

THE PRACTICE OF ARGUING ABOUT AN UNCERTAIN FUTURE

Case Study: Apple's Acquisition of Beats Electronics

For illustration, we turn to Apple. Here we examine Apple's strategic decision to acquire Beats Electronics in 2014 and the subsequent introduction of the Apple Music streaming service in 2015. With this example, we contemplate how Apple's competitors in the streaming business—such as Spotify or the now-defunct Rdio—might have analyzed the potential strategic logic of Apple Music, and how formulating a strategy argument could lead to actionable implications.

In 2003, Steve Jobs had strong opinions about subscription-based music streaming services. In an interview with *Rolling Stone*, he said: "The subscription model of buying music is bankrupt. I think you could make available the Second Coming in a subscription model, and it might not be successful."[2] Similarly, he argued forcefully that people wanted to own, not rent, their music:

> We think subscriptions are the wrong path. One of the reasons we think this is because people bought their music for as long as we can remember. . . . They're used to buying their music, and they're used to getting a broad set of rights with it. When you own your music, it never goes away. When you own your music, you have a broad set of personal use rights— you can listen to it however you want.[3]

Jobs's comments were timed to the launch of Apple's iTunes Music Store, which pioneered the sale of digital music. Paired with the iPod, the introduction of the Music Store dramatically transformed the music industry by generating revenue from digital distribution. In 2004, digital music sales accounted for 1.5 percent of industry revenue in the United States; by 2008 that share had grown to 30.1 percent.[4] Already in early 2008, Apple was the second-largest music retailer in the United States, second only to Walmart, with more than 50 million customers.[5]

By 2013, however, revenue from downloads began to decline, and in the first half of 2014 music sales through iTunes had fallen more than 13 percent globally.[6] The seeds of this change were sown, perhaps ironically, by the smartphone revolution begun with Apple's introduction of the iPhone in 2007. Among the apps and services that emerged to take advantage of the smartphone's always-on internet connectivity were music streaming services such as Spotify, Pandora, and Rdio. The success of these streaming services challenged Jobs's key assumption that customers wanted to own their music.

Apple, the original disruptor in music just a decade earlier, was suddenly facing the potential disruption of a core part of its own business model. This was not just because streaming services like Spotify and Pandora threatened a key profit engine for Apple. They also threatened to weaken the appeal of Apple's core smartphone product. When consumers owned large libraries of music in the iTunes format, their loyalty to Apple's iOS platform over Android was higher because of the greater switching costs. Streaming services undermined this by reducing the importance of the library, and hence ultimately threatened Apple's ability to profit from smartphones.

In this context, Apple announced its acquisition of Beats Electronics for $3 billion in May 2014. In acquiring Beats, "Apple [wa]s getting a music-streaming service, high-end headphones and music-industry connections"[7] in the form of Beats's cofounders, rap star Dr. Dre and music industry veteran Jimmy Iovine. The move surprised many, and led to fevered speculation as to what Apple's strategy might be. Some speculated that the idea was to "make Apple 'cool' again by uniting Mr. Iovine's feel for 'the culture of young people' with Apple's 'many millions of young people's credit card Apple's iTunes business, and as the largest acquisition in Apple's history to that point, there is no doubt the stakes were high.

By the summer of 2015, the picture came into greater focus: despite the derision that Jobs had directed at music streaming a dozen years earlier, Apple launched a new streaming service, branded Apple Music, as the cornerstone announcement at its annual Worldwide Developer's Conference. Renowned music producer Jimmy Iovine would lead Apple's push into streaming.[10]

Making Sense of Apple's Music Streaming Strategy

But what was Apple's strategy for the streaming business? If the goal was to beat back the advance of Spotify and other streaming services, then what was the intended logic of success? This question was dramatically relevant, of course, to the established streaming services: no one takes competition from Apple lightly, and the company's entry into the streaming market posed a potentially existential threat. The leaders of established competitors like Spotify, Rdio, and Rhapsody needed to devise strategic plans for how best to respond to Apple Music. To do so, they needed insight into how Apple was planning to succeed with its streaming service. They needed to articulate a plausible strategy argument for Apple's entry into the streaming business.

In what follows, we describe an attempt to formulate a strategy argument for Apple Music that we constructed at the time of Apple's announcement in 2015. Our goal in this analysis was to put ourselves in the shoes of Apple's streaming competitors and simulate how they might have used a formalized strategy argument to guide their responses to Apple Music. We imagined that the competitors' executives might have asked themselves: What is the narrative being told within Apple that suggests this strategy will succeed? We had no inside information about Apple Music, and instead relied on publicly available information and our own understanding of the industry. Executives at rival streaming services surely had more insight into what Apple was doing than we did, thanks to their industry connections, but given the scale of the Beats acquisition and subsequent media coverage, we did have lots of information to work with.

Where did we begin? As we have discussed, when formulating a strategy argument, it is often best to start by stating the conclusion that one is trying to support with the argument. In this case, we presumed that Apple's goal was to halt the advance of Spotify and other streaming services, at least among Apple consumers. In order to do this, Apple Music needed to add subscribers more rapidly than other services—especially since those other services had a head start. So, we started with the following conclusion as the outcome that we thought Apple hoped to see:

> *Conclusion A1:* Apple Music grows its user base faster than other music streaming services.

Notice that in stating our conclusion, we did so in the *present tense.* This may seem somewhat odd at first, because (when we were formulating this argument) we were trying to develop an argument about a future outcome. As a result, some may think that the argument should be stated in the future tense or future perfect tense—this would be more accurate grammatically, and would more appropriately acknowledge the provisional nature of our argument. Nonetheless, we *strongly advise formulating strategy arguments in the present tense,* for two reasons. First, using the future tense makes the logic itself much more difficult to develop and harder to deal with, and we think little is gained. Second, when using the present tense, our conclusion becomes a concise statement of the future we want to see. In fact, one trick for formulating a strategy is to imagine that one has reached that future state, and then think of the process of formulating the argument in the same way as we approached the strategy identification for Southwest and Walmart. In other words, imagine that you will achieve the same level of success as those companies and have been asked to explain why.

Let's now return to the Apple Music argument and work backward from our conclusion. How could Apple Music grow faster than other streaming services? What needs to be true for that to happen? Here we relied on two ideas. First, we noted that a basic principle of economics and strategy is that buyers make decisions between competing products based on the consumer surplus available to them. Consumer surplus is simply the difference between the customer's willingness to pay (or perceived utility that a product generates) and its price. This means that if Apple Music wanted to grow more rapidly than other streaming services, it had to generate more consumer surplus—either by offering lower prices for the same willingness to pay or by generating greater willingness to pay the same price.

Second, we observed that Apple Music was launched at the same price point as other streaming services—neither higher nor lower (unlike Apple's iPhones, which were typically priced at a premium relative to Android phones). It thus did not seem that Apple Music was trying to increase consumer surplus by offering lower prices; instead, our intuition was that Apple's strategy was to generate growth by increasing willingness to pay relative to the other services, but allowing customers to capture that value in the form of consumer surplus.

We formalized this initial reasoning in the following simple strategy argument:

> *Premise A1:* IF a streaming service offers the same price as its rival, but generates greater willingness to pay, THEN it will grow faster than the rival.
>
> *Premise A2:* Apple Music is priced the same as other streaming services.
>
> *Premise A3:* Apple Music generates greater willingness to pay than other streaming services.
>
> *Conclusion A1:* Apple Music grows its user base faster than other music streaming services.

Together, these three premises imply our conclusion. Importantly, this argument meets the minimum criterion for a coherent argument, because it is logically valid: if one accepts each of the premises as true, then one must accept the conclusion.

Of course, some of these premises may be easier to accept as true than others! In particular, while premise A1 is an expression of basic economics, and premise A2 is an empirical claim that we could verify, it was less clear, as an empirical matter, that Apple Music would generate greater willingness to pay than other streaming services. In fact, the gist of most of the outside evaluation at the service's grand unveiling in June 2015 was an expression of mild disappointment. Critics, as well as many Apple fans, were somewhat underwhelmed. *Forbes* went so far as to declare, after four months, that Apple Music had failed. It was, in the eyes of one critic, "horribly mainstream. . . . It feels like Apple's subscription music ambition is not be a leader, but a follower. It's just not very good at being a follower, missing all the reasons why the competition can produce a better product."[11] This was not because the service was bad or showed any serious flaws or design errors; in fact, minor exceptions and preferences aside, the new service compared fairly well with Spotify in most assessments. However, many people expected more from Apple and had hoped that its streaming music service would contain one or more new, greatly enhanced features.

Perhaps the unveiled service was really all that Apple had in mind—to do as well as Spotify on the combined package of features, perhaps inching ahead on some features and falling a bit short on others. If so, executives at the rival streaming services might breathe a huge sigh of relief! After all, if premise A3 is false, then by this argument, conclusion A1 does not hold. In other words, while the argument was logically valid, it was not clear that it was sound.

Should these executives draw this conclusion? In other words, should they act on the idea that Apple—universally known for its ability to generate high levels of perceived quality and associated greater willingness to pay—for some reason is unable to deliver a superior streaming service, and that therefore Apple Music will not grow faster than them?

A wise leadership team would not jump to this conclusion, appealing as it might be. There are at least two reasons. One is that Apple surely wants Apple Music to succeed, and thus even if its initial strategy (as represented in our strategy argument) fell short, it would likely try to adjust the strategy to ensure that its $3 billion investment pays off. So even if we were to accept the claim of the most negative reviewers that Apple Music did not generate superior willingness to pay, there may be other ways by which Apple Music might grow more rapidly than its rivals.[12] To figure out what Apple was up to, executives at rival firms might therefore be wise to consider other possible valid strategy arguments.

The second possibility is that the initial reviews of Apple Music are off the mark and focus too much on the specific streaming experience and associated features. If so, we should not be too quick to conclude that Apple Music will be unable to generate higher levels of willingness to pay. In other words, perhaps the executives should not overreact to the initial lack of soundness of the strategy argument and should instead deepen the argument for the potential sources of a willingness to pay advantage. We will discuss each of these possibilities in turn.

We start by considering the alternative strategy. Recall our reasoning that Apple Music can generate rapid growth by allowing customers to capture more consumer surplus. If Apple is only able to match, but not exceed, its rivals on willingness to pay, then the alternative way to increase consumer surplus is to lower prices. This alternative low-price strategy that Apple might pursue can then be represented in the following strategy argument:

> *Premise A4:* IF a streaming service generates the same willingness to pay as its rivals, but offers lower prices, THEN it will grow faster than the rivals.
>
> *Premise A5:* Apple Music offers lower prices than other streaming services.
>
> *Premise A6:* Apple Music generates the same willingness to pay as other streaming services.
>
> *Conclusion A1:* Apple Music grows its user base faster than other music streaming services.

As with our first argument, this strategy argument is logically valid. At the time of the launch, of course, premise A5 was false—Apple Music was priced the same as its rivals. But prices are a lot easier for a company to control than the willingness to pay, as buyers are often fickle. This alternative argument suggests that executives at Spotify and elsewhere should be concerned about Apple cutting prices.

How worried should they be? To us, it seemed hard at an intuitive level to imagine Apple pursuing a low-price approach: the approach clashes with its general corporate identity. It was thus tempting to dismiss the idea out of hand. But one advantage of clearly articulating strategy arguments in this way is that it gives people with alternative points of view a starting point for building their cases. It does become incumbent on them, however, to articulate clear arguments supporting the claim that Apple will have lower prices. They might start by noting that Apple has a massive war chest, thanks to the steady stream of profits generated by the iPhone, iPad, Macintosh, etc., and can therefore afford to sustain a price war in order to gain entry into the market.[13] And perhaps they could point out that if Apple views the threat posed by Spotify and other streaming services as an existential one, it would be more willing to sustain such losses.

While we will not fully articulate this alternative argument here, it is clearly possible to develop a logically valid argument to support the claim that Apple will have lower prices (premise A5). If we are the leaders of a rival streaming service, this suggests that we should not merely dismiss the idea out of hand, even though it might be hard for us to imagine Apple pursuing a low-price approach. Great strategic moves often defy expectations; perhaps Apple has a trick up its sleeve. Taking the time to articulate a strategy argument carries a real benefit in this case, because it clarifies what we believe would have to be true for Apple to make such an unexpected move. Moreover, the alternative strategy argument becomes a foundation for constructive engagement among those on the leadership team with different perspectives.

Think of the various perspectives as forming the basis of different narratives guiding the development of the strategy arguments. Narratives attempt to offer coherent accounts of conditions or sequences of activities that might produce an outcome. So, the chief marketing officer might offer one narrative, while the chief financial officer may propose a different one altogether, both based on different assumed developments or expected conditions. As narratives, these will be more than proposed actions, they will be proposed actions based on a coherent set of expectations that lead to the outcomes. Articulation of the expectations provides the basis of a more rigorous formal strategy argument.

We now return to our original argument and try to flesh out how Apple Music might generate higher willingness to pay in ways that might not be appreciated by the reviewers considering only the specifics of the streaming service experience. The executives at leading streaming rivals such as Spotify might wish to do the same in order to identify how they can best anticipate Apple's actions and respond appropriately. After all, if the executives believe that the strategic threat is that Apple Music will generate higher willingness to pay, then they need to understand how this will happen before they can take the right counteractions.

To do so we start by expressing our original premise as an "intermediate conclusion." This is just a way of denoting that we will be using additional premises to construct an argument for why the premise should hold:

> *Intermediate Conclusion A1:* Apple Music generates greater willingness to pay than other streaming services.

In trying to think about why Apple Music might generate greater willingness to pay, there are a number of different processes that might come into play. For the sake of brevity, we focus here on exploring two. First, Apple Music might have greater appeal because Apple would be able to integrate the service into the iOS operating service and thereby create interoperability benefits. Because other streaming services do not have access to the source code for the operating system, they would not be able to follow suit.

Second, based on press coverage suggesting that music industry veterans Dr. Dre (a rapper) and Jimmy Iovine (a producer) would play an important role thanks to their connections to the industry, we thought that Apple Music might be able to rely on their personal relationships to create an advantage through exclusive deals with popular artists.

We start with our interoperability subargument to support intermediate conclusion A1:

> *Premise A7:* IF a firm controls an operating system, THEN it can create a streaming service with greater interoperability and integration with that operating system than rivals.
>
> *Premise A8:* Apple controls an operating system.
>
> *Intermediate Conclusion A2:* Apple's music streaming service possesses greater interoperability and integration with its operating system than rivals.
>
> *Premise A9:* IF a streaming service has the same basic features as rival services, AND greater interoperability and integration with the operating system than rivals, THEN users of that operating system will have greater willingness to pay for that streaming service.
>
> *Premise A10:* Apple Music has the same basic features as rival services.

Together, intermediate conclusion A2 and premises A9 and A10 imply the intermediate conclusion we are trying to support, namely that Apple Music will generate greater willingness to pay than rivals. It is a valid argument.

These executives might, in light of this argument, debate two issues. The first is whether interoperability and integration really will generate greater willingness to pay among consumers. In other words, is the theory of the world articulated in premise A9 correct? If not, then Apple's control over the operating system does not, by this reasoning, provide a competitive advantage. This might then lead executives at these firms to design and carry out studies to test this theory. The precision of the argument makes clear exactly what needs to be tested.

Assume that these tests support the claim that interoperability increases willingness to pay. Should this be a cause for despair among executives at rival streaming services? We think not, although it would clearly be preferable if interoperability did not influence customers. The question for executives at companies like Spotify would now turn to considering whether control of the operating system is the only way to deliver greater interoperability, or whether some of the benefits of control over the operating system can be accomplished in different ways. At the time Apple Music was released, it may not have been clear what these alternatives would be. But the formalization of the strategy argument makes clear what is required to overcome Apple's advantage in this domain and can therefore focus the attention and perhaps investments of the rival executives. The subsequent growth of viable third-party virtual assistants such as Amazon's Alexa and Google Assistant presented an opportunity for rival streaming services in this regard.

Next, we turn to the subargument about the benefits of having exclusive acts, as a way of capturing much of the speculation in the popular press about the roles of Dr. Dre and Jimmy Iovine after the Beats acquisition. Let's state it as though it were true:

> *Premise A11:* IF a streaming service's top employees have strong relationships with leading musical artists, THEN they will be able to sign artists to exclusive streaming deals.
>
> *Premise A12:* Dr. Dre and Jimmy Iovine are top Apple Music employees.
>
> *Premise A13:* Dr. Dre and Jimmy Iovine have strong relationships with leading musical artists.
>
> *Intermediate Conclusion A3:* Apple Music will be able to sign exclusive streaming deals with leading musical artists.

Premise A14: IF a streaming service has exclusive streaming deals
with leading musical artists, THEN customers have higher
willingness to pay for the service.

Again, intermediate conclusion A3 and premises A10 and A14 constitute
a valid argument that Apple Music will have higher willingness to pay than
other streaming services.

As with the interoperability argument, this line of reasoning highlights
two issues that executives at rival streaming services like Spotify must confront. The first and most important is the causal claim articulated in premise
A14, that exclusive deals will lead customers to have higher willingness to pay
for the service. As with the interoperability claim in premise A9, this is a test-
able claim, and executives at firms like Spotify would be well served to focus
their attention on devising convincing tests of it. The results of these tests
will determine the strategic response: if exclusive acts do not increase willingness to pay, then attention can be directed elsewhere, but if they do, then a
response may be needed.

Attention would then turn to the second issue, which is Apple's ability to
sign exclusive acts. If exclusive acts do, in fact, increase willingness to pay, then
a chief goal for rivals would be to undermine Apple's ability to sign them. One
route would be to focus on artists. The fact that Dr. Dre and Jimmy Iovine
remained at Apple after the Beats acquisition made it plausible that part of
their role was to help with signing exclusive acts. But would personal relationships be sufficient to convince the biggest artists to sign exclusive deals?
Streaming was a growing distribution medium with multiple players, and stars
could potentially be leaving a lot of money on the table by going with only
one of them. Executives at Spotify or other streaming services might therefore wish to emphasize this narrative to leading artists and their managers and
labels. Alternatively, they could denigrate and try to stigmatize the act of signing exclusive acts in the eyes of consumers.

Indeed, this is more or less how things played out with respect to exclusive acts. While Apple Music did make some exclusive deals, they were not
with the most prominent artists and generally seemed less of a differentiator.
Universal Music banned its artists from signing exclusive deals, and other
labels soon followed suit. Similarly, many fans got annoyed that they might
have to subscribe to several services simultaneously in order to hear their
favorite artists. Spotify encouraged this view and announced that it did not

like exclusivity, because "artists want as many fans as possible to hear their music, and fans want to be able to hear whatever they're excited about or interested in—exclusives get in the way of that for both sides."[14] As a result of the backlash, Apple backed off on its attempts to make exclusive deals. As Jimmy Iovine put it in May 2017: "We tried it. We'll still do some stuff with the occasional artist. [But] the labels don't seem to like it and ultimately it's their content."[15]

What we have illustrated in this section is the value of clearly articulating, in a formal way, valid strategy arguments. We have done so from the perspective of an outsider trying to understand Apple's strategy in streaming music, much as executives at rival streaming services might have done (although they would surely have had more information). We asked: What is the narrative that was likely told within Apple to justify this strategy, that envisioned it ending in strategic success? As with the role of visualization in the Southwest example, these arguments are particularly valuable to executives in defining the key questions that need to be researched and debated. Most fundamentally, will Apple pursue a low-price or a high-willingness-to-pay approach? What would we have to believe in order to think it will go in one direction rather than the other? Similarly, if we believe that it will generate higher willingness to pay, what are the mechanisms or processes through which we think it will do so? Identifying these processes allows executives to isolate the key claims about causes and effects that these arguments rely on and to use these insights to collect data to assess how plausible the arguments are and, critically, whether they demand a response. Finally, the explicit nature of the strategy argument helps clarify what an effective response might look like, as in Spotify's denigration of exclusive deals.

CLOSING THOUGHTS

Recall that we developed the strategy argument for Apple Music in 2015, soon after the launch of the service. What actually happened?

As of 2019, prices for an Apple Music subscription were similar to those of rivals, although at its launch Apple Music did not have a free tier (effectively making its average price higher, not lower, than its rivals who had a free tier). Apple Music had a somewhat larger music library, and received praise for its ability to integrate users' preexisting iTunes libraries of purchased music. It did have a larger number of exclusive acts (in part because it lacked a free tier, which some stars resisted), but as noted earlier, these were largely from lesser-known acts, and Spotify responded with exclusive live performances. Other music features, such as playlists, recommendations, and radio channels, seemed largely similar across the two services. Likewise, while Apple Music's interface and design had initially been viewed as cumbersome, it was largely viewed as comparable to Spotify's, in terms of ease of use and visual appeal, by 2019. Finally, Apple Music was integrated with Apple TV and Apple's Siri intelligent assistant, which Spotify and other music services were not. However, Spotify offered integration with Amazon's Alexa assistant service.

In many respects, then, Apple Music was similar, in terms of features and functionality, to when it launched. Yet Apple Music has done very well. According to one 2019 report, it was "the hottest service on Spotify's heels."[16] Since launching in 2015, Apple Music had acquired over 40 million monthly subscribers in 2019 and had taken the lead over Spotify (the world's largest streaming service) in the United States.

In short, Apple Music has grown spectacularly, even though it is not clear that it has a radically superior product compared with rival streaming services. In other words, Apple Music succeeded in accomplishing the goal we had ascribed to it, but not for the reasons we expected (although interoperability may have favored Apple at first, before the voice-assisted devices appeared). How did this happen?

Looking back, it is clear to us that we missed a key element of what drove Apple Music's success: the power of defaults. In other words, Apple included Apple Music on all of its devices, and included free, ninety-day trial memberships. This meant that someone buying a new iMac, iPad, or iPhone would get the software already installed. It also meant that existing users who installed the (free) update of their operating system would see their iTunes app replaced by Apple Music, with their existing libraries included. When they opened Apple Music, they would immediately be offered the free trial membership. It is not clear what the take-up rate is on these new subscriptions after the free trial ends, as Apple does not release the data. However, we suspect that a lot of Apple Music's growth can be accounted for through this channel—in other words, users who may not ever actively have considered Spotify or other streaming services, which would require them to go the App Store, download the app, and create an account.

Technically, we could consider this an example of our interoperability and integration argument, because Apple's control of the operating system is the root of the dynamic. But if we are honest with ourselves (and with you), the truth is that we simply missed this aspect of the strategy. We do not know whether the strategy was intended by Apple, or whether it was discovered. But what lessons can we draw from our failure to anticipate this aspect of the strategy?

The first lesson is the importance of having a good process when formulating a strategy, whether you are trying to understand the plans of another firm or are formulating a strategy for your own company. What is particularly important is ensuring that a diversity of perspectives and information is included. The parts of Apple Music's strategy that we missed were knowable: in particular, we were aware of the ninety-day free trial that the service offered, and it was simple background knowledge that Apple at the time had an enormous installed base across all of its different devices. In retrospect the relevance of these facts seems obvious. They should have caused us to consider the power of defaults as an alternative process for generating rapid growth. Instead, we locked in on a particular line of argument that emphasized increased willingness to pay. While we briefly considered the argument that Apple would pursue a low-price strategy, this was basically a simple variant of our original intuition, as it also focused on ways in which Apple might generate greater consumer surplus. The facts that we missed—the ninety-day free trial and the large installed base—faded from view because they did not fit neatly into this way of thinking about things. We did not appreciate the significance of either of them for our strategic formulation, likely because we did not include enough different voices in the process.

The consequences of failing to see such a key element of Apple's logic of success were trivial for us, but they would not have been for Apple's competitors in the streaming business.[17] A key matter of concern for executives in these situations is therefore to ensure that the environment for formulating strategy arguments is a constructive one, such that it generates a robust consideration of a wide range of possibilities. In our view, the starting point for creating such an environment is adopting two principles: first, that the strategies worth considering are the ones that can be expressed as logically valid arguments; and second, that any strategy argument that is logically valid deserves a fair hearing. Generating a variety of valid strategy arguments in turn requires including people who are likely to have differing views, and in particular people whose views are known to conflict. Furthermore, it requires a strong orientation among the executives participating in the process that the goal is to *learn*—to arrive at a clearer understanding of the challenges and opportunities the firm faces—and not, as is so often the case in modern companies, to win support for one's point of view at all costs. As we explained in more detail in chapter 4, executive teams that are able to adopt these principles and engage in constructive arguments will reap the benefits in the form of better strategic analysis, formulation, *and* execution.

The final lesson is that once a strategy argument has been formulated, the work has only begun. As Cynthia Montgomery notes, seeing a strategy as fixed once formulated, "misrepresents the strategist's challenge. It encourages managers to see their strategies as set in concrete and, when spotting trouble ahead, to go into defensive mode, hunkering down to protect the status quo instead of rising to meet the needs of a new reality."[18] The goal should not be viewed as defending the original strategy argument. Rather, the goal is to use the process of formulating and revising strategy arguments as a way of iteratively discovering the right solutions. Embracing the distinction between validity and soundness is critical to this process.

KEY TAKEAWAYS

- Strategy formulation should be primarily about forging a logical argument for how the firm will accomplish a desired goal. Clear strategy arguments allow leaders to confidently chart a path through an uncertain future. Developing such arguments forces executives to surface and state their assumptions about the future and helps them to identify what needs to happen for a proposed course of action to succeed.

- When formulating a strategy, concentrate on the logical validity of the argument: Do the premises necessarily imply the conclusions? Validity is a necessary, but not sufficient, condition for great strategies. Avoid debates about soundness—whether or not the assumptions about the future are accurate predictions. Novel strategies demand more speculation than analyzing an existing strategy and less reliance on established facts.

- Focusing on validity pays off by surfacing the requirements for success, by being able to identify what needs to happen for the strategy to work.

Knowing necessary future conditions allows executives to undertake appropriate actions or investments and monitor important environmental conditions. Identifying the things that have to be true for the strategy to succeed also gives executives insight into how to measure and track progress toward the goal and assess the strategic health of an initiative.

- When formulating strategy, the debate process matters. Be sure to incorporate a diversity of perspectives and information, and include people with conflicting views. Success requires a commitment to the principles of constructive argumentation, a familiarity with the tools required for constructing valid arguments, and a strong orientation toward learning from the strategy formulation process. Discover the right solutions iteratively.

CHAPTER 6

||||||||||||||||||||||||||||||||||||||||||||||||||||||||||||||||||||||||||||||||||||||||||||||||||||||||||||||||||||||||||||||||||||||||||||||||||||
||||||||||
Formulating Strategy

THE BENEFITS OF LOGIC IN STRATEGY FORMULATION

The internet has transformed and disrupted countless industries since its usage became widespread in the late 1990s. In the early 2010s, many people—and the press—thought that higher education's disruptive moment had arrived. Suddenly, online classes and educational programs seemed capable of overturning the traditional residential model of college education.

The spark, at least in terms of garnering widespread attention, came from the launch of three free online courses from Stanford University in 2011. The most visible of these was Introduction to Artificial Intelligence, cotaught by Peter Norvig, a computer scientist at Google, and Sebastian Thrun, a professor of computer science at Stanford. Surpassing even the wildest expectations, the course registered an initial enrollment of more than 160,000 students. In a university where two-thirds of courses enroll fewer than twenty students, the sheer scale of the class was simply unthinkable. Pundits announced the arrival of a new model for the delivery of higher education—the so-called massive open online course (MOOC). The new online technology was, seemingly, ready to revolutionize higher education, a sector long resistant to change.

Instructors and universities scrambled to enter the online education space and exploit the emerging opportunities, as did many entrepreneurs. Thrun left Stanford to develop and offer MOOCs through Udacity, a company he founded for that purpose in February 2012. His former colleagues in the Stanford computer science department, Andrew Ng and Daphne Koller, founded another company, Coursera, with the aim of partnering with universities to offer MOOCs. Harvard and MIT formed a partnership to establish the non-profit edX consortium; it collaborated with more than thirty universities to offer online courses and developed an open-source platform that others could use for such courses. Many other universities jumped in or at least contemplated doing so.

The defining characteristic of a MOOC—what made it potentially massive—was that enrollment did not need to be limited to students at a particular university. Anyone could sign up and take a course from Thrun, a leader in artificial intelligence who helped develop autonomous vehicles for Google. Other universities took a different tack, using online education to expand their reach beyond the constraints of geography and physical infrastructure. This approach allowed them to massively increase the size of their student bodies, or simply to enter a market without having to invest in classroom space, dormitories, or the like. Those taking this route to ramp up scale included both for-profit universities such as the University of Phoenix and Kaplan University (subsequently acquired by the nonprofit public Purdue University) as well as the nonprofit University of Southern New Hampshire, all of which historically focused on adult learners with families and jobs. By contrast, the Minerva Project, a new venture launched with $25 million in venture capital funding from Benchmark Capital (at the time the largest seed investment by the leading Silicon Valley investor), aimed to create an elite liberal arts undergraduate education to compete with Harvard, Yale, and Stanford. The idea was to draw students from around the world who were capable of performing at an elite level but for whom full-time physical access to an elite college was difficult.

The froth of activity around online higher education sparked vigorous debates about the future, both within the halls of universities and in the popular press. The lower cost structure of online education, as well as the ability of students to pick and choose the elements of a college education most important to them, changed the game in the eyes of many. Harvard Business School professor Clayton Christensen, famous for his theories of disruption in *The Innovator's Dilemma*,[1] confidently predicted that the days of traditional residential colleges were numbered. He also conjectured that "a host of struggling colleges and universities . . . will disappear or merge in the next 10 to 15 years."[2] President Barack Obama celebrated the promise of "blending teaching with online learning to help students master material and earn credits in less time" and thereby increase access to quality educations.[3]

Other analysts suggested more cautiously that online education's promise—and threat to established colleges and universities—might be limited. Many pointed to an experiment by San Jose State University, a public university in California that worked with Sebastian Thrun's Udacity to offer new online-only courses that covered basic introductory material—elementary statistics, introductory psychology, entry-level math, and the like. Unfortunately, between 56 and 76 percent of students who took the final exams in these courses failed them.[4] Reihan Salam, a blogger for Reuters, suggested that this experience showed that online education could be "good or cheap, but not both," because those students not currently gaining a college education would need online courses to be supplemented by the more labor-intensive aspects of traditional face-to-face teaching.[5] Others argued that online education could never fully substitute for a four-year residential college experience, since it would not be able to offer the same opportunities to create meaningful, long-lasting relationships with classmates or provide the rich opportunities to learn from peers, mentors, and experts in one's field that physical co-location offered.

Almost a decade after Norvig and Thrun's MOOC, the early claims about online higher education appeared overhyped—until the Covid-19 pandemic caused colleges and universities around the world to send their students home, and rapidly transition classes online. During the pandemic, *everything* was online, and the debate about the future of residential higher education was reignited. There is therefore no doubt that the internet exerts real and continuing effects on how colleges and universities approach their educational missions. It also opened new opportunities for entrepreneurs. So-called "flipped classrooms" emerged and spread rapidly throughout the higher educational landscape. This class format typically consists of "chunked-up" lectures provided in advance through online videos, while classroom time is devoted to exercises and experiential learning. Some universities, like Southern New Hampshire University and Arizona State University, developed and maintain large online-only undergraduate degree programs. Other ventures, such as Coursera and Udacity, offered so-called microcredentials designed to certify to employers that students possess certain skills based on the completion of specific courses. Harvard Business School, the Stanford Graduate School of Business, and others developed and offered online-only executive education programs with credentials and in some cases university credit.

Yet much remains in flux—the uncertain long-run impact of online technologies on higher education keeps sowing anxiety among established educational institutions. It also keeps tempting nascent entrepreneurs with the dream that they might transform the educational landscape and thereby reap riches by doing good. Accordingly, university presidents and school deans cannot afford to ignore online educational technologies; they do so at their potential peril. Sitting still with the status quo makes them look antiquated as well as unconcerned with rising costs and ineffective teaching methods. Entrepreneurs and investors risk missing out on the next big opportunity.

These leaders need to make difficult, thorny strategic decisions with long-term consequences. The decisions cause angst, because so much is unknown, and yet the pressure to respond quickly is palpable. State legislatures and boards of trustees want to know what the strategy is to "modernize" their universities. The rapidly changing markets and technologies often require significant investment in money, staff, and time to even attempt to participate.

In our view, the use of strategy arguments can go a long way toward surmounting these challenges effectively. The most obvious case for mapping strategy arguments and focusing on logical validity lies in the analysis of established strategies and the consideration of specific changes, as we saw in the case of Walmart in chapters 2 and 3. In the case of online higher education, a basic question should ask how much of a real threat online education poses to most colleges and universities? (For example, for many students, the online classes taken during the Covid-19 pandemic made clear how much they valued the residential, in-person college experience.) While the internet has radically transformed some industries, such as newspapers and retail, its impact in others has only led to incremental changes. So, perhaps a college's best response is to do nothing. A deep understanding of a university's strategic logic will help its president determine to what extent online education poses a threat. To the extent that online education invalidates key assumptions in the university's strategy argument, a response is needed.

Yet strategy is about more than playing defense or responding to shifting conditions. It is also, and perhaps most fundamentally, about imagining and pursuing new opportunities. Events like the rise of online education technologies should be viewed as singular opportunities for growth and strategic discovery. This is true whether you are an entrepreneur like Sebastian Thrun or the president of an established university. What new markets might emerge? What actions can an organization undertake to further its mission that could not be done before? Transformational external developments may undermine existing strategies, but they also present opportunities for the formulation of new strategies. Growth-oriented thinking can even potentially save cases where the established business model feels severely threatened; it can provide a sorely needed plausible alternative growth path.

Perhaps counterintuitively, the activities developed in this book can play an essential and productive role here as well. In other words, strategy argumentation plays a critical role when formulating new strategies, even (and perhaps especially) when leaders are starting with a blank canvas and trying to imagine wholly new opportunities.

The role of logical rigor in strategy formulation is not obvious to many, especially those who see strategy formulation as largely a question of vision or of imagination and creativity. Yet as we detail in this chapter, the pillar of a successful strategy formulation process is the ability to construct and assess logically coherent strategy arguments. It is an essential complement to tools like design thinking or lean start-up methods that are meant to encourage divergent thinking. Executive teams possessing strong strategy argumentation skills will develop better strategic alternatives, will be clear about the critical assumptions underlying their strategies, will know which metrics are most essential to assessing strategic progress, and will be better positioned to learn and adapt to unexpected events as the strategy is put into practice.

In this chapter, we continue the discussion of formulating strategy initiated in chapter 5. Formulating strategy for the future always involves some uncertainty. In chapter 5 we considered strategic contexts in which the strategist needs to assert what needs to be true to understand a new strategy of a competitor. What does the competitor need for its proposed strategy to succeed? We then suggested monitoring those required conditions as a way of determining whether the strategy is on track. Validity today, soundness tomorrow was our mantra. In this chapter, we continue to advocate that manner of thinking, but here we adopt the posture of the focal firm rather than competitors. How does a firm facing an uncertain future devise and test a new strategy? In addition to using our previous activities of visualization and logic, we also add some ideas about ways to open up and evaluate future possibilities even more. Whereas before we implicitly relied on individual genius or brainstorming among teams to generate and evaluate new ideas, in this chapter we offer some more specific activities and principles about how to germinate, develop, and evaluate strategies for the future. As we explain later, a key part of our analysis hinges on assessing the *consequentiality* of premises in an argument about the future.

Stages of the Strategy Formulation Process

Countless executives dread their organizations' official strategy processes. Often conducted once a year, usually as a prelude to the budgeting process, the strategy process is viewed by many as an elaborate corporate ritual with little substantive payoff—and limited impact on the firm's actual strategic priorities. Such a situation is tragic, really. The strategy process should be an opportunity for leaders in the firm to imagine a better future and get excited about it.

Yet the dread expressed by many is well founded, given how the official process often plays out. Early in the cycle, executives are pressured to come up with creative and bold new initiatives. They are told that no good ideas will be ignored, no matter how outside the box they may be. Many experienced managers approach this stage with a certain weariness, as well as wariness. That's because they know that by the end of the strategy and budget cycle, all of the exciting new ideas will likely have been dropped, and the organization will enunciate a series of incremental, safe proposals. The chief virtue of the surviving initiatives is often that few leaders in the company see any big risks associated with them, and thus do not feel threatened by them. In other cases, bolder ideas do win out. But the reasons why they win are often opaque and get attributed by many to corporate politics rather than to substantive superiority.

As a result, lots of executives feel little enthusiasm for the new strategy or any strong commitment to making it happen. Ultimately everything goes back to business as usual. And having seen this happen, executives become naturally hesitant to stick their necks out and propose anything ambitious the next time around. No wonder so few executives express confidence in their organizations' strategies.

These pathologies occur despite the fact that most leaders of well-run companies have a good intellectual understanding of how a strategy process should, in principle, be structured. They know that the decision-making process should distinguish clearly between two phases: a divergence phase and a convergence phase.[6] Research on decision making clearly supports this process for the difficult, high-stakes, and potentially irreversible decisions that strategy entails.

During the *divergence phase*, the goal is to surface as many different possibilities or options as possible. Once a full range of options has been generated, attention can turn to choosing among the different options in the *convergence phase*, when each option is considered on its own merits and the alternatives are then compared.

Generating great strategies relies heavily on the divergence stage. Creativity and vision are essential to effective strategy formulation, and executive teams need to create environments where a wide range of options will be generated and formulated. Without a wide range of options, the best opportunity will likely not be identified and pursued, and the confidence of leaders in the path ultimately chosen will be lower.

Yet, in formulating strategy, many firms fail to consider a wide range of different possibilities. Research shows that when teams only consider one option, the decision fails more than half of the time, but if they consider multiple options, the failure rate drops to under one-third. Yet decision makers only seriously consider more than one option 30 percent of the time![7]

For these reasons, much contemporary strategy advice focuses on using tools and practices—such as brainstorming techniques, design thinking, and rapid prototyping—that stimulate teams to generate and explore a wider range of strategic alternatives. These tools can be important and valuable; they often help teams break out of their incremental thinking. Similarly, incorporating the voice of the customer or the perspectives of critical suppliers can do a lot to improve the divergence phase of the strategy formulation process.

But strategy formulation should be about much more than generating wild and crazy ideas in the divergence phase. For at least two reasons, the convergence phase is the more critical. First, and most obviously, a careful and robust convergence phase will—provided that a wide range of alternatives has been generated through the divergence phase—help executives choose those strategic initiatives with the greatest promise and potential. Second, people's behavior in the divergence phase will be shaped by their anticipation of having their ideas go through the convergence phase. If selection among the different options involves an opaque and poorly understood process—or worse yet, one that typically results in fierce, ad hominem fights—then executives will hesitate to stick their necks out and provide truly divergent ideas. Instead, they will try to read which way the wind is blowing and limit their ideas to relatively uncontroversial options.

By contrast, if executives anticipate that they will be given the opportunity to present logically valid arguments—and see those arguments calmly and rationally assessed—they will be more willing to propose truly divergent options. They will also be willing to develop the rationales behind their proposed options, to turn their proposals into fuller narratives that make the expected outcomes seem like natural developments based on conditions they have assumed will prevail. Evaluating competing narratives and the arguments based on them is far easier and more rational than simply choosing among proposed courses of action.

The benefits of a widely shared, logical reasoning framework in the strategy formulation process, and of an ability to argue constructively, come from creating more structure and confidence in the convergence phase of decision making. In other words, the belief that the convergence phase might be characterized by calm, dispassionate reasoning can free people to be more creative in generating strategic options.

We find it useful to break the strategy formulation process into four distinct phases, summarized in figure 6.1. The first of these phases is the divergence phase, when the objectives for the executive team are to start with a blank piece of paper, cast a wide net, and generate as many different ideas for strategic initiatives as possible.[8] (In figure 6.1, we represent these different ideas with circles and letters.) We first discussed ways to do this in a strategic setting in chapter 2.

We envision the convergence phase not as a single stage, but as three distinct substages of sorts, each of which poses distinct challenges for leadership teams. Note that while we discuss these substages in a linear, sequential way, the actual convergence process generally involves iterating or cycling between the different substages as teams make initial decisions, explore them further, and then revisit earlier decisions as they learn more.

The first substage of the convergence phase, which we call "filter and develop" follows immediately after the executive team has cast a wide net for ideas. The purpose of this stage is to choose some of the proposed ideas for further development and initial exploration. The reality is that many of the ideas that come out of, say, a brainstorming process will be underdeveloped, fragmentary, and even ill-conceived. Some of the ideas will be, quite frankly, bad ideas; that's the cost incurred when searching for good ideas. Moreover, even if all of the ideas are good, the leadership team's time and resources are limited. The ideas need to be prioritized.

Yet filtering is a delicate matter. Given that many ideas coming out of the divergence phase are likely to be incompletely or vaguely articulated, the filtering stage is often one when intuitions and biases can play a large role. This is problematic in its own right, as it may lead teams to reject promising ideas just because they don't feel right or to pursue flawed suggestions because they

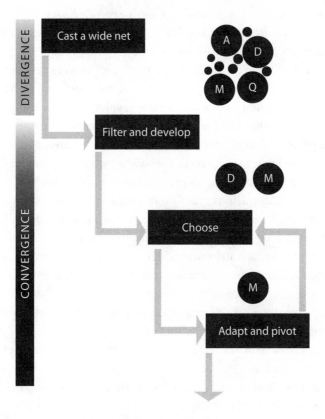

6.1 The phases of strategy formulation

fit with someone's agenda. Moreover, seemingly arbitrary decisions at the filtering stage have downstream consequences for the strategy process. If the prioritization (or rejection) of ideas is not viewed as legitimate, then people are more likely to disengage from the strategy process. We call this dilemma the *filtering challenge*. This challenge is, as we elaborate later, best addressed by focusing on the core distinction between validity and soundness introduced in chapter 3. Filtering, in short, can be best done by insisting that all proposals take the form of a valid strategy argument.

Once a small handful of potential strategic initiatives has been identified (perhaps two to four), the next substage of the convergence phase involves making an initial choice between the remaining alternatives. This means settling on the proposal that will receive first priority for implementation.

This choice is not necessarily final and may be revisited after implementation has begun, as we discuss later. But this stage is critical, because it involves fundamental resource allocation decisions.

Choosing is made more difficult when successful divergence and filtering phases generate strategic options that are quite different from one another. In fact, if executives find themselves making apples-to-apples comparisons—deciding whether they like Fuji apples or Red Delicious—they have failed at the divergence or filtering stages, or both. Ideally, executives at this stage are not comparing apples to apples, or even different kinds of fruit, but instead wrestling with choices between apples, bicycles, and bottles of wine.

This kind of comparison creates problems for many leadership teams who are accustomed to using standard decision-making tools, like those based on modern decision theory. Such tools involve generating a single metric for comparing different alternatives; they rely on being able to compare the different options according to a common set of variables. For example, strategists are often encouraged to calculate the financial net present value (NPV) of each option by projecting cash flows and expenses over time, applying appropriate discount factors, and making different assumptions about the cost of capital. Whatever the tool, this approach is problematic because a lot of implicit assumptions typically go into assigning values to the different variables. And, implicit assumptions are the enemy of good strategic decision making!

A more fundamental challenge is that what makes choosing between truly different strategic options difficult is that they are often difficult to reconcile with one another. Even though they might ultimately each be reduced to a single, perhaps monetary metric, an enormous amount of important information is lost in the process—information about what would have to be true about customer preferences, the firm's resources and capabilities, what needs to be true about the state of the world, etc. These factors will all go into projections of what revenues and costs look like, but they also have an independent importance: being explicit about these factors forces the leadership team to confront whether *they* can deliver on the proposed strategy, as opposed to opining on what the revenue would be if *someone* could.

What is needed, then, is a process for assessing and comparing different strategic options that preserves the unique features of the different options while still allowing the leadership team to be clear about the strategic bets they are being asked to make in each case. We call this the *choice challenge*. As we discuss later, overcoming the choice challenge requires focusing on what we call the consequentiality of different premises in strategy arguments; in other words, the extent to which premises are simultaneously critical to the structure of an argument and highly uncertain. Consequential premises reveal the core bets associated with a specific strategic alternative. Comparing the most consequential premises for different strategy arguments does not tell leadership which bet to make, but does clarify what the bets are.

Once a preferred strategic alternative has been identified, the last substage of the convergence phase involves implementing the chosen strategy. It is tempting to view the strategy formulation stage as completed once the executive team has made a choice between the different alternatives on the table. Yet the initial strategy argument constitutes only the beginning. Any new strategy is a provisional theory, consisting of assumptions about what it will take to succeed and what will happen in the future. No executive team trying something novel can perfectly predict what will happen.

For the higher education context, the questions may come in many forms. Will students learn as well through online instruction? Will faculty members be capable of teaching effectively if they never see their students face to face? Will parents be satisfied with their children's education if the children attend a virtual college, or is moving away from home and living on campus an essential part of the value proposition? This type of uncertainty is inherent to formulating new strategies, because strategy formulation is about the future. If there is not much uncertainty associated with a new strategy, you can bet that the strategy is not very novel.

Here's the hard reality. As they put a new strategy into action, an executive team needs to monitor its progress closely, adapt to unforeseen circumstances and new discoveries; if necessary, they need to abandon the initial strategy and return to other strategic alternatives that were under consideration in the choice phase. We refer to this as "Adapt or pivot" in figure 6.1 in order to emphasize the iterative nature of this stage of the strategy formulation process.

This stage has a strong inductive element to it, wherein the executive team needs to be open to discovery as its initial assumptions are proven wrong and to make sense of the feedback received from the market. Most importantly, leaders need a means of assessing the health of the chosen course of action. This is more difficult in the case of a new strategy than an established strategy, for which the executive team often has a set of well-established financial and operational metrics that will reliably measure strategy performance. But part of formulating a new strategy is discovering what the right metrics are for the new course of action and using those metrics to make the right call as to whether to adapt or pivot. We call this the *learning challenge*. Overcoming the learning challenge is greatly aided by the use of clearly formulated, valid strategy arguments. These arguments become a lens through which leaders can identify which of their original premises turned out to be true, and which turned out to be false. Evaluation of the premises become the basis for revising the strategy argument.

The three challenges of the convergence phase are core obstacles to successful and productive strategy formulation. If leaders cannot effectively manage the three challenges (filtering, choice, and learning), the likelihood of discovering a compelling strategy is far less likely and becomes more a product of luck—stumbling into something that works—than deliberate action. While each of the three challenges we have identified has unique difficulties, strategy argumentation skills are critical to surmounting each challenge. A leadership team with a strong commitment to the principles of logical validity and to arguing constructively will be strongly positioned to overcome these challenges.

THE PRACTICE OF LOGIC IN STRATEGY FORMULATION

Filter and Develop: Focus on Validity

Imagine you have just been appointed to the role of chief strategy officer at a major multinational corporation. While you have never worked for this particular firm before, it has long been your dream to lead strategic initiatives in such a large, market-leading company. At the same time, you can see how you can make a difference for this company and strengthen your own career prospects: while the company's long-standing core offerings remain strong and viable in the market, its recent attempts to deliver sustained growth have come up short and include a variety of attempts that seem, to an outsider, somewhat hit or miss. Investors are applying pressure, and recent initiatives show uneven performance. That is why, you suspect, that the company has turned to an outsider to lead the strategy office.

Upon starting your job, you eagerly await your first meeting with the CEO and the board, where the main topic will be the company's strategic priorities. As the meeting starts, you are handed a document with the company's list of strategic priorities. There are thirty-six priorities on the list! Suddenly, the magnitude of the challenge facing you becomes clear. Most people would say that such a long list of priorities demonstrates, in fact, a *lack* of strategic priorities. Indeed, you see that the proposed initiatives on the list—ranging from new product categories, to operational improvements, to new distribution channels and marketing messages—are all over the place. What do you do?

This scenario is not hypothetical; it reflects the (disguised) firsthand experience of an executive at a *Fortune 500* company who shared his story with us. This executive suddenly found himself in a very delicate and difficult situation. It seemed likely that each of the thirty-six "priorities" had one or more advocates in the senior leadership or the board, and that the list itself resulted from a series of political compromises among powerful actors in the company. As a newcomer to the firm, this executive had little sense of who favored which proposal or of the structure of the political coalitions in the company. One false step in the minefield, and what once seemed like a dream job could quickly come to an abrupt end.

This scenario may seem extreme, but the basic structure of the challenge faced by this executive is endemic to the strategy formulation process—even a healthy one. As noted earlier, the strategy process is only as good as the quality of its divergence phase, and in particular the ability of this phase to generate a wide range of creative options. Call it human nature: people grow attached to their own ideas. Such attachment may reflect a sincere belief that they hold the best idea for the firm or it may reflect a set of self-interested concerns. People understand that not all ideas can be pursued, but they still want to see their ideas treated fairly.

How to overcome the filtering challenge? Part of the answer—although certainly not the complete answer—is to use a logical validity criterion as the main filter. All successful long-term strategies are based on sound strategy arguments, valid arguments whose premises have proven true. Validity is a necessary—but not sufficient—condition for a strategy to be successful. The implications for the filter and develop stage of the strategy formulation process are twofold:

- First, to receive further consideration, all strategic proposals need to be presented in the form of a logically valid argument. Stated more strongly, strategic proposals that cannot be articulated as valid arguments do not deserve further consideration and should be filtered out. When first articulated, ideas need to be in the form of complete, valid arguments. Rarely do novel ideas emerge in this way. But someone who wants his or her idea to be given serious consideration should take the next step and translate it into a valid argument that clearly identifies what needs to be true for the proposal to succeed.

■ Second, *all* proposals that meet the logical validity standard must be given full consideration. In other words, the advocates of a proposal must be heard and taken seriously if they can articulate a logically valid argument. Ideas cannot be rejected simply because they seem implausible or rest on assumptions that strike others as fanciful or false at first glance.

In our view, starting the convergence phase of the strategy formulation process by insisting on logically valid arguments carries a number of benefits.

One benefit might best be called "self-filtering," a process by which the people who initially generated an idea come to their own realization that their initial proposal rested on a flawed—i.e., logically invalid—argument. Most often, this occurs when people's initial ideas depend on implicit or unstated assumptions, as in the iPhone example discussed in chapter 3. In the process of reformulating their initial idea into a valid argument, people may realize that their casual argument relied on common logical fallacies such as affirming the consequent or denying the antecedent. The discipline of formalization may make them realize that their initial conclusion requires accepting a theoretical or empirical premise that, on closer inspection, they do not want to defend. In short, once an invalid argument has been made valid, its original proponents may conclude that its assumptions seem too strong.[9] Self-filtering means that those with more authority and influence do not need to reject the ideas. This benefit is powerful, as most people would rather dismiss their own ideas than have them dismissed by others.

A second benefit lies in the objectivity of the logical validity screen, which protects leaders from allowing their own biases and preferences to influence the filtering process. Just as an executive does not get to decide arbitrarily whether two plus two equals four, he or she does not get to decide arbitrarily whether a conclusion follows necessarily from the premises as stated. Rather, the rules of deductive logic prevail. Moreover, when those rules are widely known and accepted in an organization, there is accountability built into a filtering process that relies on logical validity; others can use the same rules to "check the work" of the leaders performing the filtering. As a consequence, leaders cannot reject a proposal at this stage simply because they do not like it or their gut instinct says it will not work. Accordingly, they are less likely to mistakenly reject ideas that later turn out to be good because they could not see their potential initially. Similarly, leaders will have more difficulty advancing logically invalid proposals simply because they feel right or are preferred for political or other reasons. At the very least, advocates of such proposals will need to state their assumptions—as unrealistic as they may be.

A third and related benefit of using logical validity to filter proposals coming out of the divergence phase lies in the legitimacy of validity as a criterion. Consider, as an analogy, the role of math in executive decision making. Organizations make countless organizational decisions based on mathematical calculations, whether they involve simple arithmetic or complex formulas. Rarely do people argue with the math, and never successfully. They might disagree about the numbers entered in the different cells of a spreadsheet, or whether the right formula was used, but they do not argue with multiplication and division. Logical validity has the same character: whether a formal argument is judged valid depends on a set of widely accepted, universally shared rules (i.e., the rules of first-order logic). As a consequence, decisions at the filtering stage based on logical validity are not only less likely *to be* arbitrary but are also less likely *to be seen as* arbitrary.

This legitimacy is important, because it sets the tone for the rest of the convergence process and for the next round of strategy formulation. If proposals survive the filtering stage for apparently arbitrary reasons, then engagement with the rest of the strategy formulation process will suffer. People become cynical and focus on figuring out what the boss wants rather than what might be the best option for the firm. Moreover, this cynicism may carry over to the next strategy formulation cycle. If your ideas were not treated fairly the first time around, why take the risk of offering imaginative proposals the next time? Instead, people will focus on trying to guess what the boss will like. By contrast, team members who expect their ideas to be given a fair hearing as long as they are logically valid are, in our view, more likely to offer creative and risky ideas.

Focusing on logical validity helped the executive we met who was faced with thirty-six different strategic priorities. By constructing a logically valid argument for each of them, he was able to start a constructive dialogue with the various stakeholders and proponents of the different proposals. This dialogue focused on what had to be true for each proposal in order for it to succeed, because the process of constructing valid arguments surfaced these assumptions. As so often happens, many of these assumptions had previously been unstated or implicit premises. Once they were made explicit, the nature of the dialogue changed and a fair amount of self-filtering took place as advocates of specific priorities realized what it would actually take for their proposals to succeed. Furthermore, the objectivity of the focus on valid arguments meant that the newly hired executive avoided many of the political landmines and became viewed as a fair broker.

In summary, the filtering stage should center on asking, for each of the articulated strategic alternatives, the basic question, "What has to be true for it to succeed?" As A. G. Lafley and Roger Martin put it in *Playing to Win*,

> [At this stage] there is absolutely no interest in opinions as to whether the conditions pertaining to a given possibility are true. In fact, expressing such opinions is counter-productive. The only interest is in ferreting out what would have to be true for every member of the group to feel intellectually and emotionally committed to the possibility under consideration.[10]

The visualization and formalization tools we have used in this book are particularly important for addressing the filtering challenge and for getting the rest of the convergence phase of the strategy formulation process off to a good start. We wish to emphasize two things about this stage. First, this step may take significant analysis—and associated time—for the arguments to gel in a way that the strategy-making team believes makes each of them fully valid. In our observation, at this stage executives too often become impatient. As a result, they then reach and announce a decision (pro or con) about an argument or option without rigorously vetting its validity. Second, at this stage leaders must resist the temptation to debate how reasonable the assumptions in a given argument appear: reasonableness concerns the soundness of the argument, not its validity. This advice is particularly important when one executive assesses an argument proposed by another, and even more so when the evaluator holds more authority than the proposer. A failure to accept the proposer's premises "for the sake of argument" can all too easily be seen as an arbitrary exercise of power.

Choose: What Has to Be True

Emphasizing validity in the filtering stage sets the stage for a productive choice stage, for two reasons. First, it ensures that diverse but logically consistent alternatives enter into the choice stage. These alternatives might have varying degrees of plausibility (i.e., their assumptions might be more or less believable) and appeal, but they meet the minimum criterion for being a good strategy by being logically coherent. Confronting multiple viable strategic options is critical to getting everyone's buy-in. As Lafley and Martin emphasize, "Until a real choice (e.g., should the company go in this direction or that one?) is articulated, team members can't understand cognitively or feel emotionally the consequences of the different ways to resolve the issue."[11] Second, the emphasis on validity ensures that the leadership team has identified, to the best of their ability, what needs to be true for each strategy argument to hold. While these necessary premises may differ radically across different strategic alternatives, clearly identifying what needs to be true sets the table for making better strategic choices. It helps the leadership team be clear with themselves about which bets they are making and to consider how the bets differ across the different strategic alternatives.

Ultimately, these strategic choices will reflect a mix of the leadership team's risk tolerance, beliefs about the future, and strategic vision. Strategy is unavoidably about making bets on an uncertain future. But the choice stage should not just be about what feels correct or comfortable to the leadership team at a particular moment. Instead, choices about where to invest time and resources should be based on an informed prioritization among the options.

This prioritization is not simply a matter of comparing what has to be true across the different options and deciding which premises or bets the leadership team feels most comfortable endorsing. In fact, premises play different roles in different arguments, depending on the structure of the argument.

To see this, recall from chapter 3 the difference between AND and OR connectors in argument structures. Imagine that the filtering stage of a strategy formulation process results in two different strategic options. Also imagine that the arguments for each option are very similar; the arguments contain the same number of premises (let say, three: premise A, premise B, and premise C), and they seem equally likely to be sound in the future; they also generate conclusions that seem of roughly equal future value. The only difference is that in the first argument, two of the premises (B and C) are connected by an

AND operator, and in the second, the two premises (B and C) are connected by an OR operator. In chapter 3 we noted that a square bracket in a diagram indicates an AND relationship, meaning that both premises connected by the square bracket need to be true for the conclusion to hold. By contrast, if the premises both imply the conclusion, but do so independently of each other, they are joined by an OR connector. We represented this argument structure with separate arrows leading directly to the conclusion and joining it at the exact same point.

Assume now that premise A is the same in both arguments, and premises B and C seem equally likely to be true. Which strategic option would we prefer, based only on the difference in argument structure emanating from the operators?

The option with premises B and C connected only by OR connectors would be preferred to the option with the same premises connected by AND connectors. Why? Because in this option, there are two simple independent routes (any single premise) to securing the conclusion, while in the other option there is only one relatively difficult route (both premises simultaneously). This is true even though we have assumed that all of the premises are equally likely to be true. While this exact dilemma may be unlikely to actually occur, it does illustrate how overall argument structure comes into play and should be considered in conjunction with the next consideration, *premise consequentiality*.

Perhaps the natural tendency in comparing different strategic alternatives involves assessing how much we believe in their assumptions about what has to be true. But the difference between these two argument structures illustrates that the *structure* of arguments and the roles of different premises in them should also inform how we prioritize among the alternatives. One strategic proposal may make a number of very reasonable assumptions, each of which we might think is quite likely to be true. This may create the impression that the strategy is very likely to succeed. But if all of those reasonable assumptions are joined through AND connectors—in other words, if they all have to be true simultaneously—the likelihood of success may actually be quite low.[12] By contrast, another proposal may be more likely to succeed, even if the premises, taken individually, are less likely to occur, if the argument only requires that one of the assumptions needs to hold.

This hypothetical example points to the importance of identifying, for each strategic alternative, the most *consequential* premises in the strategy argument. The consequential premises of a strategy argument encode the most important bets of the proposed strategy. These premises serve as the hinge upon which the strategic decision turns. If leaders are uncomfortable with these premises, then they should not pursue the strategic option.

What makes a premise in a strategy argument more or less consequential? We see two main factors:

1. the extent to which the argument's conclusion depends uniquely on that premise, or how *critical* the premise is; and
2. the leadership team's *uncertainty* about whether the premise's assumption will hold true in the future.

We will consider each of these in more detail. Before doing so, it is important to note that assessing how consequential a premise is along these two dimensions is inherently difficult. Leadership teams must embrace the fact that they have limited knowledge about both the correct structure of the strategy argument and the truth value of the premises. The process of working through the different strategic options should be viewed as a learning process. A premise initially viewed as critical to the strategy argument may, upon discussion and reflection, come to be understood as less critical, because other premises may also support the conclusion. Similarly, an assumption that is at first considered outlandishly uncertain may, following further research and investigation, be seen as more plausible than first thought.

In short, the choice stage of the strategy formulation process is iterative, not a one-shot decision; it should be focused initially on prioritizing the different alternatives. In this respect, the choice phase and the adapt and pivot phase of the strategy formulation process (which we discuss next) are highly interdependent. Leaders are well served to first make an initial prioritization among the strategic alternatives, select a limited number to explore further, and then use what is learned to further inform the ultimate choice of which strategy to pursue.

Consider now how criticality and uncertainty shape a premise's consequentiality. We turn first to criticality. Once the strategy argument has been clearly laid out, its premises can each be assessed in terms of how critical it is within the structure of the argument, or the extent to which the conclusion depends uniquely on the truth of the premise. Generally, premises will vary in the extent to which they are critical to the conclusion. A highly critical premise is one where the conclusion will not hold if the premise is false. This is most obvious when a conclusion depends on a single premise, even if such a scenario is unlikely in a real-world strategy argument. At the other extreme, premises are not critical if they are "redundant" with a host of other premises, meaning that the same conclusion can be reached by ignoring this premise and using another one.

One simple way to see the difference between a critical and a redundant premise is to consider yet again the difference between AND and OR connectors in figures 6.2 and 6.3, respectively. When the premises are connected by AND, all premises need to be true for the conclusion to hold, and each of those premises becomes more critical. As we add more independent reasons for why the conclusion should hold, i.e., premises connected by OR statements, then the criticality of any given premise or assumption will decline.

The existence of AND statements does not automatically make premises highly critical, however; it depends on where they fall in the structure of the overall argument. This can be seen in figure 6.2.

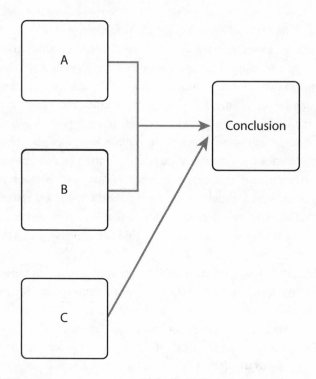

6.2 Argument structure with both AND and OR connectors

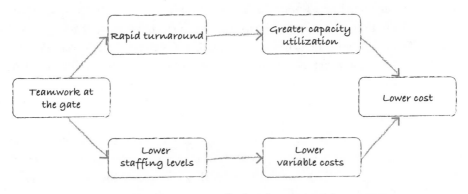

6.3 Strategy map for Southwest

Here, the presence of an independent cause of the conclusion (C) reduces the criticality of premises A and B. Premise A in figure 6.2 is still more critical than premise A in an argument with all OR connectors, but it is less critical than premise A in the all AND connectors argument.[13]

Another form of criticality arises when a single premise factors into multiple branches of a strategy argument, such that if the premise is false, then all those multiple subarguments are false. An example of this form of criticality can be found in our original strategy map for Southwest Airlines in chapter 2 and reproduced in figure 6.3.

If we were to formalize this argument, using the principles in chapter 3, then we would have two subarguments: one supporting an intermediate conclusion that Southwest has greater capacity utilization, and one supporting an intermediate conclusion that Southwest has lower variable costs. Both of these subarguments would contain a premise relating to teamwork at the gate. So, teamwork at the gate is a critical premise because, per the argument, in the absence of teamwork, Southwest would not be able to deliver rapid turnarounds and lower staffing levels, which in turn contribute to Southwest's cost advantage.[14]

Identifying critical premises is the first step toward isolating the most consequential assumptions in a strategy argument, but it is not sufficient. After all, an argument's conclusion may hinge on a particular assumption, but there may be little doubt that the premise will hold. Our confidence in whether a given premise will hold is the second dimension relevant to assessing how consequential an assumption is. For example, we might be very confident that in five years there will be demand for travel between New York and San Francisco, less confident in how greenhouse gas regulations will affect an airline's cost structure, and highly skeptical that teleporting will be a viable option. Similarly, if you are starting a delivered meal subscription business like HelloFresh or Blue Apron, there is little doubt, in the age of cloud computing providers like Amazon Web Services or Microsoft Azure, that you can launch a website that can take orders, manage inventory, and the like. What is far more uncertain is whether potential customers have sufficiently high willingness to pay for the service, or whether they instead will subscribe for a short period and then quit.

We are now in a position to identify the most consequential premises in a strategy argument by simply considering a premise along the two dimensions—criticality and uncertainty—simultaneously. Figure 6.4 illustrates the different possible combinations that might arise.

The most consequential premises in a strategy argument are those that fall in the upper right-hand quadrant of this figure: these are assumptions that are simultaneously highly uncertain and highly critical within the structure of the argument. In essence, the premises that fall in this quadrant constitute the

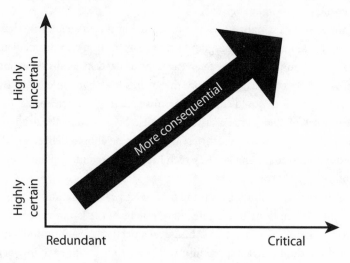

6.4 Consequentiality of premises

core bets that the firm would be making in pursuing a given strategic option: these are the risky assumptions that will make or break the success of the strategy. These most consequential assumptions—the big bets—are the ones that should be debated and researched most carefully.

Identifying the most consequential premises for each strategic alternative under consideration gives leadership teams different ways of comparing what may otherwise be incommensurable alternatives. One basis for comparison involves simply counting the number of highly consequential premises associated with each alternative's strategy argument. Other things being equal, strategic alternatives with fewer highly consequential premises will be preferable, because a strategy argument that relies on multiple highly consequential premises has multiple points of potential failure. This assessment assumes, of course, that the expected payoffs associated with each alternative are the same. A second basis for comparison is the leadership team's assessment of the relative consequentiality of the most consequential premises for each alternative. For example, two strategic alternatives may be similar in the criticality of their most consequential premises (i.e., their placement on the horizontal axis in figure 6.4) but differ in the relative uncertainty of those premises (i.e., their placement on the vertical axis). If the expected value of the two alternatives is the same, then the alternative with lower uncertainty associated will be preferable ex ante. The same reasoning applies to cases in which the premises for two arguments have similar levels of uncertainty but differ in their criticality.

Unfortunately, these rules are not hard and fast, but rather are rules of thumb. In many situations, identifying the most consequential premises will not lead to a clear rank-ordering of the alternatives based on the number or consequentiality of their premises. Leaders will still need to make choices among strategic options that rely on very different assumptions about the future but seem equally consequential. Yet identifying the most consequential premises in each strategy argument still advances the debate and improves the decision-making process. By knowing each option's most consequential premises, leaders can isolate and clarify the precise nature of the different bets that each strategic option entails. Having identified these highly consequential premises, the leadership team is in a better position to discuss, debate, and decide between the different strategic options identified in the divergence phase.

The leadership team's intuition, risk tolerance, beliefs, and values enter into the picture here, by shaping the bets they are willing and motivated to place. Logical analysis will not tell leaders which strategy to pursue. In fact, no strategy formulation process can guarantee that the right strategies will be chosen; the future is too uncertain for that to be possible. But the analysis of consequentiality will improve the odds of making a good bet, and one that the leadership team as a whole will embrace. It does so by laying bare, for everyone on the leadership team to see, what exactly those bets entail or what the team is assuming by pursuing one option and not the other. This is an important accomplishment.

Learn: Adapt or Pivot

Maintaining a clear distinction between the validity and the soundness of strategy arguments is an essential part of successful strategy formulation. Throughout the filtering and choice stages of the strategy formulation process outlined in figure 6.1, any considerations of the soundness of the strategy arguments should be avoided to the greatest extent possible. While the choice stage involves some assessment of the leadership team's subjective sense of confidence in different premises, there should ideally be no testing of the truth value of the assumptions. Wild and crazy ideas are good!

During the adapt and pivot stage, leadership teams begin to assess the soundness of their strategy arguments. Here's their learning challenge: trying to get a better sense of whether or not the premises underlying the strategy arguments will turn out to be true and adjusting the strategy accordingly. If the assumptions underlying a valid strategy argument are supported, then a viable logic of success has been identified. If not, then either the strategy needs to be adapted to reflect the reality that has been discovered, or it should be abandoned, and the firm should pivot to an alternative strategy.

In our view, the adapt and pivot stage can be seen as playing out over different timescales. On the one hand, a version of this learning stage plays out relatively rapidly, particularly when leaders are debating a number of different strategic alternatives that could be pursued. On the other hand, testing the critical assumptions of a strategy argument is also essential once a strategy has been chosen and has proven successful. Here we aim to ensure that critical assumptions that were once true do not suddenly become false, for example, because of regulatory changes, competitor actions, or technological advances that undermine a core part of a firm's strategy. We consider each of these in turn.

Consider first the role of testing the soundness of premises when debating between strategic alternatives. In this case, the leadership team should generally be rapidly iterating between the choice stage and the adapt and pivot stage. The learning goal: to gain more insight into the relative likelihood of success of the different alternatives that are being considered, by assessing the likely soundness of their most consequential premises. In other words, the team should be moving from a purely subjective sense of the uncertainty associated with the most critical premises in each argument to a judgment grounded in facts and data. As new data are gathered, some alternatives may be eliminated and the team's prioritization among the remaining alternatives may change.

In other words, the leadership team should take action to resolve the uncertainties surrounding different assumptions during the adapt and pivot stage; this is when the team's beliefs about the key assumptions underlying a strategic alternative should turn from speculation and intuition to something grounded in evidence. This research and discovery process should be undertaken for all the different strategic alternatives that might be under consideration, as a means of providing better information to inform your choice.

In many cases, uncertainty about a premise reflects a simple lack of information or knowledge and can be resolved through research. Often low-cost data gathering, forecasting, and analysis can play an important role. Surveys, experiments, and prototypes can also shed light on whether new product features increase the willingness of customers to pay. Government statistics and demographic data can be used to forecast trends. Calls to suppliers can illuminate their ability to deliver critical components at a reasonable cost.

In other cases, the uncertainty can only be resolved through more substantial commitments of resources, as when we try to assess the likelihood that an engineering team will make a fundamental advance in chemistry or bioengineering. Conversations with experts can generate estimates on the likelihood of making a technical breakthrough in a particular domain, but if the challenges are at the frontier of technological knowledge, expert opinion will also be highly speculative. In some cases, this type of uncertainty can be resolved only by taking action and seeing whether a given problem can be solved.

Data gathering and analysis are, of course, often time-consuming and expensive. How to best prioritize these efforts? In our view, the highest-leverage investments at this stage come from focusing on the most consequential premises for each strategic option. This focus is valuable in two ways. First, and most obviously, we gain little additional insight by testing a premise that is not consequential to a strategy argument. For example, the premises in the upper-left corner of figure 6.4 are not essential to the success of the strategy, even though uncertainty about them is high. If a premise here turns out to be false, redundancy with another premise means that the strategy can still succeed. In this quadrant, we might find assumptions about things that are "nice to have" but not essential. For example, perhaps the firm is considering a new process technology that is thought to lower the firm's costs. If successful, this process would allow the firm to create more value. But if the firm already is able to create sufficient value with existing technologies, then worrying about whether the new technology will work when deciding whether to pursue that course of action is not essential.

Premises in the lower-right quadrant of figure 6.4 are somewhat different, but also should not generally be a first-order priority for further testing, particularly when formulating new strategies. A premise located here is critical to the strategy argument; at the extreme, the whole strategic initiative fails if the premise is false. Yet at the same time, the leadership team is quite confident that the premises here will hold. There is some value, of course, in determining whether the leadership team is deluding themselves, and so the soundness of these premises should not be ignored given that they are so critical. On the other hand, if there are critical assumptions that are also highly uncertain, these should likely be tested first. Lafley and Martin similarly suggest that an executive should

> first test the things you're most dubious about. Take the condition the team
> feels is the least likely to hold up, and test it first. If the team's suspicion is
> right, that possibility will be eliminated without the need to test any of the
> other conditions.[15]

We agree with this suggestion, with one important caveat: test first the most consequential premise, i.e., the one that you're most dubious about *and* that is also most critical to the strategy argument. Little value comes from eliminating dubious premises that are redundant with premises you are confident about.

If a strategy has been chosen and the firm is actively pursuing it, then do strategy arguments still play a role? This question is relevant both when we are thinking about an established strategy that the firm has long pursued and when we are considering a relatively new strategy that has emerged as the winner from the choice stage of the strategy formulation process. In both cases, we believe that a deep understanding of the argument underlying the strategy is essential to effective learning and to the ability to adapt (or abandon) the strategy in the face of changing conditions.

A fundamental challenge that leaders face in this situation is knowing what they should be paying attention to. Changes occur all of the time, with rapid developments in technology, consumer tastes, regulation, and competition. Which changes matter and which ones do not? Good leaders know that they cannot afford to respond to every little change in the world around them, but they also live in fear that some seemingly inconsequential change will fundamentally undermine their success. They want to track changes and learn about new threats and opportunities. How do they learn smartly?

The answer, in our view, is for leaders to return to their strategy arguments and focus on the most critical premises in these arguments. The fact that the logic of success depends strongly on these assumptions means that things will go wrong if an assumption no longer holds. The danger lies in taking the truth of these premises for granted—something that is more likely to happen when the strategy overall works, and other, more uncertain, critical premises receive the lion's share of attention. These assumptions require monitoring to ensure that conditions have not changed so as to render them false. Leaders who have identified the most critical assumptions know exactly which things need to be monitored to assess the health of the strategy. Doing so in turn helps clarify when a strategic initiative needs to be adjusted or abandoned.

CLOSING THOUGHTS

Our goal in this chapter has been to outline a process for generating novel strategic alternatives and to provide a structure for choosing between them. When leaders seek to consider how to react to new threats or opportunities, it is important to adopt a disciplined and structured approach. This approach involves, first, creating an environment in the divergence phase where a range of genuinely diverse strategic possibilities are generated. In this divergence phase, the goal is not to assess, but rather to be creative and consider as wide a range of alternative combinations of customer and product or service as possible.

The skills in developing and evaluating strategy arguments—as arguments per se—are particularly valuable in the convergence phase, when the leadership team needs to debate and evaluate the different options on the table. The convergence phase is not just about exercising choice; it is about making an informed choice. Strategic decision making is, unavoidably, about making bets about an uncertain future. But success becomes more likely if one knows which bets one is making—in other words, if one has identified the premises that are required to hold—and if one is clearly aware of the consequences of specific bets not working out. Focusing on identifying the most consequential premises required for each strategic option to succeed is essential to making an informed strategic choice.

Our efforts in this chapter show how the activities developed above—particularly logical formalization—can be adapted to aid in this crucial stage of strategy formulation. The task relies on many of the same techniques deployed in the strategy analysis chapters but uses them under different conditions. That, in turn, leads to different points of emphasis and different kinds of tasks for managers. In particular, rather than stating the conditions or premises that produced an effective strategy, strategists designing a new strategy for the future are asked to imagine and specify what conditions or premises or assumptions need to be true in the future for the strategy to succeed.

This seemingly slight tweak makes the task much harder, because strategists are now asked to consider future states of the world, and even predict them, as opposed to evaluating current or past conditions. The shift in thinking can derail the strategy formulation process: it is easy to get hung up on debating what the future might look like, and there is often no natural stopping point. We recognize that it is difficult to think about a future world without getting lost in debates about how it will look. It is all too easy to revert to debating the soundness of a strategy argument. But this is precisely what is needed to formulate strategy effectively: one must imagine a future world and then devise a strategy that would plausibly succeed in it.

The mental challenge of this task resembles the mindset often required to read fiction: the willing suspension of disbelief. Without a temporary suspension of one's critical abilities with respect to the depiction of incredible events (or characters or situations), the reader will not have the pleasure of exploring an unusual idea. Similarly, if executives are unwilling to make bold assumptions about what the future might hold, they are unlikely to generate compelling new strategic approaches.

Suspending disbelief is critically important when formulating novel, creative, and potentially disruptive strategies. Imagine proposing something that has never been tried before—not just by your firm, but by anyone. Perhaps that means introducing a new technology or a fundamentally new way of reaching customers—like, say, Amazon's idea to deliver packages with drones. The strategy will hinge, critically, on whether or not this new idea will work out—but before trying it, one cannot know whether it will. As a result, assumptions about this new idea will play a central role in the strategy argument.

To return to the fiction analogy, one can think of these ideas as the work's *central conceit*, the core assumption that must be accepted. For instance, the central conceit of *Winnie the Pooh* is that stuffed animals can talk to each other much as humans do and that they engage in many of the same social activities. Likewise, in formulating future strategy, there will be a central conceit upon which the whole effort rests. For example, a central conceit of the early pioneers of the personal computer movement was that semiconductor processing power would increase dramatically and rapidly at the same time that costs dropped. Similarly, the central conceit of Uber was that customers would be willing to get into the unregulated personal cars of strangers instead of taxis.

When serious contention arises about the central conceit of a strategy, two steps are in order. First, it may be advisable to develop several plausible strategies based on different sets of assumptions about the future. Second, to do so, one should focus on ensuring the validity of the strategy arguments. Do not focus on their soundness, as this is precisely where the contention lies. Of course, developing multiple strategy arguments adds to the work involved, but it may wind up that the different conceits do not imply radically different strategies. And, if they do, then the organization is somewhat better prepared to deal with alternatives for the future.

Ultimately, bold strategies rest on assumptions that are difficult to accept at face value. The bolder the strategic vision, the more it asks you to suspend disbelief in order to accept the central conceit. This ironic situation, in our view, is the primary reason to focus on validity and not soundness when formulating strategy. Doing so does not mean one has to act on crazy assumptions, or that every strategy with outlandish premises is worth pursuing. But a refusal to entertain untested assumptions and an insistence on soundness at the formulation stage guarantees timid, incremental strategies.

Approaching strategic choices about the future in this way is unfortunately not, in our experience, very common in modern firms. Rather, a more common approach is to identify a set of options (as in the divergence phase) and then move directly to placing a bet. It is like betting everything on a sporting event without knowing anything about the teams. In practice, this often happens by creating a "pro-con" matrix, where the pros and cons of each alternative are listed. This is particularly likely to happen when executives realize, perhaps implicitly, that it is difficult to make apples-to-apples comparisons between the options. Unfortunately, the pros and cons for different options are often qualitative assessments that are difficult to reconcile and compare with one another, because they lack a common metric. In particularly egregious cases, the pros and cons of different options will be symmetric, in the sense that the disadvantage of option B is that it lacks the advantages of option A, and vice versa. As a result of this ambiguity, the decision-making process is often opaque and subject to the arbitrary dynamics of the discussion among the people in the room. Intuition and subjective judgments substitute for rational analysis, rather than complement it.

In light of these dynamics, it is no wonder so many executives lack confidence in the strategic decision-making process or that such decision-making processes yield poor results.

Our hope is that the process outlined in this chapter demonstrates how a culture and process of strategy argumentation can ensure greater strategic confidence in the leadership team, and ultimately throughout the firm.

KEY TAKEAWAYS

- Argumentation can help fix the broken strategic planning process of many organizations. Tools exist for generating new ideas in the divergence phase, but a principled process by which some ideas get chosen in the convergence phase remains a neglected area of focus. The three main activities of this book allow leaders to develop a superior process for choosing the most promising alternatives.

- Making the convergence phase productive requires applying the logical validity standard to all strategic proposals. To be considered, any proposal must be presented as a logically valid argument, and all logically valid proposals must be given full consideration, no matter how dubious some of the assumptions may appear. As an objective and widely accepted criterion, logical validity sanctifies the decision process. Decisions emanating from such a process are not only less likely to be arbitrary, but also less likely to be seen as arbitrary.

- Consequential assumptions—defined as the combination of their criticality in the structure of the argument and the uncertainty associated with the assumptions—represent the key bets involved in each strategic alternative. Instead of debating what will be true in the future, focusing on the most consequential premises allows leadership teams ways of identifying what needs to be true for each alternative to succeed. Assessing consequentiality facilitates difficult apples-to-oranges comparisons.

- Strategy formulation requires a willingness to suspend disbelief about what might be possible in the future. Too often, executives are too impatient and rush to make a choice between alternatives based on gut instinct. Leaders must resist the temptation to move quickly or debate the reasonableness of different assumptions. The belief that the convergence phase might be characterized by calm, dispassionate reasoning can free people to be more creative in generating strategic options.

CHAPTER 7

|||||||||||||||||||||||||||||||||||||||||||||||||||||||||||||||||||||||||||||||||||||||||||||||||||||||||||||||||||||||||||||||||||||||||||||
|||||||||||

Communicating Strategy

THE BENEFITS OF EFFECTIVELY
COMMUNICATING STRATEGY

In May 2017, Mark Fields was replaced as CEO of Ford Motor Company by James Hackett, the former CEO of the office furniture maker Steelcase. The move came as a surprise to many, because Fields had long been groomed for the CEO role yet led the company for less than two years. The reasons given varied, but several factors clearly came into play: although the company made money, Ford's stock price had declined precipitously, and car sales were dropping 25 percent, far more than the industry-wide average. One critical factor, observers suggested, was that Fields had not done enough to position Ford for the newly emerging technologies such as autonomous vehicles (AVs), electric vehicles (EVs), and ride-hailing and ride-sharing services that many thought would disrupt the automotive sector (or, as many increasingly referred to it, the mobility sector). By contrast, crosstown rival General Motors was considered by many to be better prepared for the future, having acquired AV start-up Cruise among other actions.[1]

The new CEO, James Hackett, worked as the head of Ford's efforts in emerging mobility services, but his arrival had been recent. While he had served on Ford's board of directors, he was essentially an outsider. Company statements at the time of the appointment made clear that the company wanted a more forward-looking leader than Fields, someone who would set a new direction for them in developing new technologies. "This is a time of unprecedented change," Bill Ford said. He continued, "A time of great change requires a transformational leader."[2] It seemed clear that Ford's board of directors wanted a new strategy for the company to be developed, specifically one incorporating new mobility technologies, and the board had appointed the new CEO to lead them through the process.

The challenges Hackett faced, especially as a relative newcomer to both the industry and the company he was tasked to lead, were immense. Given the fundamental transformations besetting the industry, the strategic issues were complex and highly uncertain. In addition to the difficult task of charting a course forward, Hackett faced an additional leadership challenge: communicating the strategy to stakeholders, both inside and outside the company. Hackett could not be expected to communicate a plan from day one—good strategy arguments take time to develop. But once a coherent strategy began to take shape, communicating at least the broad outlines of Ford's new approach was essential to assuaging shareholders, Ford executives and frontline employees, and other stakeholders. Hackett recognized how important this was at the time of his appointment: "The way we're going to win the hearts and minds of everybody is to have great ideas that work, and Ford has put a decade into the AV development and it's really coming along. And [when] we're ready to talk about it, we're going to be really clear about it."[3]

Eighteen months later, the press and analysts' comments suggested strongly that the outside world was still waiting to learn about the new strategy. In October 2018, Ford's share price was at a six-year low. While analysts attributed Ford's downward trajectory to several factors, a big cause for many was the uncertainty about Hackett's strategy and associated restructuring plan. Two years after his appointment as CEO, Hackett had not yet delivered on his promise to be really clear about what the company's new mobility strategy would be. One auto analyst at Morningstar said, "There's still a lot of uncertainty about Hackett's plan and vision," while another analyst at CFRA Research complained, "There's really no visibility about their strategy. There are also no real catalysts on the horizon."[4]

Analysts and investors are, of course, privy to less information about a firm's strategy than people inside a company. Perhaps a clear strategy was in place, but it had not yet been communicated (well) externally. How was this strategy communicated within the rest of Ford?

Not, it appears, very clearly. According to an August 2018, report in the *Wall Street Journal*, Ford's strategy was not well known or well understood in the ranks, even among top lieutenants. For example, Ford's finance chief, Bob

Shanks, was quoted as saying some of Hackett's concepts made his "head hurt." The *Journal* reported that "some executives have taken to asking Mr. Hackett's chief of staff, Clare Braun, to clarify his comments or diagrams following a meeting." A significant number of Ford's top executives left early in Hackett's term, which some saw as a response to the internal confusion.[5]

It was against this backdrop that, in November 2018, Ford announced, "We are in the early stages of reorganizing our global salaried workforce to support the company's strategic objectives, create a more dynamic and empowering work environment, and become more fit as a business. The reorganization will result in headcount reduction over time and this will vary based on team and location."[6] No specifics were provided, but the restructuring would affect Ford's white-collar workforce of about seventy thousand employees worldwide.

News of a substantial corporate restructuring generates anxiety and often anger within almost any company. Yet the agitation felt by Ford's employees was likely exacerbated by the absence of a clearly communicated strategy for the company. While a well-communicated strategy would surely not eliminate the stress and uncertainty of a restructuring, it would at least focus the issues. A clear strategy statement would let some know they were not under the gun and would assure everyone inside and outside the company that there was a coherent plan to bring the company around. Saying that the changes will "support the company's strategic objectives" is not enlightening when those objectives are unclear. Cutting jobs in a sector undergoing disruption without explaining the plan for the turnaround can only heighten tensions and create ill will.

There can be little doubt that Ford's strategy was the central concern of executives within the company. They were not ignoring the strategic challenges; indeed, the company worked to make the ongoing strategy process visible to executives. In the company's headquarters, offices formerly occupied by corporate officers were transformed into strategy rooms. In these rooms, the *Wall Street Journal* reported, "Rather than sit through PowerPoint presentations, executives meet surrounded by walls packed with charts, diagrams and other materials outlining the strategy for various models and business units. The goal is to allow everyone to view different parts of a plan, from manufacturing to marketing, in one place and make decisions quickly."[7]

Whether this engagement and activity resulted in a clear consensus among executives on Ford's strategy argument is unclear to us as outsiders. For current purposes, let's stipulate to the idea that a consensus had emerged, and that Hackett was correct when he claimed, "Things are actually gelling now in the way we're thinking and doing. . . . It's not clear to the market yet, but I see it."[8] Even so, consensus in the senior leadership team is not enough. A great strategy needs to be communicated clearly and widely. Failure to do so cripples the strategy. In many cases, the problems caused by a poorly communicated strategy are indistinguishable from the problems caused by not having a great strategy or by having no clear strategy at all. Indeed, Hackett retired unexpectedly from Ford in August, 2020.

Ford was not alone in communicating its strategy poorly. Far from it: four out of five senior executives say that the overall strategy is not well understood within their companies.[9] What's worse, this is not only a problem with the rank and file or middle management. In our own experience with executives, we have on occasion been shocked to discover that in some companies, even top leaders do not always know or agree in their understanding of their companies' strategies. Or they are simply incapable of explaining the strategy in plain and simple language. If the leaders-in-charge can't explain the strategy, then it will likely be a monumental challenge for their employees to know it!

In this chapter, we present and discuss various methods and principles for communicating organizational strategy. We discuss both the content of the strategy message, as well as its general form, and modes of communication. Communicating strategy is essential in every organization, so we offer some tried and true ideas for doing so effectively from social science and the field of communications.

While we think all of these principles are worthwhile and would work in most any organization, we recognize that some are better in some organizations than others. In some organizations, the communication effort will need to be much stronger and more pervasive than in others. For instance, if an organization has a culture that encourages the strategy being widely discussed and debated as it is being developed, then employees will already be familiar with much of it. In that case, perhaps all that is needed is a clarifying summary message that reminds them about the final agreed-upon strategy. On the other hand, if a limited number of people in the organization were involved in strategy formulation and debate, then much more information about the strategy and its rationale will need to be communicated. Accordingly, someone will need to decide what is going to be done, and how much effort needs to be applied when communicating the strategy.

Make the Strategy Visible

An effective strategy message communicates the essential, core elements of the strategy. Someone who hears it or reads it should be able to walk away with a clear mental image of how the organization works, and how it intends to succeed. That is, the message should explain the *why* behind the choices the organization made. How much detail is provided, as well as which details are shared, depends on the audience in question, of course. The message for the general public may be articulated at quite a high level, while internal audiences and important external stakeholders might receive more detail and insight.

That may sound simple, and in many ways it is—but the potential impact is powerful. Take, as an example, Walmart's statement of its enterprise strategy on the company's webpage: "Price, access, assortment & experience drive a customer's choice of retailer. Historically, Walmart led on price and assortment. Retail environments are more competitive today, especially with e-commerce. To win, Walmart will lead on price, invest to differentiate on access, be competitive on assortment & deliver a great experience." Walmart also explicitly states its approach to the market in an easy-to-comprehend customer value proposition: "We help our shoppers live better because we deliver low prices on the brands they trust, in an easy, fast, one-stop shopping experience."[10]

As this example illustrates, a clear basic strategy message communicates the organization's primary goals to its employees. It conveys the basic value proposition to customers, so that they understand why the organization should be preferred. Finally, it tells potential suppliers, regulators, and other stakeholders what kind of organization they are dealing with and what to expect from it during interactions. A good strategy message sets goals and expectations for the organization, and it provides guidance to others about how to behave.

Unfortunately, organizations typically do a poor—often terrible—job of communicating their strategies, even when they may have a well-defined one that they rely on regularly for guidance. Strategy is, instead, one of the most misused and misunderstood words in the business world. CEOs will routinely say something like, "Our strategy is to win" or "Our strategy is to be No. 1" or "Our strategy is to outdo our rivals" or "Our strategy is to always work harder."

Strategy messages of this sort typically confuse goals and determination with a plan for how they will win, and how the hard work will pay off.[11] It is like saying that your strategy for winning a football game is to score more points than your opponent or for winning a race is to run the fastest time. As Richard Rumelt argues in *Good Strategy, Bad Strategy*:

> Strategy cannot be a useful concept if it is a synonym for success. Nor can it be a useful tool if it is confused with ambition, determination, inspirational leadership, and innovation. . . . Strategy is about *how* an organization will move forward. Doing strategy is figuring out *how* to advance the firm's interests.[12]

In many cases, organizations do not even try to communicate their strategies. In researching this book, we attempted to find the strategy message for a wide range of companies, including those we have featured in earlier chapters, like Southwest Airlines, Walmart, and Apple. We searched mostly for publicly available materials, as one main purpose of the strategy message should be to communicate with the outside world. Of course, in some cases, the internal materials could be very different. Still, a company that only communicates its strategy internally misses a great opportunity.

The results were surprising. First, and most obvious, corporate strategy messages typically were not easy to find. We looked at company websites, annual reports, and 10k filings with the Securities and Exchange Commission (SEC). These searches usually uncovered something that could be considered a corporate strategy statement, but it was never clear where we would find it. Moreover, the statement itself was often terse and incomplete. If these messages had been student responses to a class assignment, they would not have been given good grades! Many companies, including those that we considered otherwise quite transparent, say very little about their strategy.

Given the quality of managerial talent in these companies, this is unlikely to be an oversight. Rather, we suspect that either of two reasons can explain the dearth of clear, visible strategy statements. First, management may assume that everyone knows the organization's strategy, and there is no need to repeat it. Yet as surveys show time and time again, this is almost always a mistaken belief. Many employees either do not know the strategy, misunderstand it, or are uncertain. Second, there may be an intentional effort to hide the strategy, or at least keep its details under wraps. This latter impression is confirmed by our experiences with various companies and learning what they consider confidential about their strategies—namely almost everything.

Of course, certain things about strategy should, at certain times, be kept under wraps and not revealed to the outside world. This is especially true for plans to launch new products, to change prices, or to engage in similar actions that are intended to catch competitors by surprise. But most of the time—the vast majority of the time—the veil of secrecy is extended to the most trivial or obvious facts. Often, the things companies think they should keep secret are already very well known. Almost certainly investors, analysts, consultants, and competitors already possess this information and have scrutinized it thoroughly. Don't believe it? Then try an internet search with just two words—a company's name and the word "strategy." You will likely be amazed at all the descriptions and analyses you will find, often quite detailed, accurate, and illuminating. Except that is, the one from the company itself.

Whom do companies think they are fooling? What is the big secret, if everyone knows? And, most importantly, why do companies want to let third parties tell the world their strategies when they could tell their stories better themselves? Leaders should consider whether they actually want their subordinates, or their most important stakeholders, to base their understanding of what the organization is trying to do on the opinions of bloggers and industry analysts, rather than a thoughtfully composed statement from the leaders themselves.

The consequences of these failures in communicating strategy are substantial. They take the form of poor market valuations, missed opportunities, wasted effort, bad decisions, lack of internal alignment, and employee disengagement and even cynicism. How can this problem be overcome?

The foundation for effective strategic communication is clear, well-reasoned strategy arguments. At one level this point is obvious: you cannot hope to communicate a strategy well if the strategy itself is flawed and incoherent. And we are sure that in many cases, the confused strategy messages emanating from corporate public relations departments merely reflect a strategy in disarray. For strategic communication to make sense, the strategy has to make sense.

Yet the importance of articulating clear, well-reasoned strategy arguments for effective communication goes deeper. The reason is simple: the key to effective strategic communication is to give audiences a clear narrative, one that allows them to imagine a sequence of interconnected events that will lead to a chosen aspiration.

Consider, as an example, Elon Musk's famous blog post announcing (to the whole world) "The Secret Tesla Motors Master Plan (Just Between You and Me)." Musk noted that while Tesla's initial product was a high-performance electric sports car, many people did not understand how making a low-volume, expensive car made sense, given that Tesla's stated goal—its reason for existence—was to reduce global carbon emissions. As Musk acknowledged,

> Are we really in need of another high performance sports car? Will it actually make a difference to global carbon emissions?
>
> Well, the answers are no and not much. However, that misses the point. . . . Almost any new technology initially has high unit cost before it can be optimized and this is no less true for electric cars. The strategy of Tesla is to enter at the high end of the market, where customers are prepared to pay a premium, and then drive down market as fast as possible to higher unit volume and lower prices with each successive model. . . . In keeping with a fast growing technology company, all free cash flow is plowed back into R&D to drive down the costs and bring the follow on products to market as fast as possible. When someone buys the Tesla Roadster sports car, they are actually helping pay for development of the low cost family car.[13]

Musk ended the blog post as follows:

> So, in short, the master plan is:
> Build sports car
> Use that money to build an affordable car
> Use *that* money to build an even more affordable car
> While doing above, also provide zero emission electric power
> generation options
> Don't tell anyone.[14]

Tesla's remarkable record of success since that blog post in 2006 is due to many factors, including its innovative capabilities, rapidly advancing technologies, fast expansion in China, as well as growing concerns about climate change. But in our view, a major factor has also been the company's ability to communicate its strategy quite clearly, albeit at a high level. Tesla and Musk provide an effective narrative through which investors, employees, and customers can understand the choices the company makes. Thanks to this narrative, audiences can see how events are connected to one another, how past investments and current choices shape future outcomes. This clarity has likely served Tesla well as it encountered bumps in the road, such as those surrounding the delayed release of the Tesla Model 3.

Tesla's "secret master plan" might be viewed as something of an anomaly, given that it is the statement of a young, Silicon Valley start-up. What about, say, a large, complex, established corporation working in a highly regulated environment?

Consider Roche, a pharmaceutical and diagnostics corporation, founded in 1896 and based in Switzerland, with 2018 revenues close to $60 billion worldwide. Despite operating in multiple geographies and product categories, Roche's strategy statement on its public website makes very clear statements of focus and of contestable claims, such as:[15]

- "We will continue to concentrate our energies entirely on prescription medicines and in vitro diagnostics, rather than diversify into other sectors like generics and biosimilars, over-the-counter medicines and medical devices."
- "With our in-house combination of pharmaceuticals and diagnostics, we are uniquely positioned to deliver personalized healthcare."
- "Our distinctiveness rests on four key elements: an exceptionally broad and deep understanding of molecular biology, the seamless integration of our pharmaceuticals and diagnostics capabilities, a diversity of approaches to maximise innovation, and a long-term orientation."
- "Our structure is built for innovation. Our autonomous research and development centres and alliances with over 200 external partners foster diversity and agility. Our global geographical scale and reach enables us to bring our diagnostics and medicines quickly to people who need them."

While written in a very different style than Tesla's "secret master plan," Roche's strategy statement does an excellent job of explaining succinctly what Roche plans to do, what it does *not* plan to do, how they aim to do it, and why. Overall, the Roche strategy message impresses us with its crisp statements.

Both of these examples are good illustrations of the connection between clear, well-reasoned strategy arguments and effective strategic communication. A good strategy argument articulates the leadership's theory of success, its beliefs about how certain investments and actions will lead to desired outcomes, how inputs will lead to outputs, and how causes will lead to effects. With this theory of success in hand, leaders can much more easily craft an effective strategy message, because the logic of the theory forms the backbone of the narrative conveyed by the strategy message.

The lesson for leaders is that the beautiful, well-reasoned strategy argument that they have crafted—through painstaking research and constructive, but difficult, debates and decisions—*should not be hidden from view*. While the work of formulating the strategy argument may primarily be performed by the executive leadership team, it is not enough for those leaders to keep the logic in their heads, or on a whiteboard in the executive boardroom. Others need to understand leadership's way of thinking. Without clear communication, those entrusted with responsibility for making the myriad decisions required to execute the strategy will be at a loss for what, exactly, to do. The organization will quickly turn incoherent, as different managers make conflicting decisions based on inconsistent understandings.

By contrast, in an organization with clear and consistent strategic messaging, everyone marches to the same beat, understands the connection between what they do and the organization's success, and is capable of providing critical insights on how the strategy might be improved to tackle unexpected challenges or opportunities. Achieving such concerted action requires sustained effort on the part of the organization's leaders. The story needs to be told, and it needs to be told again and again. As Jack Welch urged, great business leaders should "never get bored telling their story."[16]

THE PRACTICE OF EFFECTIVELY COMMUNICATING STRATEGY

Crafting the Strategy Message

How do you craft a strategy message intended for wide distribution inside and outside the organization? What should the message say?

When tasked with describing a strategy, executives will often turn to the many off-the-shelf templates for strategy description that are available online and elsewhere. Avoid this at all costs. Useful as some of these templates are for stimulating thinking and initial discussions, the cookie-cutter style of them is obvious and can convey the implicit message that the organization's leaders have not thought hard about the strategy. More importantly, the generic nature of such tools leaves little room for the distinctive elements of an organization's strategy to be identified and communicated. What is needed is a strategy message that reflects the distinctive elements of the organization's approach, and one that captures the hard-won insights generated by the iterative application of the three activities of strategy mapping, logical formalization, and constructive argumentation.

This observation might lead some to the conclusion that the work product generated by all those efforts should be what is communicated. Given the many hours put into creating strategy maps and logical syllogisms, why not share those more widely? After all, these will best capture the subtleties of the strategy!

We think this approach would be a mistake. Do not, for example, broadcast the formal logical syllogisms developed in the processes described in chapter 3. The form of the syllogism does not lend itself to mass circulation, because the formal structure makes syllogisms difficult to read. A syllogism will likely not be comprehended or appreciated, and it could very likely generate ridicule from the intended audiences.

Similarly, while highly simplified versions of the corresponding strategy maps (chapter 2) can be effective visual tools for communicating the relationships between concepts, they cannot do the work of effective communication on their own. Strategy maps are, as we have emphasized, subject to varied interpretations, especially when presented in a very simplified form. Instead, visuals need to be complemented by carefully written text that clarifies the ideas.

The key, in our view, is to use the maps and logical syllogisms as the *foundation* for crafting an effective strategy message. The strategy argument captures the essential elements of the strategy, and hence the essential content of the strategy message. Moreover, the argument articulates the connections between ideas; it serves as an outline for communicating those cause and effect relationships to others. The clarity of thinking generated through the application of the three activities lays the foundation for clarity of communication.

But communicating a strategy argument is a separate step in the process, one demanding a different set of skills and considerations. Formulating a strategy argument is an act of thinking; communicating it is an act of rhetoric and persuasion. In what follows, we offer some brief observations on what makes for effective strategy messages, particularly as they relate to message content, structure, and presentation. These observations should be treated as a starting point, not as a comprehensive guide to effective rhetoric and persuasion.

Message Content

Focus first on the content of the message. Ideally, a strategy message should hit all of the essential core elements of the strategy, the high-level abstract aspects of the strategy that convey its essence and also seem relevant to people throughout the organization.

What does this mean? It means that, above all, the message should clearly convey the core logic by which the organization succeeds. Recognizing that there are a number of different ways to do this effectively, we believe that the best messages contain four elements:

1. a concise description of the strategic *opportunity*;
2. a forthright acknowledgment of the primary *obstacles* to success;
3. an articulation of the *logic* by which the organization will overcome those obstacles; and
4. a clear connection between the strategy and the organization's *actions*.

We discuss each of these in turn.

Opportunity. An effective strategy message needs a clear description of the value creation opportunity pursued by the organization. How does the organization create value? This includes relatively high-level statements of the purpose of the organization, such as answers to the question "How does the organization make the world a better place?" But most importantly it should include a clear statement of how the organization creates economic value. Who are the organization's customers, and how do the company's products and services generate willingness to pay among them? What are the critical assets and activities required to create this value? Why does (or will) the organization have a superior ability to create value relative to others?

Obstacles. A convincing strategy message is clearheaded and realistic about the obstacles to realizing a strategic goal. In many strategy messages we have seen, organizations are good at describing the enticing potential of the value creation opportunity, but are less than frank and transparent about the challenges associated with capturing that value. As a result, many strategy messages come across as wishful thinking or as suggesting that success will be easy. But the realities of market forces in modern economies mean that sustainable success is hard won. Failing to acknowledge the obstacles to capturing value does not make them go away. Moreover, the audience for a strategy message—both internal and external—is often well aware that these obstacles exist, so there is little to be gained by sending a message that does not acknowledge the elephant in the room. Doing so suggests the leadership is out of touch with reality.

Logic. The strategy message should provide an explanation for how the organization will overcome the obstacles it faces and realize the opportunity. It is here that the core logic of the organization's strategy argument takes center stage, where the reasoning that has been honed through the use of the three activities is put on display. It is here that people see the connection between actions and consequences and begin to perceive the mechanisms through which the organization will succeed. This is perhaps the most important content dimension, because it explains why certain behaviors are important. It is also the dimension most often missing in the strategy messages we have reviewed.

Action. Strategy messages are often communicated in conjunction with strategic decisions, whether large or small. Such decisions present an opportunity for leaders to illuminate the logic of a strategy, and thereby reinforce people's understanding of how the strategy works. More generally, effective strategy messages use actions as concrete manifestations of the rather abstract ideas embedded in the strategy argument. Because actions are concrete, they provide a firmer basis for people to grasp how the strategy works. While in some settings (such as a strategy statement on a public website) a strategy message will be general and abstract, on many occasions the strategy message should explicitly link the abstract argument to specific decisions. Communicating clear connections between the strategic logic and actions are particularly important when leaders are assigning tasks to subordinates. Action disconnected from strategy and strategy disconnected from action encourage the mistaken perception that strategy and execution are separate tasks.

Message Structure

For effective communication, the structure of the message matters. By structure, we primarily refer to the rhetorical features of the message—how the content is presented and how the text reads.

How do you evaluate structure? A simple test is to ask yourself after reading the message whether you can tell what the organization does, who it might compete with, and how it intends to win. It may seem obvious that a strategy message would pass this test, but this is surprisingly rare in practice. Strategy messages instead often seem to be exercises in intended obfuscation.

Many books have been written on effective rhetoric and writing, and we will not try to repeat their lessons here. We focus instead on three issues that we think are particularly relevant to the communication of strategy arguments: forensic-like focus, clarity without clichés, and unassailable credibility.

Forensic-like Focus. The temptation with any public message is to add more, to provide one more detail, to sneak in one additional (seemingly) important message. Don't do this with the strategy message. It only serves to distract and confuse. The audience should have no doubt or ambiguity about the core strategy after reading it. The message must be distilled to its essential spirit, condensed and edited to be gulp-sized yet flavorful. The iterations and editing required to get there require hard work and discipline. As the writer Arthur Plotnik said, "You write to communicate to the hearts and minds of others what's burning inside you. And we edit to let the fire show through the smoke."[17]

In principle, the strategy message will be more effective if some element of it is concrete, making it vivid. For example, consider the value proposition statement offered by start-up Zūm, which provides transportation services for young children. The company says, "Zūm is the leader in safe rides for schools and busy families—when and how they need it—7 days a week, with hyper-vigilant safety and security."[18] Do you need to know much more to understand at a basic level how Zūm tries to create value?

We suspect that badly structured strategy messages often come from organizational processes of review and approval in which too many different people and units have editorial influence, in part because crafting the strategy message is viewed as a minor, low-stakes part of the strategy process. For instance, the team developing the strategy may very well craft a sharp pointed message indicating that the firm pursues a high perceived quality strategy, because its products last longer than competitors' products and break down less frequently. As a result, the company charges more for its products, because they appeal to customers on these specific aspects of quality. But then someone with a financial orientation complains that the message mistakenly gives the impression that the company doesn't care about costs, is inefficient, and will alienate investors. Rather than resolve the dispute and clarify the strategic claims, in goes a phrase about lower costs. After all, it is "just" the messaging.

Then someone in sales and marketing chimes in to say that the message should also let people know that the firm cares about customer service. So, in goes a phrase about better customer service. And on and on.

The end result is an unfocused, confusing strategy message. For those who have been most invested in formulating the strategy, this may not seem like a big deal. The strategy message is not for them, and they understand what they are doing anyway. But an unfocused, everything-but-the-kitchen-sink message has real consequences. New people will join the organization and look to the strategy messages for guidance, only to become confused. The same thing goes for people lower down in the organization or stakeholders outside the firm. With messaging that confuses rather than guides, strategic incoherence is sure to follow.

Clarity Without Clichés. A strategy message should be accessible and comprehensible to all, which means it needs to be simple and direct. One tendency to avoid in particular is the tendency to use highly technical language. Such language has many benefits, particularly in the process of formulating precise and rigorous arguments, because technical language is typically more precise. But when communicating strategy, big words are often deployed primarily as a means of projecting authority and credibility and serve more to obfuscate than to clarify. Moreover, complex, technical language exacerbates the sense that strategy is a topic that only specialists can engage with. It thereby serves to reify the false distinction between strategy and execution.

The danger of simplifying, however, is that it is very easy to devolve into clichés or to employ widely used words and ideas that are not elaborated but appeal because they have widespread resonance. The problem with clichés is that they don't communicate. People hear them but don't take them seriously enough. They gloss over them, and they do not resonate as real messages. Or worse, people misunderstand their meaning and application.

Making the message simple but cliché-free is essential but hard to do. To many managers, the effort requires a facility with the subtleties of language that is not normally part of the job. As a result, it can take many iterations to get the message pared down but to remain meaningful. This is a task where seeking expert assistance may be useful.

Regardless of the method used, it is very hard to appreciate the way a message you crafted will be received by others and its potential impact without doing some field testing. Try the message out on some people who have not seen it before and then debrief them. Find out what they heard and what it meant. Revise your message accordingly and then do it again. It is surprising how much effort it sometimes takes to make things simpler and simpler—to cut through the smoke and edit for fire, as Plotnik says.

Unassailable Credibility. To have impact, the strategy message needs to be credible, by which we mean believable. People who read the message must believe that what is being proposed and expected can actually be accomplished.

Credibility can come from many sources. If a company or a leader has a proven track record of success, the strategy message is likely to be viewed as more credible. The credibility of a strategy message can also be established through reference to unassailable facts, to known truths about the world or the organization. Yet such claims to credibility are rooted in the past and the present, and should not be the only source of credibility when the concern is how the organization will thrive in the future. They also have less force when communicating an ambitious, visionary strategy. In an organization with a highly aspirational strategy, it can be difficult sometimes to make the strategy message credible. Tesla's "secret master plan" is a compelling example of a message that combines radical ambition with a high degree of credibility. After all, Tesla had no track record at the time, and its technologies were still unproven on a mass scale.

We think the most effective and powerful source of credibility in a strategy message is a well-reasoned, logical argument. The story being told has to make sense to people, and logical coherence is a powerful way to cause a story to make sense.

A common and effective way to introduce credibility in the strategy message is to use an analogy. Analogies are effective because they usually refer to something that exists and is successful or at least well known. For instance, the company Dectar promotes its Dogise service as an "Uber like on-demand dogwalker application."[19] Analogies are effective when they rely on people's implicit understandings of another organization's strategic logic. If they find the analogy apt, it quickly gives them insight into a firm's proposed strategy. However, analogies can also be overly seductive and subject to many implicit assumptions. They should, as a result, be employed with care.

Message Projection

Once the content and structure of the strategy message have been settled on, attention turns to actually communicating it. This process involves deciding how and where the message should be projected. The efforts put into crafting compelling strategy messages will be wasted if the message is restricted to a strategic planning document or a short discussion in the company's annual report. The benefits of clear strategic messaging only come about if the message is widely diffused, vivid, and memorable, such that it effectively shapes thought and action inside and outside the organization.

Here we touch briefly on three issues related to the effective presentation of strategy messages: the use of visual images and graphics, the need for relentless repetition, and the value of many different messaging modes.

Visual Images and Graphics. It is common for a company to attempt to summarize its strategy in a graphic—often a one-page graphic intended to show the essence of the strategy at a glance. Indeed, the shorthand graphical summary can be very useful in communicating to many audiences and often serves as a useful reminder or guide about the strategy. We have seen lots of these graphics, and they almost always look enticing, with nice geometric forms and colors—they look cool!

Our emphasis in chapter 2 on the value of visualizing strategic issues leads us to naturally be sympathetic to the value of graphic representations of strategy. But visually arresting graphics can easily substitute for clear thinking and, most importantly, rarely are able to speak for themselves. Unfortunately, visual appeal is often all that a graphic delivers. In the most egregious cases they fail to capture the fundamental trade-offs and choices inherent in a great strategy. They show everything as connected to everything, or imply that everything comes together seamlessly through the magic of nested circles and recursive loops.

To be useful on its own, the strategy graphic needs to be self-explanatory—it needs to tell the viewer the basics of the strategy all by itself. And that is a tall order—perhaps too tall. A good test of a strategy graphic is to show it to a person who has never seen it before and who does not know much about the company in question. Then ask that person, "What is the strategy of this organization?" If he or she can't tell you, then the graphic is not doing its job. In most cases, a graphic representation of the strategy should be a complement to a clear, written explanation of the strategy. The strategy is not a logo or a trademark.

Relentless Repetition. The core ideas in a strategy message need to be communicated over and over again. And then some more. All too often, organizations devote substantial effort to devising a compelling new strategy, work hard to get the strategy message just right, announce the new strategy to great fanfare—and then move on. But this is a flawed approach, for at least two reasons. First, people in organizations are constantly inundated with news of different initiatives, new priorities, and the like. But the most important thing they should understand is the strategy, because the strategy defines the framework for all of the decisions they will need to make, and it will define what success looks like for the organization and for their careers. Second, strategy arguments are often difficult to grasp at first reading. Great strategies incorporate non-obvious elements and specific approaches to difficult trade-offs. These choices take time to sink in, and people need to be exposed to the strategy message repeatedly.

As a result, the best approach is to send the strategy message out many times, in many different ways. Repeating the same idea over, and over, and over, may quickly strike the leadership team that crafted the strategy as overwhelmingly boring. But it is usually the only way to reach all the intended recipients and to give them the opportunity to fully absorb it.

Many Message Modes. In addition to relentless repetition, strategy messages are more effectively communicated if they are transmitted through many different modes of presentation. In any given form or mode, or through any given channel, the message will connect only with certain people and not others. Moreover, varying the mode of presentation challenges people to engage with the strategy message in different ways. One more email summarizing the company's strategy is easily deleted, but unexpected visual treatments, stories, and the like are more likely to maintain people's interest. So, make the message appear in many different modes and forums and with many different angles. Use images, stories, logic, graphics, logos, icons—don't use just a single medium. Broadcast the message in person, by posters, by email, by photos, by meetings, by example, and any other way that can be imagined. The goal is for people to encounter the message in many different forms on a regular basis.

The message will be better received if some versions of it arouse emotion among the recipients. A sterile and abstract message may be informative, but it is not inspiring and memorable. If you can connect with the reader on an emotional level, the message will be more powerful. For example, at the peak of the holiday shopping season in 2011, Patagonia garnered strong reactions when it ran a stark ad in the *New York Times* showcasing one of its jackets and telling customers, "Don't Buy This Jacket" and "Don't Buy What You Don't Need."[20] The ad generated strong reactions both for and against, with some accusing the company of hypocrisy and others lauding it for its commitment to improving the environment by reducing mass consumption. The message forcefully communicated the company's hard-and-fast commitment to environmental sustainability and directed attention to its unique lifetime product repair service as well as its line of recrafted clothing.

It also helps to embed a story in some renditions of the strategy message, a simple but compelling human narrative that conveys something central to the strategy. It is much easier for people to relate to and remember a story than an abstract set of ideas. The story should be specific and memorable—it can be about an executive, a customer, or even a technology or a product. The more the story can be grounded in the details of someone's life, the better it will communicate. Storytelling is a craft and it may be worthwhile to bring in a professional to help your organization come up with a story and articulate it.

Return to the example of Zūm, mentioned earlier. On their web page, the company tells us:

Our founder's mother sacrificed a thriving career to raise her four children. Years later Ritu found herself in the same predicament—how could she advance her career while making sure her two kids had trustworthy and reliable care?

With this simple question Ritu started an incredible journey with her two brothers. Together the trio—Ritu; a visionary Silicon Valley product leader, Abhishek; a 100x technologist and a programmer and Vivek; an operational go-getter with military discipline—meticulously set out to create a solution that met and exceeded the needs of parents.[21]

In four sentences, you have a vivid and touching personal story about why the company was started and what they hope to achieve.

Ultimately, the aim of strategic messaging is to change the way people think and the way they see the world, and to help them understand their roles in execution. Messaging takes effort and time. But it has a powerful benefit, because it is the most effective means of driving sustained strategic engagement and consistency.

Communicating Within the Organization

Most of what we have advised addresses strategy messaging without considering the social context. Much of the time, this is what is called for, and the approach has the advantage of consistency. People hear the same message no matter where or how they hear it.

The one context that may require some additional communication work is the organization itself, the setting where the strategy applies. It's not that our earlier advice is not appropriate here—it is, rather, that some additional considerations also likely come into play, and addressing these may be critical.

A common problem organizations face is that information and beliefs get trapped in silos. What people in one unit know and believe differ from what those in another unit know and believe. In the worst case, siloed parts of the same organization work at cross-purposes, sometimes deliberately undermining each other. Fights pitting manufacturing against marketing and sales are legendary, for example. The marketing and sales people are attuned to customer wants and needs and pay strong attention to revenue, often because it determines their compensation. By contrast, manufacturing has constraints on its capacity and flexibility; they want to be efficient and safe, and stability often helps ensure that. Strategy is an opportunity to align these units, but if not done carefully, it can actually pull them apart, because their immediate interests and incentives may pull them in opposing directions.

Organizations differentiate themselves into distinct units in order to control and coordinate specialized work better. The units might be organized in any manner of ways, including, of course, by function (manufacturing, marketing, R&D, etc.) or by product or by place. Whatever the basis of the grouping, putting a set of people and activities together helps them coordinate without the difficulty that would be encountered if these same people and activities were located in separate units. People within the same unit recognize their common problems and fates; they begin to identify with one another and develop interests that they purport will make them all better off. That's fine and what we want in an organization.

The problem occurs when the unit and its interests become the dominant driver of people and activities in the unit and the rest of the organization is forgotten, ignored, or defied. An important function of a good firm strategy is to align and prioritize the activities and interests of the various units so they work together rather than in opposition.

Any able executive knows that an articulated firm-wide strategy only applies so well to any given specific unit. The activities and interests of the unit need to be recognized and incorporated into the strategy for it to be compelling and meaningful at the local level. The challenge of the strategist is to make consistent translations, interpretations, and adaptations of the broader strategy to the specific problems of the unit. That is, the unit may need and want to develop a unit-specific strategy, and this may be encouraged. But that unit-specific strategy must start with a recognition of the broad overarching company-wide strategy and find a way to address its needs in a manner consistent with it. The unit-specific strategy needs to be subordinated to the firm-wide strategy.

While advocating such consistency is easy, achieving it is often hard. In many organizations, people in the various units resist and argue vociferously to be allowed to pursue their own independent strategies, ones that optimize their needs and interests. The debate should be encouraged, and it may even bring up matters that induce revisions to the firm-wide strategy. But at the end of the day, there must be a resolution that makes the strategies consistent. If push comes to shove, then leadership may need to exercise authority.

Volumes have been written about organizational communication, and we do not want to digress from strategy too much in emphasizing the importance of this context. In starting to wind up this discussion, let us make several basic points instead.

First, executives possess enormous power to communicate and send messages. Executives control the forums and articulate the challenges facing the firm. Everyone pays attention to what they hear the executives say, at least initially, because they understand authority and appreciate the resources attached to it. Executive communications do not usually need to be amplified—they are by nature high amplitude. In our experience, the problems begin when messages get confused and garbled. Then people read inconsistency in the messages they hear. The rational reaction in such situations is often to start ignoring the messages and read behaviors instead. In doing that, they then look for inconsistency in behaviors compared to the message. Nowhere is this more keenly examined than in compensation and resource allocation. Accordingly, it is crucial to make sure that the implicit messages that behaviors send do not contradict or undermine the official message.

Second, good communication is a two-way street. The slogans and the images and the official messages may all be telling concise, nifty stories. The executive's job is to not only be sure they are well crafted and widely available, but also to make sure that they are received and received right. By this we mean that executives need to be in touch with those receiving the message, engaging them in dialogue about what they are hearing, how it is being interpreted, and what it means to them. Is the message being received what was intended? If not, then engage in dialogue to figure out what's wrong and how to do it better.

Third, perhaps the best opportunities to convey the message and to determine how it's being heard comes during performance reviews. Annual performance reviews are increasingly being discarded in favor of more frequent and regular check-ins with employees conducted around specific topics. These interactions are great times to reinforce official messages and to gauge reactions from colleagues and employees. Performance reviews, whatever they are called and whatever form they take, almost always garner employee attention. And the typical one-on-one format can be conducive to authentic conversation and dialogue, especially if done in a positive and nonthreatening way.

CLOSING THOUGHTS

The world's best strategy—the most innovative, clever, and unassailable strategy—is worth little if no one knows about it except those who devised it.

Think about this. The essential point of strategy in the first place is to provide a guide for action, decision making, and resource allocation. Within a modern organization, scores of managers, if not hundreds or even thousands, are tasked with the responsibility to make decisions and to allocate resources. And, virtually everyone in the organization is expected to act judiciously in performing his or her job.

How can managers and other employees carry out these responsibilities effectively if they do not know what they are supposed to do?

Strategy is central to concerted coherent action within any organization. Managers and employees usually want to act in accordance with the strategy. But, for that to happen, they need to know the strategy and to understand it well. Most members of the organization will not—cannot—reach this state of understanding unless the strategy has been explicitly communicated to them. Effective communication requires the executive(s) sending the message to take responsibility for its receipt, to appreciate the distractions involved, and to use the many tools available in the modern digital world. We have tried in this chapter to review some of basic criteria and methods typically associated with effective communication.

KEY TAKEAWAYS

- Failing to clearly and widely communicate a great strategy causes problems that are almost indistinguishable from those caused by the lack of a clear strategy. While some elements of the strategy may require secrecy, effective strategic messaging provides guidance to, and defines expectations for, stakeholders both inside and outside the organization.

- Effective strategic communication provides a clear narrative, one that allows audiences to imagine a sequence of events that lead to a clearly stated goal. Strategy arguments serve as the foundation for such narratives, because they articulate the organization's theory of success, or its leaders' beliefs about how actions and investments will lead to desired outcomes.

- A good strategy message explains the *why* behind the strategic choices of the organization. The best messages convey four core elements: a description of the strategic opportunity; a clearheaded recognition of the main obstacles to success; a simple articulation of the core logic through which the obstacles will be overcome; and a clear connection between the organization's choices and its strategy.

- Leaders must consciously invest in translating their well-formulated strategy arguments into compelling strategy messages for different audiences. Clear argumentation does not suffice; distinct effort needs to be devoted to rhetoric and persuasion. Organizations only reap the benefits of strategic messaging if those messages are widely diffused, vivid, and memorable.

PART IV

Arguing Deeper

CHAPTER 8

||||||||||||||||||||||||||||||||||||||||||||||||||||||||||||||||||||||||||||||||||||||||||||||||||||||||||||||||||||||||||||||||||||||||||||||||||||||
|||||||||||
Elaborating the Strategy

THE BENEFITS OF ELABORATING
THE STRATEGY ARGUMENT

With the widespread proliferation of online digital mapping tools like Google Maps, Waze, and the like, just about everyone has experience zooming in and zooming out on a map. You type in the location you want to see on a map, say Copenhagen, Denmark. The first image you see typically is a high-level "bird's-eye" type of view of the whole place or entity you searched for. For Copenhagen, we see an outline of the entire city situated on a piece of land jutting out from the west (left-hand side of map) and near a body of water to the east (right-hand side). We can see a narrow body of water running through the city from the north to the south, spreading out some into a bay near the southern outskirts of Copenhagen. Within Copenhagen, we see several outlined districts or neighborhoods with names, including Frederiksberg, Vanløse, Nørrebro, Østerbro, Sundbyøster, and Sydhhavnen. The map is a good depiction of the entire city, but it does not show much detail.

In the pre-digital era, the usual way to get increased detail on the streets and places in Copenhagen involved finding another series of maps of the various parts of the city, each depicting its own defined space and showing more detail. In fact, a company named Thomas Brothers operated a healthy business for decades selling Thomas Guides of various cities, consisting of an atlas of places within the city, shown in varying grades of detail. Today, of course, the way to get greater detail is much easier—it requires only a click of your computer mouse or pinching your fingers on the screen of your smartphone.

You can zoom in (or out) on any part of the map, and if you keep zooming, you can get an amazing degree of detail about any particular place.

Why do we zoom in on maps? Because doing so reveals details that are obscured or omitted at higher levels of abstraction. High levels of abstraction are powerful in terms of giving us a sense of the overall structure, but what they leave out can be consequential. In a new city, what looks like a convenient way to cross the river and drive from point A to point B may turn out to be a one-way bridge in the opposite direction. Only by zooming in do we discover the right way to go.

As with maps, strategy arguments can be developed and articulated at different levels of abstraction. To this point, the arguments we have developed have been at reasonably high levels of abstraction, akin to what one would get if one typed a city name like Copenhagen into Google Maps. There is enormous value in generating a strategy argument at this high level of abstraction, because (with fewer moving parts) it is easier to communicate, and because it provides an overarching structure for strategic debates. Moreover, the right place to start will almost always be at a high level of abstraction, so that everyone agrees on the basic contours of the strategic landscape.

Yet a complete understanding of a firm's strategy will require diving deeper into or zooming in on particular aspects of the argument and fleshing out the details. In our view, this process of elaborating the strategy argument has three potential benefits, which we illustrate in this chapter. First, elaborating the argument will often result in the discovery of necessary but unstated or hidden conditions (premises) for the argument. Second, diving deeper into background assumptions and premises will—just as we saw in the transition from a strategy map to a formal argument—often surface unstated differences in interpretation or a recognition that people are looking at the same statements and thinking different things. And finally, elaborating the argument can lead to a reconsideration of the logic behind intuitions developed (and perhaps rejected) at a higher level of abstraction.

In this chapter, we illustrate these benefits by returning to the Walmart case study and elaborating different aspects of the arguments developed in chapters 2 and 3. We try to both deepen the argument by delving further into background assumptions and premises, and elaborate the argument by extending it to other phenomena. There are many ways to do this; the way you should proceed ultimately reflects both your taste and artistry as a strategist. Still, we think a good next step almost always involves trying to identify and specify causes (or conditions) of the listed premises. In mapping terms, we are suggesting coming up with insights that can be placed to the left of the current list of premises and drawing arrows to the existing premises. In doing so, we are turning the current premises into intermediate conclusions that need to be justified in a formal argument. In short, we are going back further in the causal chain.

THE PRACTICE OF ELABORATING THE STRATEGY ARGUMENT

Zooming in on Walmart

In the Walmart map we developed in chapter 2, we started our analysis with the ideas about its strategy from table 2.1 (please see table 2.1 to refresh your memory).

We then took some of these ideas, those considered to be among the most important, and built a map of cause and effect (or premise and conclusion) in figure 2.7, presented again in this chapter as figure 8.1.

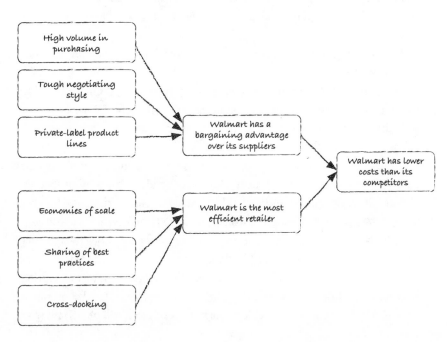

8.1 Expanded visualization of cost argument for Walmart

In chapter 3, we then turned a component of this map into a formal argument using some of these ideas. It read as follows:

Premise W4: IF a firm has a bargaining advantage over its suppliers, THEN it will have lower per-unit input costs.

Premise W2: Walmart has a bargaining advantage over its suppliers.

Intermediate Conclusion W2: Walmart has lower per-unit input costs.

Premise W1*: IF a firm has lower per-unit input costs AND at least comparable other costs, THEN it will have lower costs than its competitors.

Premise W3: Walmart has at least comparable other costs.

Conclusion W1: Walmart has lower costs than its competitors.

Notice that in our attempt to explain how mapping and argument construction goes, we dropped some ideas and focused on others. In particular, we zoomed in on Walmart's bargaining advantage over its suppliers, and we left the other ideas in the table and the map out of the analysis, most notably the argument branch about Walmart's efficiency as a retailer. We also did not go backward in the causal chain about bargaining advantage, which in the map contains ideas about purchasing volume, negotiating style, and private-label lines.

So, in attempting to elaborate the argument, the first question is: Where should we start? We have several options. Obviously we could go back to table 2.1 and pull out ideas like "own trucking operations." Or we could try to improve the "efficient retailer" branch of the argument. Or we could stay with the bargaining advantage branch of the argument and develop it more precisely. What to do?

Our view is that the best place to start is with a critical premise (as discussed in chapter 6) that is important to the overall conclusion but that also appears either opaque or complex. Why? Three reasons. First, we are trying to unpack the argument behind the strategy in order to make it as clear and comprehensible as possible—and an opaque or complex cause does the opposite, it obfuscates. Second, we think breaking down an opaque or complex cause allows us to isolate and to monitor the simple straightforward assumptions buried in the cause. Third, breaking down the cause into isolated components should help to uncover actionable managerial levels that will be helpful when executing the strategy.

Of course, deciding which premises are critical as well as opaque and complex is a matter of judgment in many cases. Think of this judgment as part of the art of doing strategy with logic. With Walmart we think most of the causes depicted in the map could benefit from unpacking. For illustration purposes, we choose here to develop first the one we worked with in chapters 2 and 3, the premise about buying from suppliers at lower costs because Walmart has a bargaining advantage. Why? The criticality of this cause is clear, as without lower supplier prices, Walmart could likely not sustain its lower costs of operation relative to competitors, the primary conclusion. And, while it is easy to state this premise, it is not obvious to many how you can do it, as suppliers usually don't want to (and won't) lower their prices just because a customer asks. Moreover, there are many ways to try to get your suppliers to do this, and it is important to understand the strategy to know whether Walmart has any special or unique practices.

Uncovering Unstated Premises: High-Volume Purchases

Our map for Walmart initially contained three sources of the bargaining advantage: high volume, tough negotiating style, and private-label products. In chapter 3, we more or less dismissed tough negotiating style and dropped it from the analysis. However, we will return to this idea later. First, however, we ask: how do high volumes and private-label products give Walmart a bargaining advantage over its suppliers? What are the causes, conditions, or assumptions needed for this to happen? What we want to do in this step is to *treat the bargaining advantage as an intermediate conclusion to explain.* Let's call it intermediate conclusion W3. That is, we are now focusing on the problem you might map simply as follows:

High volume in purchasing → Walmart has a bargaining advantage over its suppliers

The rationale for this causal link will likely be intuitive to most people—if we buy more, then we can likely get a lower per-unit price. That's a common occurrence, and it takes no further explanation, one might say—it's common sense.

"Common sense" assumptions can often generate misunderstanding and get us into trouble. For instance, in the Walmart case, several different mechanisms might plausibly convert high-volume purchases into a bargaining advantage, ranging from enhanced familiarity with the supplier and its economics (arising from repeated high-intensity interactions) to high dependence of the supplier on the buyer (because the purchase is a large chunk of its output). Among a group of strategy analysts contemplating the issues, each may be thinking of a different mechanism and assuming the others think as he or she does, even though each may have a very different mechanism in mind. Yet it is imperative for the analysts to know whether they agree on which mechanism is operative here and whether the mechanism Walmart uses is a common one and easy to implement elsewhere, or if it is something unique. Moreover, even when people are thinking of the same mechanism, they may not understand the conditions that allow it to work successfully—fleshing out these conditions may show the limits of the strategy as well as provide additional strategic advice, as we will show later. Formalization can help surface these issues and make the mechanism and its conditions more transparent.

So, what is behind the claim "High volume in purchasing → Walmart has a bargaining advantage over its suppliers"? How could it be true for Walmart? Conceptually, what we aim to do is to unpack the main premise into a set of more specific premises that highlight the bargaining effects of high-volume purchasing. We want to break things down analytically. So, we start with the (now) intermediate conclusion W3 that states "Walmart has a bargaining advantage over its suppliers" and work backward, attempting to break down the premise about high-volume purchasing into a more insightful series of assumptions.

In doing so, we begin with a simple observation about the basic economics of the supplier, economies of scale. An economy of scale occurs when the per-unit costs are lower at high production volumes than at small production volumes. This is a familiar and widespread phenomenon, true of many manufacturing processes in which firms must make substantial fixed cost investments before producing the first unit of output. For example, before producing its first car, an auto manufacturer needs to build a factory. As output increases, these costs are spread out over the larger volume, thereby lowering per-unit costs, as long as the firm does not have other variable costs that increase with volume. So, we specify the premise:

IF a supplier has substantial fixed costs of production AND variable costs do not increase with production volume, THEN increases in the volume of production generate lower average costs per unit produced.

Actually, this premise is true by definition, so we might call it a "definition" rather than a premise. It will not matter for our derived conclusion which way we specify it, but calling it a definition does make it clear that we do not have to worry about its truth value as a premise. So, we rewrite it as (where "WV" stands for "Walmart volume"):

> *Definition WV1:* Economies of scale: A supplier with substantial fixed costs of production and variable costs that do not increase with production volume will show lower average costs of production at higher production volumes.

Now let's think about what this means for a specific supplier with multiple customers. If, for any reason, the supplier increases production volume, its average cost will be lower for all its output of the product. So, if the supplier has multiple customers for the product, an increase in demand from any one of them will result in lower average costs for the supplier's total production. Note furthermore that anything that lowers the supplier's average cost of the product creates the potential for the supplier to increase its margin (average price-average cost) with all of its customers, provided the price remains constant. Price may not remain constant, however, so we specify the premise as follows:

IF a supplier's average costs of production decline, THEN the supplier's possible margins increase for all the supplier's customers of that product.

Alternatively, we could again write this as a definition and not worry about its truth value:

> *Definition WV2:* When a supplier's average costs of production decline, its possible margins with all its customers of that product will increase.

Now, let's consider what this means for the supplier in terms of its relationship to a high-volume buyer. The high-volume buyer is attractive to the supplier, because the economies of scale generated by that buyer would substantially lower average per-unit costs and increase possible margins, and this benefit would be spread over other buyers as well, even if they have small purchasing volumes. By contrast, a small-volume buyer has less of an impact on the supplier's economics. With lower overall average costs thanks to the high-volume buyer, the supplier could either reap the reward by taking higher returns, lowering its prices to gain more market share, or a combination of both, and improve its competitive position against other suppliers. This situation can be specified with a premise that combines the insights of definitions WV1 and WV2:

> *Premise WV1:* IF a supplier has economies of scale, THEN a high-volume buyer allows the supplier EITHER to reap higher margins for each sale OR to lower the prices of its product to buyers.

If there are multiple buyers, some will clearly be more important to the supplier than others simply because they are bigger and have a larger impact on its economics—the larger buyers are the ones who really drive the costs down because of the volume they add. So, we can again see a truth simply by definition:

> *Definition WV3:* For a supplier with economies of scale, the buyer who purchases the greatest percentage of a supplier's output for a product will contribute the most (of all buyers) to lowering the average cost of production (greatest downward effect on average costs).

Now, finally, think about the bargaining situation that occurs between a supplier and its highest-volume buyer, especially if that high-volume buyer is a supplier's largest customer. For the supplier, the highest-volume buyer is the most important buyer, and the relative importance of the buyer increases as the volume demanded by that buyer increases relative to other buyers. The supplier really needs this customer, for the simple reason that losing the highest-volume buyer will have the largest impact on the supplier's overall margins, especially if there are no alternative buyers that could take up the volume. Keeping this customer is critical, because doing so allows the supplier to increase its margin with other customers. Accordingly, the supplier is typically willing to accept a lower price (and lower margins) from this high-volume buyer than it might from a smaller buyer. Conversely, if the buyer is aware of the fact that it has this impact on the supplier's cost structure, it is in a better position to demand a price discount relative to other buyers. This mechanism is at the heart of the bargaining advantage. We specify it as follows:

> *Premise WV2:* IF suppliers can maintain higher margins with other customers AND the demand of the supplier's highest-volume customers is difficult to replace, THEN suppliers will be willing to accept lower prices (margins) from their largest customers.

Putting together the three definitions WV1–WV3 with the premises WV1 and WV2 yields the intermediate conclusion W3 we seek, explaining how high-volume purchasing gives a bargaining advantage over suppliers. To make it applicable to the Walmart case, we need to add a few more empirical premises:

> *Premise WV3:* Walmart buys many products in high volume from its suppliers.
>
> *Premise WV4:* Many of Walmart's suppliers have production systems with substantial fixed costs.
>
> *Premise WV5:* For many suppliers, Walmart represents the highest-volume buyer in their portfolios, and there are few alternative buyers with the same demand.
>
> *Premise WV6:* Suppliers can charge different prices to different customers, and therefore maintain higher margins with other customers, even if they give their largest customers a price discount.

So, definitions WV1–WV3 along with premises WV1–WV6 (connected by AND operators) yield the intermediate conclusion W3 (Walmart has a bargaining advantage over its suppliers, previously premise W2) we want about Walmart holding a bargaining advantage over its suppliers.

What exactly is gained by this exercise? For many readers, the logic of this argument is straightforward; countless executives are familiar with the concept of economies of scale, either thanks to training in economics or through experience. For many, this is what they implicitly mean when they claim "High volume purchasing gives Walmart a bargaining advantage over its suppliers," and indeed the logic seems so obvious that it may seem there is little point in spelling it out.

In our view, however, there are almost always gains to being explicit about the underlying logic. In part this is because everyone in the organization may not have the same grounding in economics and may not think of this particular logical argument when seeing the initial claim relating purchasing volume to bargaining advantage. Clarity about the elaborated logic will ensure superior communication and make reliable execution more likely. But more importantly, the benefit of spelling things out is that doing so helps to surface unstated assumptions. In this case, spelling things out makes it clear that a condition for the bargaining power over suppliers is the existence of economies of scale in the supplier's production process. If almost all of the supplier's costs are variable, then it makes far less sense for Walmart to try to push hard with other suppliers or markets. Frontline negotiators therefore need to understand the economics of the suppliers they are negotiating with. Similarly, premise WV2 makes clear that it is not enough to be the largest supplier; in order to extract a bargaining advantage, it must be difficult for the supplier to replace Walmart should it walk away from the negotiating table. Isolating this requirement generates a useful insight: Walmart's bargaining advantage likely has deteriorated somewhat with the growth of Amazon.

The lesson of this exercise is that elaborating an argument can help surface implicit assumptions, even in situations in which members of the leadership team accept the basic claim. In fact, it is precisely when the leadership team agrees that elaborating the argument can play this useful role. When there is disagreement among team members, constructive argumentation is more likely, and implicit assumptions are more likely to come to the surface. But when there is apparent agreement, these assumptions are more likely to remain submerged.

Discovering Differences in Interpretation: Private Label

The second branch of the map concerns an argument about private-label product brands. These are brands that the retailer owns, designs, and sources itself and uses a "private" label to market. Private labels are attractive to consumers because they typically provide reasonable quality for lower prices than branded goods, although there is often uncertainty in the consumers' eyes about the extent of the quality difference. At Walmart, an estimated 84 percent of its customers purchase at least one of its private-label products.[1] Private labels are popular among large retailers, because they offer potentially higher margins and can be started and discontinued quickly, because manufacturing is outsourced. Amazon launched its AmazonBasics line with a small number of products (such as batteries) in 2009, and offered more than 1,500 products in the category ten years later.[2] Walmart's many successful private-label brands include Ol' Roy (a top-selling dog food), Equate (health, beauty, and pharmaceutical items), Parent's Choice (baby products), Mainstays (home décor and utensils), as well as a variety of apparel brands, including Time and Tru (women's clothing), Terra & Sky (plus-size clothing), Wonder Nation (children's clothing), and George (men's clothing).

In our strategy map about Walmart, we showed a premise indicating that private-label product lines gave Walmart a bargaining advantage over its suppliers. We now ask: Why is that the case? What is it about private labels that provide a bargaining advantage? As with the high-volume purchasing branch, what we seek to do here is to unpack the causal link, and make explicit and transparent the mechanism and conditions that foster this advantage. The intended outcome is again the bargaining advantage stated in intermediate conclusion W3, but now private labels are the pathway. We distinguish private labels from broader consumer brands such as Coke or Pepsi, which we refer to here as "third-party brands."

We start the formalization by reconsidering the intermediate conclusion we wish to support, namely that Walmart has a bargaining advantage over its suppliers. This leads to a confession—one that demonstrates the value of trying to elaborate arguments: in discussing between ourselves why we think private labels generate a bargaining advantage, we realized that each of us was thinking of a different process! The problem is that the intermediate conclusion is stated imprecisely, in a way that only becomes clear when one thinks about the effects of having private-label goods. When we say "suppliers," do we mean the suppliers of private-label goods, or the suppliers of third-party brands like Coke and Pepsi? Our intuitions on this matter were different, it turned out: one of us was referring to suppliers of private-label goods, while the other had third-party brands in mind. This is not, in this case, a problem; because it seems that both could be true, and because we wish to preserve a harmonious relationship as coauthors, it simply means that we need to construct two subarguments related to the effects of private-label goods. Yet even before we began, this realization illustrated that one value of elaborating an argument is to reveal differences in people's interpretations of more simply stated claims.

With this clarification in place, we are ready to begin by considering why Walmart might have a bargaining advantage over its private-label suppliers. One set of reasons relates to those elaborated in the prior section; it seems likely that Walmart is the highest-volume buyer for many of the suppliers of private-label goods. But is there something more to the dynamic when it comes to private-label suppliers? We think there is. With private-label sourcing, the manufacturer is not revealed to the customer. As a result, a private-label owner like Walmart has greater flexibility. They can buy from multiple suppliers at the same time, can buy opportunistically in market cycles, and (as just mentioned) can buy with guaranteed high volumes, all of which serve to provide a bargaining advantage to the private label when sourcing its products.

These tactics may not always be successful, so again we ask: When would they be? Under which conditions? An obvious condition is when the product carries low switching costs, meaning that the owner can move its production from one manufacturer to another without great difficulty or investment in start-up costs. Another condition is when the supplying industry has excess capacity, meaning idle equipment and resources can be deployed for some positive return (as opposed to losses when idle). Putting all this together gets us the following argument (where "WP" stands for "Walmart private label"):

> *Premise WP1:* Private-label production entails low switching costs for the buyer.
>
> *Premise WP2:* Private-label manufacturers collectively hold excess capacity.
>
> *Premise WP3:* IF a buyer can switch manufacturers with low costs AND a buyer can buy from producers with high excess capacity, THEN the buyer will have a bargaining advantage over the manufacturers.
>
> *Premise WP4:* Walmart is a private-label product buyer.
>
> *Intermediate Conclusion W3:* Walmart has a bargaining advantage over suppliers (manufacturers of private-label products).

These conditions would definitely push prices for private-label goods downward, but how might owning private labels help in bargaining with third-party brands? One possibility is that owning a successful private label puts the retailer in a better position to walk away when negotiating with the third-party brands, because any loss in revenue from losing the brand can be at least partially made up by customers switching to the corresponding private-label products. For example, Walmart will drive a harder bargain with Purina if it is confident that most customers will be satisfied with Walmart's own Ol' Roy brand dog food, and that any reduction in revenue from Purina products will be largely made up by higher margins on the private-label product. We can state this intuition as follows:

> *Premise WP5:* IF a private-label product has higher margins for a retailer than a third-party brand, THEN the retailer will have more of a bargaining advantage over the supplier of the third-party brand.

The key for this argument, then, is whether the antecedent of premise WP5 holds: we have to demonstrate that private-label products have higher margins than third-party brands. One reason to believe this is the bargaining advantage that the retailer has over the private-label manufacturers, as just elaborated. But are there other reasons to expect margins to be higher? Yes. One major factor is that the private label carries almost no advertising and marketing costs, while third-party brands invest heavily in maintaining brand awareness. Of course, public labels are also often higher volume too (think of Coke versus a chain grocery's private-label cola), so they may enjoy economies of scale in production and have lower per-unit production costs. This means advertising and marketing costs might trade off against scale advantages. For products manufactured at the same scale, the private label should be less expensive, because it does not involve advertising and marketing costs. So, it matters whether the private label can be sourced at high volume.

> *Definition WP1:* Private labels entail no or very low advertising and marketing costs.
> *Definition WP2:* Third-party brands have substantial advertising and marketing costs.

Premise WP6: IF a third-party brand's scale economy savings do not exceed its advertising and marketing costs, THEN a private-label product can be supplied at lower cost than a third-party brand.

Premise WP7: For the third-party brands in product categories in which Walmart has a private-label product, the third-party brand's scale economy savings do not exceed its advertising and marketing costs.

Intermediate Conclusion WP4: Walmart can source private-label products at lower costs than a third-party brand.

Now, let's move to the consumer side of the transaction, as consumers' willingness to pay for private-label goods will determine the margins of those goods. How much are consumers willing to pay for private-label goods, relative to third-party brands? This will obviously vary from consumer to consumer and product category to product category. However, in general it seems reasonable to assume that customers will have lower willingness to pay for a private-label good, because they typically do not have the same confidence in the quality of the private-label product relative to the third-party brands (in part thanks to the marketing by those brands, which emphasizes quality ingredients, product innovation, etc.). But how much lower—enough to offset the cost savings associated with private-label goods?

It seems difficult to provide a precise answer to this in the abstract, but we can consider some of the reasons why third-party brands might command a price premium. One simple way to bring this subargument to a close is to assert an empirical premise:

Premise WP8: The reduction in prices for Walmart's private-label goods relative to third-party brands will be less than the reduction in costs.

Taken together with intermediate conclusion WP4 and premise WP5, this generates our desired targeted intermediate conclusion:

Intermediate Conclusion W3: Walmart has a bargaining advantage over its (third-party brand) suppliers.

At one level, relying on an empirical premise like premise WP8 at such a critical stage of the argument is very unsatisfactory, because as outsiders we have no basis on which to assess whether it is true. Even for people within the company, who might be able to measure the differences in prices and costs, the premise is somewhat unsatisfying, because it short-circuits any insight we might be able to gain into *why* premise WP8 holds, or when it should hold. At another level, however, there is some value in the stark nature of premise WP8: it forces us to recognize what has to be true empirically for there to be a bargaining advantage over third-party brands. In our judgment, this premise is less likely to hold than the intermediate conclusion about the cost advantages of private-label brands. By its starkness, the premise gives leaders an opportunity for a gut check about the conditions under which a private label creates a bargaining advantage. We can imagine some product categories—such as wine—where premise WP8 is generally unlikely to hold, and other categories—such as dog food—where it is much more likely to hold. Spelling out the logic behind these intuitions is beyond the scope of this chapter, however.

We close this section by emphasizing again one of the true benefits of elaborating one's initial, often simplified arguments: surfacing fundamental differences in interpretation. Only upon elaborating this strand of argument did we fully realize that private-label products can have two different kinds of effects on bargaining power over suppliers.

Reconsidering Intuitions: Walmart's Negotiation Process

Now let's return to the Walmart negotiation process. In chapters 2 and 3, we dropped the initial premise "tough negotiating style," because we thought it too facile and unconvincing. Still, when you look at the company's beliefs and the suppliers' experiences, there seems to be something important about the way Walmart negotiates with suppliers. The experience of negotiating with Walmart is an important part of the lore surrounding the company in popular media, business cases, and more sophisticated analyses, and appears to have been so for decades. From an analytical perspective, when a pattern repeats itself like this, it is reasonable to believe that there is a systematic reason for it. So rather than discard our initial intuition, as we did in chapters 2 and 3, perhaps we need to rethink the logic that might be at work.

Why might Walmart want to cultivate a reputation for tough, no-nonsense bargaining? One reason, we speculate, is to limit favoritism, influence, and petty corruption. The actual bargaining and price setting is carried out by individual Walmart buyers who interact with the suppliers' sales staffs. High-volume purchases make the staff who control the negotiation process with high-volume suppliers not only powerful but also susceptible to influence and favoritism. The suppliers' sales staffs, on the other hand, will typically have very strong incentives tied to the margins of a sale, which, given Walmart's volume, are potentially quite large. There is a reason, in short, that salespeople like to wine and dine their clients. Moreover, it is difficult to monitor the buying process when it involves such volumes on a regular basis. A company that is able to prevent such influencing tactics will have lower costs than a company that cannot do so. We can formalize this argument as follows (where "WN" stands for "Walmart negotiation"):

> *Premise WN1:* IF an organization's buyer makes high-volume purchases and controls a large budget, THEN the buyer and organization face potential influence and favoritism problems from suppliers eager to win their business.
> *Premise WN2:* Walmart's buyers make high-volume purchases and control large budgets.
> *Intermediate Conclusion WN1:* Walmart and its buyers face potential influence and favoritism problems from suppliers eager to win its business.
> *Premise WN3:* IF an organization can eliminate influence and favoritism by suppliers in its buying process, THEN its purchasing costs will be reduced.

How does Walmart eliminate influence and favoritism in its buying process? Our intuition is that this has to do with its tough negotiating style. But now we have to be specific about what we mean by a tough negotiating style. In the popular lore, this is less about Walmart buyers yelling and screaming, and more about requirements that suppliers come to Walmart headquarters at a specified time, meet in a bare-bones Walmart office, and present offers in a prespecified manner. In other words, suppliers and buyers are given very standardized ways of interacting. We build this observation into our argument, even though we do not specify all the techniques Walmart uses. The key causal claim is premise WN4:

> *Premise WN4:* IF an organization requires potential suppliers to follow standardized, depersonalized, and transparent procedures in making offers and negotiating, THEN it lessens the chance that influence and favoritism affect the negotiation with suppliers.
>
> *Premise WN5:* Walmart carefully controls and monitors the buying process by requiring potential suppliers to follow the same standardized, depersonalized, and transparent procedures in making offers and negotiating.
>
> *Intermediate Conclusion WN2:* Walmart's negotiating style lessens the chance that influence and favoritism by suppliers affect its buying process.

With this intermediate conclusion, we have now justified the antecedent in premise WN3 and can conclude that, thanks to its negotiating style, Walmart is able to reduce its purchasing costs.

> *Intermediate Conclusion WN3:* Walmart's purchasing costs will be reduced (thanks to its negotiating style).

This argument could be elaborated further, although we will not do so here. One natural avenue of inquiry would be to ask why it is that Walmart can impose these strict negotiation procedures on its suppliers. The answer likely has to do with its purchasing volume, but we leave the development of this argument to the reader.

This example illustrates another virtue of elaborating one's arguments. Recall that in chapter 3, we rejected our initial intuition that a tough negotiating style played a role in Walmart's success. The reason we did so was because our initial formulation relied on a simple causal claim that seemed too implausible: "IF a firm has a tough negotiating style, THEN it will have a bargaining advantage over its suppliers." It seemed easy to imagine exceptions to this claim, and so we rejected the premise as false, even though the argument that we had developed was logically valid. Yet intuitively we continued to suspect that Walmart's negotiating style played a role in its success. Returning to this intuition and adopting a different argumentative approach generated a better insight into an element of Walmart's logic of success.

CLOSING THOUGHTS

We have tried in this chapter to show how the logical analysis of a strategy can be elaborated at length and in depth. We did so by continuing with the Walmart formalization of chapter 3 and showing how it could be elaborated by working backward in the causal chain of conditions or premises generating the bargaining advantage of Walmart over its suppliers. Specifically, we developed three separate subarguments or mechanisms that might lead to Walmart's bargaining advantage, including its size or volume of purchasing, its use of private-label products, and its highly disciplined negotiation process.

Arguably, any of the three mechanisms could produce Walmart's advantage on its own, and so the subarguments might be properly connected by OR operators. Numerous analyses by economists and others suggest, however, that Walmart benefits from all three. So, even though we don't need all three to make the argument hold, it seems useful to recognize and monitor all three, whether you are concerned about Walmart or whether you are a competitor looking for an opening. The fact that all three seem to hold also says something about the strength and sustainability of Walmart's advantage, at least over smaller brick-and-mortar retailers.

We recognize that the kind of analysis laid out in this chapter is quite advanced, and in many cases more in-depth than is needed by many executives or companies. We say that not because the arguments are technically complex—the elaborations consist primarily of specifying longer sets of premises, including some about social and economic processes. The added complexity comes mainly in the form of greater detail and longer lists. We are confident that virtually every executive can handle that. Rather, the question is about value—how much is gained by spending this extra effort and elaborating the argument in such detail?

This question is particularly important given the fact that it is quite possible to elaborate arguments in too much detail. To return to our earlier analogy, you can zoom too far in on a map: everyone who has used an online map has had the experience of overdoing it, zooming in too far (or in the wrong place) so that you get more detail than you want. You lose track of where you are on the map and have no orientation points to situate yourself. You are lost in detail, unable to see the forest for the trees.

Theorizing about strategy, even with maps and logic, can easily result in the same experience. As we show in this chapter, formal theory has the ability to narrow the scope of analysis tighter and tighter, honing in on some particular aspect, feature, or mechanism. This is a great virtue when it comes to deepening one's understanding. Yet there may be no natural end to this increasingly tighter focus, and ultimately strategic leaders need to act. In a famous folk story, upon seeing an image of the earth positioned upon the back of a very large turtle, a child asks his father, "What is under the turtle?" The father responds, "Another turtle," and after this exchange repeats itself several times, the father finally pronounces with finality, "It's turtles all the way down." So too with theoretical assumptions—the ability to delve deeper and deeper into assumptions means there is no natural end to this tightening focus. It is a virtue of theory. But it is also a danger of theory—going too deep into the underlying assumptions and premises may take you too far away from the problem of interest. For executives doing strategy, that means taking you into a world that you have no ability to influence, making the theory vacuous and the analysis irrelevant. The art of doing both theory and strategy involves knowing precisely the right level of abstraction and detail at which to conduct the analysis.

How far should you go? How do you avoid getting lost in the trees and losing sight of the forest? Ultimately, this is a matter of judgment and is dictated by the strategic problem at hand. We realize that this may be an unsettling answer—what if you are a novice and don't have, or even know, good judgment? The answer is that this judgment comes with experience. The more you work with strategy as theory, the better your instinct will get for finding the right level of abstraction and knowing when to stop. Perhaps the easiest place to get this kind of experience is in performing strategic analyses of other companies—whether you read about them in the press or in case studies or experience them firsthand. Much of MBA teaching in business schools is founded on the same principle: cases are taught and analyzed not to provide a template for action, but to give students experience in formulating and elaborating strategy arguments to the point of understanding which premises in the argument can be accepted without needing further elaboration, and honing one's instincts for when further elaboration is likely to be fruitful.

In short, strategy theorizing is an intensely iterative process. Therefore, start with an initial theory or formalization and take it as far as you can. Then let it sit. Come back to it later and look at it again, and you may see it differently and find new openings. It also helps to show it to others, to discuss and to debate and to argue in the ways discussed in chapter 4. The questions others raise about your theory will likely lead you to see things you have not articulated well or things that you have been assuming without being explicit about it. Others will also tell you when you have gone too far, are not producing insight, and are lost in the detail. Listen to what they say.

Part of the learning you will get from experience comes from making mistakes, going too far into the details or background assumptions, or not far enough, and then realizing it and recalibrating. In any recalibration step, we also strongly believe that it is much easier to zoom out and give up detail than it is to zoom in and go deeper into the stack of turtles underlying the theory. So, our advice for those just starting to work with these tools is to develop your theory as deep as you can initially. Then go deeper. Then go even deeper. At some point you will lose your ability to go further, or you will recognize that going any further has little value. At that point you should not stop, but instead go back and look at the whole effort and contemplate where it started to get lost in the trees. Again, we advocate doing this in conversations or debates with others. Your colleagues will usually be happy to tell you when they think you have gone too far into the details, and if you can't convince them otherwise, then you probably have done so.

Purpose also determines what part of the argument to build out and develop. The biggest challenge facing Walmart as we write clearly comes from online retail in general and Amazon in particular. The great success of Walmart occurred in a different world, at least as it concerns consumer behavior. We imagine that the assumptions about consumer behavior inside Walmart's executives' heads are so deep and ingrained that they have trouble recognizing them, let alone evaluating them. If so, then we have little doubt that a deep and elaborated analysis of online and other consumers would be valuable. Walmart needs to understand what they are up against and how much of their old model works against them (surely part of their rationale for acquiring online star Jet). And, even with a valid logical analysis in hand, questions would arise about whether they could actually undertake the steps needed. These are issues about strategy formulation that we address in chapters 9 and 10. Using logical tools for formulating future strategy involves using what we have reviewed and learned so far, but also adapting it slightly to face the special problems of thinking about the future.

KEY TAKEAWAYS

- Initial attempts to visualize and formalize strategy arguments will typically focus on capturing the logic of success in broad strokes, with the core logic being represented at relatively high levels of abstraction. This powerful starting point provides a framework for agreeing on the core strategic issues and is easier to communicate. Yet what is left out can be consequential, particularly when a strategy needs to be put into action. Leaders should be willing to elaborate their strategy arguments in a focused way by zooming in on particular elements.

- Elaborating arguments benefits the strategy process in three main ways. First, it will often result in the discovery of additional necessary but implicit assumptions in the original argument. Second, elaboration can cause leaders to recognize that they may be thinking different things when looking at the same statements. Third, elaboration provides a vehicle for rethinking strategic intuitions that might initially have been abandoned in the initial argument.

- Strategy-making involves iteration, moving back and forth between concrete facts and experiences on the one hand and abstract concepts and theoretical claims on the other. Ultimately, the craft of arguing strategy involves judging exactly the right level of abstraction at which to conduct the analysis, one that provides sufficient general insight to handle unforeseen circumstances, but not so abstract as to be difficult to apply to the organization on a day-to-day basis. Leaders develop such judgment through experience with formulating and assessing strategy arguments.

CHAPTER 9

||||||||||||||||||||||||||||||||||||||||||||||||||||||||||||||||||||||||||||||||||||||||||||||||||||||||||||||||||||||||||||||||||||||||||||||
||||||||||

Perceived Quality Strategies

THE BENEFITS OF STRATEGY ARGUMENTS FOR PERCEIVED QUALITY STRATEGIES

In the fall of 2017, a thirty-second commercial appears on the television screen. The rapidly cascading sequence of images is disconcerting, if somewhat familiar—a linear montage of split-second shots and loud noises:

- a dark flashing sky with a mushroom cloud from an exploding nuclear bomb;
- a crowded room with press photographers and reporters standing and lying spread out all over the floor;
- what looks to be a bearded terrorist making pronouncements;
- an angry President Donald Trump at an official podium;
- a grainy aerial image of the top of a building disintegrating into smoke as a missile strikes it;
- a motorcyclist riding with an automatic weapon extended, firing at cars;
- an unaccompanied conga drum set on a dimly lit stage;
- a sleek modern virtual reality mask;
- members of a large crowd holding lit cellphones in the air;
- electronic equipment boards with exposed circuitry;
- a dense cluster of slim, white, modern windmills on a wind farm peacefully rotating in the breeze;
- a frantic hospital scene where an injured person is being wheeled down the hall on a stretcher;
- and so on.

This is *just* the first seven to eight seconds of the commercial.

Over the background sounds and sirens of distress, a male voice-over intones gravely: "It's a noisy, chaotic, confusing world. If only everyone could see it more clearly. Separate fake from fact. If only we all understood what's really going on. The world needs another *Economist* reader."

Few for-profit companies are so brash as to base their sales pitch on the assertion that the fate of the world depends on you buying their product. But *The Economist* is so bold, and long has been. It is an approach that has worked, particularly in recent years. Despite strong downward trends in both sales and profits for newspapers and magazines, *The Economist* stands out as a major exception. According to the Audit Bureau of Circulations, *The Economist* in late 2018 had an average world circulation per issue of over 1,650,000, with almost 800,000 of these from the printed publication and the remainder from online digital views. Within North America, its largest publication market, the weekly magazine had an average circulation of almost 900,000 (nearly 500,000 in print), with 98 percent of these actively purchased. *The Economist* continues to grow in size and show good profitability: in 2017, revenues increased by 4 percent from the previous year and reached an all-time record. Unlike newspapers and magazines that rely on a traditional business model that depends heavily on advertising, *The Economist* derives the bulk of its revenue from subscriptions, where it commands an impressive price and requires separate fees for print and online access. By contrast, other, more advertising-dependent American news magazines, such as *Newsweek*, *Time*, *US News & World Report*, and the *New Republic*, all suffered setbacks due to the rise of the internet. Some even teetered on the brink of failure. No other magazine of this scale has succeeded by building a subscription base that pays most of the bills.

At a time when access to news is free and widespread, thanks to the internet, *The Economist* stands out as a firm that has built a sustainable competitive advantage in a tough industry. Its competitive advantage is fundamentally different from the two major examples we have considered so far, Southwest Airlines and Walmart. Specifically, *The Economist* does not pursue a low-cost (LC) value creation advantage, as those two firms do; instead, its orientation is resolutely toward building a perceived quality (PQ) advantage. (For more on this generic distinction in strategies, see appendix B.) Firms that pursue PQ advantages do so by focusing on driving up the willingness to pay of their customers or finding ways to increase the benefits that customers see in their products or services relative to those of their competitors. By contrast, firms pursuing LC advantages largely try to match their competitors in terms of willingness to pay, but at a lower cost. Walmart does not try to convince you that the box of Tide detergent you buy in its stores is better than one you would buy at the corner market; instead it sells the detergent to you at a lower price, because its cost structure is so much lower than the corner market's. *The Economist*, by contrast, quite explicitly works to convince you that its news coverage is superior to that of its rivals.

The commercial spot fits neatly with *The Economist*'s business strategy; it is a nice illustration of how a specific corporate action can be guided and tailored by the strategy, once it is known and recognized throughout the organization. Needless to say, we doubt that the ad would make sense for many other magazines or newspapers, where its brash arrogance might rub readers the wrong way.

In this chapter, we apply the book's activities for developing strategy arguments to *The Economist*. In addition to providing another opportunity to demonstrate the use of the reasoning tools, focusing on *The Economist* allows us to demonstrate the specific challenges associated with developing strategy arguments for firms pursuing PQ advantages. These unique challenges derive from the nature of a PQ advantage.

The core challenge in developing a strategy argument for a PQ advantage is to articulate and develop a theory of customer preferences: a set of explicitly stated claims about how a product or service drives up willingness to pay for different types of customers. As discussed in strategy textbooks (and appendix B), a PQ advantage depends on the firm's ability to generate a higher willingness to pay among potential buyers of its products than its rivals do, for a given cost level. As a result, PQ strategies hinge critically on understanding the buyer's drivers of willingness to pay and being able to identify which features might generate greater benefits for the customer. The attention of a PQ firm is squarely on the customer. In comparison, leaders of a firm pursuing a LC advantage are, as we saw in the Southwest and Walmart cases, primarily focused on developing a deep understanding of the cost drivers in the business model and finding ways to increase efficiency without diminishing the benefit perceived by the customer.

The different focal points of PQ and LC advantages create two important consequences for the process of developing strategy arguments. First, many (but by no means all) of the central cause-and-effect claims made in LC strategy arguments are general across firms of many different types, with many different kinds of customers. As a result, they are less subject to debate. For example, many LC firms rely on economies of scale to achieve their cost advantage. As a result, their strategy arguments will contain a theoretical premise along the lines of "If fixed costs are a meaningful proportion of total costs, then average cost per unit will decline with production volume." This statement will be of critical importance for the strategy argument, but because it is a general principle of economics (and accounting), it is unlikely to carry much controversy when invoked and will hold for all kinds of firms no matter the industry.

With PQ strategies, on the other hand, many potential evaluation metrics can be called into play, and different customer segments may respond to totally different dimensions of quality. For instance, in the automobile market, some customers seek speed and handling, others seek comfort and luxury, and still others seek safety features. Each represents a different kind of perceived quality. In strategy arguments for PQ advantages, the central causal claims will be about how customers react to different product attributes or activities. These claims are more likely to be idiosyncratic to specific product categories and distinct customer segments, and therefore rely on greater context-specific knowledge.

For these reasons, in a typical consumer market, there are generally several different kinds of successful perceived quality strategies, with different strategic logics; by contrast, there is generally less variation in logic among firms competing on cost. To return to the automotive example, some would say that Toyota's logic is centered on reliability, Volvo's on safety, and BMW's on handling. We think that this differentiation makes the strategy analyst's job more difficult. Pursuing a PQ advantage implies that a company will be able to offer products/services that are not only somewhat unique but that consumers will find more appealing than competitors' also somewhat unique products/services. In other words, the strategy analyst has to figure out how to compare apples and oranges in terms of their appeal and potential margin.

Second, the claims about cause-and-effect relationships that enter into an LC strategy argument are typically easier for a firm's leaders to verify, because accurate and detailed information on cost structure is more likely to be available. Costs are highly measurable. By contrast, measuring willing-ness to pay is considerably more difficult. Particularly when firms are selling products to consumers (as opposed to selling inputs to another firm's production process), the impact of different actions on willingness to pay can be diffi-cult to assess and quantify. Recognize that when a customer buys a product at a certain price, all that can be determined with certainty is that the custom-er's willingness to pay exceeded that price—but not by how much. As a result, strategic leaders must typically rely on more indirect means of verifying the central claims in their strategy arguments. In our view, this means that leaders of firms pursuing a PQ advantage must be even more explicit about the nature of their assumptions about the relationships between the firm's actions and customers' willingness to pay.

If logical argumentation can help people appreciate and understand LC strategies, where there is essentially one dimension to the comparison, then it has even greater value in the more multidimensional world of PQ strategies. But the nature of PQ advantages also makes developing the argument harder: it is more difficult to spell out the logic, because it is more likely to be idiosyn-cratic to the firm and its context. A big part of the problem is that in addition to everything developed above for LC strategies, with a PQ-based strategy the analyst also needs to articulate the *theory of customer appeal* that is implicit in the strategy. He or she must be able to answer the question "What is it that the consumers really want?" We illustrate one such argument through an analysis of *The Economist*'s strategy.

THE PRACTICE OF STRATEGY ARGUMENTS FOR PERCEIVED QUALITY STRATEGIES

Case Study: *The Economist*

Founded in Britain in 1843, *The Economist* officially calls itself a newspaper, but to most readers it conforms better to what is considered a news magazine. Published weekly, it reports on events and trends throughout the world, with a greater focus on economic and political matters than, say, fashion or lifestyle, even though it does touch on those topics at times.[1] Most articles are short, digest-form summaries of the news on a specific topic, designed to give the reader a quick overview of the most important happenings around the world. However, the magazine is also known for its special reports on specific topics, such as artificial intelligence or the geopolitics of energy, that provide deeper than usual analysis. Many view the content as sophisticated as well as intellectually stimulating. For example, *The Economist* ran a story in 2018 about how cultural taboos in China make it difficult to build and manage health-care facilities for very sick people near the ends of their lives—not a topic that most readers would have thought about before. Each issue begins with editorials written by the magazine's staff that forcefully and often humorously articulate *The Economist*'s distinctive worldview and often contrarian ideology, which does not fit neatly into a traditional left–right spectrum.

The Economist plays to a global readership. With the bulk of its readers based in the United States and United Kingdom, the magazine has benefited from the rise of a well-educated, English-speaking middle class in Asia, Latin America, and Africa who participate in the global economy. The magazine targets a sophisticated audience, both in its content and its marketing. Its articles often cover seemingly esoteric or narrow topics, such as the political sentiments of voters on remote islands in Indonesia, the state of press freedom in Ethiopia, or the changing attitudes toward gold among Indian consumers, as well as the major events of the day. *The Economist* thus claims not to worry about what content readers might think they want, but instead gives readers what the editorial staff thinks they need. Articles do not merely summarize facts, but have a point of view. A reporter for the publication related to us that when he was hired, the magazine's editor told him that it was a "views paper" not a newspaper, and that the reporter's role was "to sit on the moon, and look at the earth" and then comment on it. The reporter expanded on this phrase by saying it means that while you should take a position and argue it, you should do so from a nonpartisan perspective (a guy on the moon), taking all other arguments seriously. Our informant also noted that *The Economist* has resisted efforts to put more data and pictures and less text in the paper, saying that it believes readers want the arguments more. The magazine is therefore densely written (and typeset); moreover, the complexity of the writing demands a higher level of reading comprehension than mass-market news magazines and newspapers.

Based on its content and its British origin, *The Economist* signifies intellectual and analytical sophistication to many. The reporter with whom we spoke noted that many people regarded the magazine as snooty, snobbish, and boring—what he called the "William" effect (in an exaggerated British accent). *The Economist* embraces this sense of exclusivity and sophistication. In addition to the television commercial described earlier, *The Economist* has a long-running series of print advertisements that in simple white type against a red background signal the exclusivity of its readership, with messages like: "It's lonely at the top. Bring something to read"; "Fueling your delusions of grandeur"; "Pressure peers"; and "For those whose photos aren't tagged on Facebook." A high subscription price contributes to the sense of exclusivity. The articles and the marketing combine to make many *Economist* readers feel pride in their association with the magazine when others think highly of them and defer to them for information and opinions. Anecdotal evidence from executives and MBA students suggests that many value the magazine in part because by reading it they acquire insights and opinions that serve as fodder for cocktail party conversations or opportunities to impress the boss. The magazine gives them not only something to talk about, but also a way of subtly showing off their sophistication by virtue of reading it. Some go so far as to suggest that reading the magazine is actually not necessary, as long as one is seen with it—perhaps carrying a copy when boarding a plane or casually leaving copies around the office. Showing others that you are an *Economist* reader can affect the way your opinions are perceived regardless of what they are or how well formulated they are.

Organizationally, *The Economist* has a distinctive structure and culture compared to many other news magazines. Our informant suggested that *The Economist* has relatively little hierarchy relative to other publications. The editor in chief is appointed by an independent set of trustees, not the parent company board. The magazine has department and section editors, but job rotation is a core principle of the organization; correspondents are regularly rotated across topic areas, and people move back and forth between business and editorial roles. The focal point of the magazine's editorial process is the so-called Monday meeting, when the editors and correspondents discuss the week's events, debate the magazine's position on the issues, and plan the upcoming issue. Influenced by an Oxford-style debate culture, these meetings are wide-ranging discussions that could touch on any issue, although the editor in chief makes the final content decisions. Unlike traditional newspapers, stories have no bylines; readers do not know who wrote a given article. This was an explicit and long-held policy, well articulated on *The Economist*'s website, which explains that the policy allows many writers to speak with a collective voice. Leaders [leading articles] are discussed and debated each week in meetings that are open to all members of the editorial staff. Journalists often co-operate on articles. And some articles are heavily edited. Accordingly, articles are often the work of *The Economist*'s hive mind, rather than of a single author. The main reason for anonymity, however, is a belief that what is written is more important than who writes it.[2]

Before going to press, articles might be read and edited at least a dozen times by various members of the staff. Ideas and claims are held to a high standard. These different elements of organization and culture combine to produce *The Economist*'s distinctive, high-quality content.

Visualizing the Argument

We begin with the visualization and mapping tools developed in chapter 2. As before, we start with the conclusion that we wish to reach, namely that *The Economist* has a PQ value creation advantage. A necessary condition for a PQ advantage is that a firm's products generate higher willingness to pay than those of its rivals. In addition, for more value to be created, the increase in costs required to deliver this higher perceived benefit must be less than the increase in willingness to pay. For our current purposes, we are primarily interested in understanding how *The Economist* generates higher willingness to pay. As a result, we will focus on this as our conclusion. We place this on the right-hand side of the board (see figure 9.1).

A full-blown analysis of *The Economist*'s strategy would, of course, need to justify the claim that the magazine's costs are not disproportionately out of line with those of its rivals.

Next, we do some brainstorming based on what we know about the magazine, generating a list of key activities, assets, and resources that we think

> *The Economist* has
> higher WTP than
> its rivals

9.1 Conclusion of strategy map for *The Economist*

Table 9.1 Brainstorm ideas about *The Economist*'s strategy

◦ Intellectually demanding writing	◦ Rising demand for intellectually challenging material	◦ Growing global middle class
◦ Unique editorial voice	◦ Correspondents posted globally	◦ Decline of print advertising
◦ Focus on arguments and analysis	◦ Dependence on subscription sales at high prices	◦ Prestige accorded to readers
◦ Trustee structure	◦ Perceived as sophisticated	◦ No bylines
◦ Use of humor	◦ Current events	◦ Middle-class status anxiety
◦ Diverse and sometimes esoteric coverage	◦ Global coverage	◦ Short articles
◦ Articles reviewed by peers before publication	◦ Association with nineteenth-century Britain	◦ Marketing emphasizes exclusivity
		◦ In-depth reports
		◦ Editorial independence

might be crucial to the PQ advantage. The informal process we conducted produced the list shown in table 9.1.

This list of elements is, as it should be at this stage, wide-ranging, with details on the nature of *The Economist*'s customers, the magazine's product features, and its organizational practices. In particular, the list includes both factors that might influence the willingness to pay of buyers and factors that shape *The Economist*'s cost structure. This is appropriate, because any value creation advantage involves increasing the wedge between customer willingness to pay and the opportunity cost of inputs. However, here we will focus on the factors that shape willingness to pay.

In the next step, we tried to cluster together related ideas from the brainstorming session. In doing this, we kept in mind that our goal was to build an argument concluding that *The Economist* has a PQ advantage over its competitors. Using the information from table 9.1 as the brainstorm input, this exercise yielded a set of idea clusters:

Magazine content

- Intellectually demanding writing
- Unique editorial voice
- Focus on arguments and analysis
- Use of humor
- Diverse and sometimes esoteric coverage
- Short articles
- Current events
- Global coverage
- In-depth reports

Organizational practices

- Trustee structure
- Editorial independence
- Correspondents posted globally
- No bylines
- Articles reviewed by peers before publication

Market context

- Decline of print advertising
- Growing global middle class
- Rising demand for intellectually challenging material
- Middle-class status anxiety

Social benefits of readership

- Dependence on subscription sales at high prices
- Perceived as sophisticated

- Prestige accorded to readers
- Association with nineteenth-century Britain
- Marketing emphasizes exclusivity

Next we took these ideas, synthesized them, and tried to fashion them into a linear argument generating the conclusion we seek.

A natural place to start was to ask ourselves, "Why do people subscribe?" One obvious answer is related to the intrinsic characteristics of the articles and coverage provided; in other words, the knowledge and information provided by *The Economist* is useful to people and superior to what is provided by others. These factors are identified in the cluster we labeled "Magazine content." Each of the factors listed in this cluster contributes in its own way to the appeal of *The Economist*, but what they share is that their appeal for a customer can be found in the pages of the magazine itself—the appeal derives from the knowledge and insight each article brings, from the depth of analysis, and from the distinctive point of view, all of which are unique to *The Economist*. For simplicity, we label this type of influence on willingness to pay as *The Economist's intrinsic appeal*.

Customers derive a second, less tangible kind of benefit, one deriving from the social signals sent by being an *Economist* reader, such as creating the impression that one is a sophisticated person, thereby conferring social status or prestige. These factors are listed under "Social benefits of readership." In our view, these factors generate willingness to pay because they help improve someone's perceived social standing or status. We label this *The Economist's status appeal*.

The two arguments about *The Economist's* strategic advantage operate somewhat independently from each other. So we depart from our default premise connector and join them with an OR connector. Accordingly, our map of the willingness to pay argument for *The Economist* looks like figure 9.2, with the two branches connected to the conclusion independently of each other.

Before we turn to formalizing our argument, we want to include more depth in our strategy map for *The Economist*. We do so by trying to relate some of the factors identified in our brainstorming about the two primary drivers of willingness to pay. At this point the mapping does not have to be perfect, but it will provide a useful starting point for the formalization of the argument. The map we came up with, again with premises linked by OR connectors, is shown in figure 9.3.

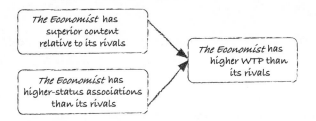

9.2 Elaborated strategy map for *The Economist*

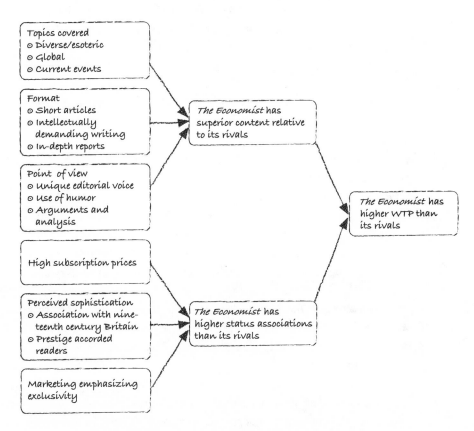

9.3 Expanded strategy map for *The Economist*

Formalizing the Argument

How do we turn this simple visualization into a formal argument? We start by trying to formalize the simple strategy map in figure 9.2. This figure contains empirical claims about the intrinsic appeal and the status appeal of *The Economist* and links each (separately) to the argument's conclusion. We need to state explicitly what each of those links (arrows) in figure 9.2 represents; in other words, we need to generate If-Then premises that are causal claims. We do this for the top branch of the map as follows (where "EC" stands for "*Economist* content"):

IF

> *Premise EC1:* IF a product has superior content relative to its rivals,
>   THEN it will generate higher willingness to pay than its rivals.

AND IF

> *Premise EC2:* *The Economist* has superior content relative to its rivals.

THEN

> *Conclusion E1:* *The Economist* generates higher willingness to pay
>   than its rivals.

Notice the AND connector here (which we usually keep implicit), which is needed to make the argument work. And for the lower branch (where "ES" stands for "*Economist* status"):

IF

> *Premise ES1:* IF a product has higher perceived status than its rivals,
>   THEN it will generate higher willingness to pay than its rivals.

AND IF

> *Premise ES2:* *The Economist* has higher perceived status than its rivals.

THEN

> *Conclusion E1:* *The Economist* generates higher willingness to pay
>   than its rivals.

Note again that the two separate content branches in figure 9.2 are connected to the conclusion independently of each other. This means that we would connect these subarguments through an OR statement rather than AND, because the truth of one subargument does not depend on the truth of the other. In other words, premises EC1 and EC2 combine to imply conclusion E1; similarly, premises ES1 and ES2 also combine to imply conclusion E1. For completeness, we can represent the whole argument as follows, with the two subarguments in parentheses, connected with an OR:

IF
    (Premise EC1: IF a product has superior content relative to its rivals,
        THEN it will generate higher willingness to pay than its rivals.
AND
    Premise EC2: The Economist has superior content relative to its rivals.)
OR IF
    (Premise ES1: IF a product has higher perceived status than its rivals,
        THEN it will generate higher willingness to pay than its rivals.
AND
    Premise ES2: The Economist has higher perceived status than its rivals.)
THEN
    Conclusion E1: The Economist generates higher willingness to pay
        than its rivals.

One implication of structuring the argument in this way is that we are claiming that the effects of intrinsic appeal and status appeal on willingness to pay are additive. Put differently, our argument claims that *The Economist* could have status appeal even in the absence of any intrinsic appeal. At the extreme, the pages of the magazine could be filled with gibberish, and it might still have greater status appeal than its rivals. We do not really believe this, but for the time being we will set this issue aside. (We return to the connection between the two below.)

Our next step in formalization is to ask how we can support premises EC2 and ES2, which claim that *The Economist* has superior content and higher perceived status. We start with superior content and then turn to social status.

Superior Content

What does it mean to claim that *The Economist* publishes superior content? To a certain extent, this question has already been answered in figure 9.3, where we connected the different features of the magazine to the superior content claim. Indeed, when we ask executives why their products are superior, they typically will give us a long list of product characteristics—"better design," "faster performance," "superior functionality," "better user interface," etc. These are partial explanations. They are not sufficient, because they do not explain why those characteristics make the product superior, as opposed to any other number of product features. For example, in the strategy map in figure 9.3, we claimed that *The Economist*'s short articles on a wide-ranging set of global events produced superior content. Why? Does every customer view this type of content as superior? That seems unlikely. But then which kinds of customers *do* value what *The Economist* offers?

Here we encounter the fundamental challenge of a perceived quality argument: *articulating and developing a theory of customer preferences*. When analyzing an existing strategy, the process for developing such a theory is somewhat inductive, at least at first. We start with the features that we identified in figure 9.3, and then ask which kinds of customers might value them. What is the narrative someone might tell that accounts for their attraction to the product? Thus, we ask ourselves what kind of person might want a weekly magazine that has broad global coverage of current events; presents a lot of short, analytical articles; but also has occasional deep dives into specific topics?

Our initial conception of these people is that they hold high-level corporate and governmental jobs or that they work closely with such people. They help set policy for large organizations. These people need to stay up to date on current world events. They also need a nuanced understanding of events, because they make a number of important decisions with wide-ranging consequences. But these people also have hectic and complex lives and do not have the time to gather and analyze information from a wide range of news sources. In the tongue-in-cheek spirit of *The Economist*, we will refer to these types of customers, who shape the policies of large organizations, as "busy, important people," or BIPs.

Let's start by formalizing the intuition that such customers value *The Economist* because they are pressed for time but want to have the best information possible due to the importance of the policy decisions that they make. We formalize this claim in premise BIP1 and write out the argument as follows (where we return to our earlier convention and implicitly assume AND connectors among the premises):

> *Premise BIP1:* IF someone is pressed for time AND needs to make important policy decisions, THEN they will view short, analytical articles as a superior form of content.

Premise BIP2: BIPs are pressed for time.

Premise BIP3: BIPs make important policy decisions.

Intermediate Conclusion BIP1: BIPs will view short, analytical articles as a superior form of content.

Now that we have established why BIPs might prefer the type of content offered by *The Economist*, we need to be explicit about our belief that *The Economist* is unique in offering this kind of content:

Premise BIP4: *The Economist* has a unique emphasis on short, analytical articles relative to its rivals.

Intermediate Conclusion BIP2: BIPs will view *The Economist* as superior to its rivals due to its short, analytical articles.

Similarly, we can develop an argument explaining the appeal of *The Economist*'s emphasis on diverse, esoteric content for BIPs.

Premise BIP5: IF someone's job requires him or her to engage in a lot of professional networking and small talk, THEN he or she will view articles covering a diverse and esoteric set of topics as a superior form of content.

Premise BIP6: BIPs engage in a lot of professional networking and small talk.

Intermediate Conclusion BIP3: BIPs will view articles covering a diverse and esoteric set of topics as a superior form of content.

Premise BIP7: *The Economist* has a unique emphasis on articles covering a diverse and esoteric set of topics.

Intermediate Conclusion BIP4: BIPs will view *The Economist* as superior to its rivals due to its articles covering a diverse and esoteric set of topics.

As a next step, we suggest how intellectually demanding writing and in-depth reports drive intrinsic appeal:

Premise BIP8: IF a person has a high level of education, THEN he or she will view intellectually stimulating articles as a superior form of content.

Premise BIP9: Articles with intellectually challenging writing are intellectually stimulating.

Premise BIP10: In-depth reports are intellectually stimulating.

Premise BIP11: BIPs have high levels of education.

Intermediate Conclusion BIP5: BIPs will view intellectually challenging writing and in-depth reports as a superior form of content.

Premise BIP12: The Economist has a unique emphasis on intellectually challenging writing and in-depth reports.

Intermediate Conclusion BIP6: BIPs will view *The Economist* as superior to its rivals due to its intellectually challenging writing and in-depth reports.

Let's now step back and contemplate this argument we have constructed. A first reaction may very well be: "Wow, that's complex!" Indeed it is. Partly this is a function of the number of ideas, and therefore the number of premises introduced. But the structure is also more complex than formalizations in prior chapters. Consider our original claim that *The Economist* has superior content (premise EC2). This is now an intermediate conclusion supported by three intermediate conclusions about why BIPs view *The Economist* as superior: because of its short analytical content (intermediate conclusion BIP2); because of its articles covering a diverse and esoteric set of subjects (intermediate conclusion BIP4); and because of its intellectually challenging writing and in-depth reports (intermediate conclusion BIP6). Each of those three (even-numbered) intermediate conclusions is in turn supported by its own subargument containing multiple premises and an (odd-numbered) intermediate conclusion.

A deeper source of complexity in this argument arises from the connectors between premises. Again, we have been following our convention that the premises in each subargument are connected with AND connectors. This means they must all be jointly true for the conclusion to hold.[3] Furthermore, our convention dictates that even the most "important" intermediate conclusions—the even-numbered ones that yield the intermediate conclusion about superior content—are joined using an AND connector. Taken literally, that means that we are claiming that *The Economist*'s superior content requires short analytical content AND diverse and esoteric subjects AND intellectually challenging writing and in-depth reports. All three have to be true at the same time.

Even more stringently, all of the premises used to justify each of the three even-numbered intermediate conclusions have to hold as well. If a single one of them fails, the entire argument supporting the conclusion that *The Economist* has superior content fails as well.

With so many premises in the argument, this seems rather severe and somewhat implausible. Does *The Economist* really always need all these things to be true in order to generate a higher willingness to pay? It seems doubtful. At the other extreme, the option is to connect at least the three even-numbered intermediate conclusions with the OR operator, as we did when connecting the content and status claims to our overall conclusion (figure 9.2). But this condition seems overly lax, because it implies that any single premise could generate the conclusion. Doubtful again.[4] The problem is that we don't know which of the even-numbered intermediate conclusions (acting as premises here) can generate the conclusion on their own and which require the joint operation of others.

We are left with this quandary because the case and surrounding verbal accounts of the intrinsic appeal of *The Economist*'s content are not precise enough. In attempting to write out the newspaper's strategic advantage in a logical format, seeing this gap can be frustrating. But we actually find it very insightful and even enlightening. Think about it. The exercise has allowed us to see and appreciate the limits of our understanding and knowledge of the strategy, something we could investigate in greater depth with systematic research if we needed to do so. The gap is also consistent with our editorial insider's understanding of *The Economist*'s appeal, which he attributed to a "secret sauce" that was hard to pin down precisely.

This example highlights the challenges one often encounters in trying to construct arguments for perceived quality strategies, because such strategies often rest on differentiation, or the idea that a firm offers a product that is unique relative to its competitors. But products usually differ from their competitors along multiple dimensions simultaneously, for intended and unintended reasons. More importantly, those different characteristics can interact in ways that are both difficult to predict and to discern. Unlike the case of a low-cost strategy, for which one can often specify the cost function quite precisely, it is difficult to specify a corresponding willingness to pay function. One potential response to this challenge would be to engage in hand-waving or at the other extreme to exhibit a blind confidence in one's knowledge of what exactly causes the PQ advantage. But in our view, a more fruitful approach—because it allows for learning and insight—is to embrace the complexity of these kinds of strategy arguments.

It is worth noting that in the process of formalizing our original strategy maps, the argument has evolved and become deeper. This is an important benefit. In the strategy map, we simply linked the characteristics of *The Economist* to the idea that the magazine had superior content. Now, we have spelled out a set of theories of why customers prefer *The Economist*'s content (premises BIP1, BIP5, and BIP8). We believe each of these three premises represents a step forward in our understanding in two respects. First, each specifies an explicit, falsifiable theory of customer preferences. This means that we could relatively easily determine whether this is really the way the world works. In our experience, having some knowledge of a wide range of esoteric topics is quite valuable when you are sitting next to someone at a corporate function (premise BIP5), but perhaps our intuition here is idiosyncratic to our own experiences.

Another advantage of the formalization of our beliefs about customer demand is that we have stated our theories of customer behavior independently of who the publication's readers are. Many executives will try to explain the appeal of their product or service by pointing to the characteristics of their existing customers. As a result, their first pass at articulating the strategy argument will rely on simple statements about what their customers like. We did the same thing as we were developing these arguments. We started with an image of who *The Economist*'s customers are—busy, important people (BIPs) and made different claims about what BIPs prefer (i.e., intermediate conclusions BIP1, BIP3, and BIP5). We could have treated these as empirical claims. However, as we thought about it, it seemed more productive to turn them into intermediate conclusions and try to articulate our argument for *why* BIPs might prefer these kinds of articles. In short, we forced ourselves to develop a more abstract argument.

The great benefit of abstracting the argument somewhat is that if our proposed mechanisms hold (as we think they do), we have a more general and abstract understanding of which kinds of people might prefer *The Economist*. For a practicing executive, this kind of insight is quite valuable, because it makes it possible to imagine new customers beyond the firm's current buyers. For example, the claim that people with high educational levels will be drawn to the intellectually challenging content opens up the possibility that the magazine appeals to highly educated people who are not BIPs as we have defined them—like college professors. In this way, even though we started with a caricature of the customer, the process of formalizing led to deeper, more general insights.

Status Appeal

Let's now work on the other argument branch in figure 9.3, the one concerning the status appeal of *The Economist*. Recall that what we have formalized to this point is the following:

> *Premise ES1:* IF a product has higher perceived status than its rivals, THEN it will generate higher willingness to pay than its rivals.
> *Premise ES2: The Economist* has higher perceived status than its rivals.

As sociologists, we don't feel the obligation here to go into the rationale behind the claim that people prefer higher-status goods (premise ES1). Recognition and praise from others is satisfying to most people and is actively sought by many.

Instead, our main task in developing this argument is to try to back up our assertion in premise ES2 that *The Economist* has higher perceived status. That requires us to articulate an argument for why a product like *The Economist* may be seen as higher status than its competitors: How do people come to associate products with different levels of social standing?

A fascinating yet challenging feature of status is that it is hard to see and measure. It is not like the weight of a product, for which there is a common metric that can be printed on the label. Absent a "status score" listed on each product, what do customers do? They draw inferences about the status of a product by paying attention to a variety of cues. For example, because occupations vary in their prestige, people draw inferences about the status of a person by the job that person has—doctors are generally held in higher esteem than garbage collectors. Similarly, people draw inferences about the status of a person by paying attention to who associates with that person. One person's status rubs off on the other: if we are regularly seen hanging out with Nobel Prize–winning scientists, others will generally start to think more highly of us, with the logic being that someone so eminent would only spend time with us if it were worthwhile. A similar effect occurs with products and firms, which are often defined socially by the "company" they keep (e.g., who their customers are). Finally, the scarcity or exclusivity of a product is often an important status cue. Being high status is about being at the top of a social hierarchy, and only a few can be at the top.

We can use these intuitions about the nature of status goods to substantiate our claim that *The Economist* has higher perceived status than its rivals. Let's start with the observation that people and objects are accorded some status by others simply by virtue of perceived association with high-status others. We then argue (where "ESA" stands for "*Economist* status association"):

> *Premise ESA1:* IF people see a high-status person with a product, THEN that product will have high perceived status.
> *Premise ESA2:* BIPs are high-status people.
> *Premise ESA3:* People see BIPs with *The Economist*.
> *Intermediate Conclusion ESA1:* *The Economist* has high perceived status.

Note that spelling out the argument in this way generates some interesting implications. For example, for the conclusion to hold, it is essential that people see BIPs (or other high-status people) with *The Economist*. This insight has strategic consequences for *The Economist*, because it implies that the print version is important to the magazine's status appeal—people cannot as easily see BIPs consuming *The Economist* if the BIPs are reading it exclusively online. Indeed, consistent with this argument, *The Economist* has maintained its commitment to print issues despite the rise of the internet, unlike many other news magazines that have ceased production of their print issues.

Before we accepted our argument, however, we decided to think more carefully about the key theoretical claim, premise ESA1. Are all products that high-status individuals consume automatically high-status goods? What happens if we see Mark Zuckerberg drinking a Diet Coke? Our intuition about status is that it rubs off, that the status associated with a product is a function of the status of the people associated with the product—whatever the status of those people is. Premise ESA1 is problematic, because it assumes that all that matters is whether a high-status person is associated with a product. Diet Coke is not high status in the same way as *The Economist*, because all kinds of people drink Diet Coke, no matter where they are on the status spectrum. This suggests that we should modify the first part of our argument. A simple way to do so is with the argument restated as follows (changes marked by *):

> *Premise ESA1*:* IF people predominantly see high-status people with a product, THEN that product will have high perceived status.
> *Premise ESA2:* BIPs are high-status people.
> *Premise ESA3*:* People predominantly see BIPs with *The Economist*.
> *Intermediate Conclusion ESA1: The Economist* has high perceived status.

In our view, this slight reformulation generates an important insight, thanks to the necessary empirical claim that people *predominantly* see high-status individuals with *The Economist* (premise ESA3*). What our argument now suggests is that for *The Economist* to generate status appeal, its readership should primarily consist of high-status people; if everyone is reading *The Economist*, then it will not have the same high perceived status.

This insight implies major strategic consequences. It creates a tension for *The Economist's* use of status appeal as a driver of willingness to pay, in the following way. On the one hand, it seems reasonable to assume that BIPs are the potential customers for whom the status appeal is least important, as they have other markers of status—like job titles, club memberships, private bankers, etc.—available to them. On the other hand, for people who are not members of the elite, yet want to appear to be legitimate members, *The Economist's* value as a status symbol has a lot of appeal. As noted earlier, some of these "wannabe BIPs" may not care very much about the content of the magazine—they just want to be seen with it. Yet if there are too many "wannabe BIPs" and everyone is carrying a copy of *The Economist*, its status appeal will disappear.

Now let's think about how some other features of *The Economist's* policies might relate to sustaining its status appeal. One obvious way to address this challenge is through marketing campaigns that emphasize its status associations. Messages like "It's lonely at the top. Bring something to read" attempt to reinforce intermediate conclusion ESA1 ("*The Economist* has high perceived status") somewhat independently of the composition of the magazine's readership.[5]

> *Premise ESA4:* IF a firm emphasizes exclusivity and status in its product marketing campaigns, THEN its product will have high perceived status.

Premise ESA5: The Economist emphasizes exclusivity and status in its product marketing.

Similarly, the magazine's emphasis on its nineteenth-century British roots are another way of creating high-status associations that do not depend on the readership—provided people associate nineteenth-century Britain and its empire with status.

Premise ESA6: IF a firm emphasizes its nineteenth-century British roots, THEN its products will have high perceived status.
Premise ESA7: The Economist emphasizes its nineteenth-century British roots.

As with premises ESA1–ESA3, these premises (ESA4–ESA7) lead into intermediate conclusion ESA1. And as with the previous BIP premises, it is not clear whether these premises are needed jointly to generate the intermediate conclusion (using AND connectors) or whether some or several of them can generate it independently (requiring only OR connectors). It is an open question that background research might reveal an answer to, but for now we assume the more restrictive statement and connect them jointly (with AND connectors).

We should also think about the rivals of The Economist, because it matters whether they have high perceived status as well—the advantage here should be relative. We think a good way to conceptualize this difference again hearkens back to the BIPs. As we understand it, the rivals are not seen in the hands of the BIPs nearly as often. So, we formulated the following premise:

Premise ESA8: People do not predominantly see BIPs with The Economist's rivals.
Premise ESA9: People do not predominantly see high-status people with The Economist's rivals.

When coupled with premise ESA1*, the following intermediate conclusion follows:

Intermediate Conclusion ESA2: The Economist's rivals do not have high perceived status.

The subargument is potentially important as a reminder to monitor the readers of rivals and to recognize that if one of them starts catching on with high-status people, it could undermine the competitive advantage of *The Economist*.

An altogether different way to sustain the status appeal of *The Economist* is through policies that affect the composition of the readership. In other words, *The Economist* can do things to ensure that premise ESA3* holds true. The most obvious of these policies is pricing and can yield a new argument as follows:

> *Premise ESA10:* IF a product has a high price relative to its rivals, THEN its buyers will predominantly be those for whom the product has highest intrinsic appeal.
>
> *Premise ESA11: The Economist* has a high price relative to its rivals.
>
> *Intermediate Conclusion ESA3:* The buyers of *The Economist* will predominantly be those for whom the product has highest intrinsic appeal.

In combination, these premises support the claim that *The Economist* will predominantly be read by BIPs and show how pricing can help sustain the magazine's status appeal.

Furthermore, with the intermediate conclusion in this subargument, we have made a connection to our earlier arguments about *The Economist*'s intrinsic appeal to BIPs! For simplicity here, we have not formalized this link, but a more complete argument might do this.

But this last observation generates another important strategic insight: to sustain its status appeal, *The Economist* needs to deliver on the intrinsic appeal of the content. In other words, it must ensure that the articles in the magazine serve the needs of the busy, important people who are its core customers.

CLOSING THOUGHTS

Value creation is the starting point for any strategy; if the firm does not create a meaningful gap between the buyer's willingness to pay and the opportunity cost of inputs, it cannot prosper economically. In our analyses of Walmart and

The Economist, we have formulated strategy arguments for different aspects of the value creation process, reflecting the different widely used generic value creation orientations—low cost and perceived quality—of the two firms. Because our primary goal has been to illustrate the application of the strategy argument tool kit, in neither case have we performed a complete analysis of each firm's strategy. In a sense, we took one side of the value creation process for granted in each case: for Walmart, we treated the willingness of buyers to pay as unproblematic, and for *The Economist* we did not devote attention to the cost structure. In practice, one may not want to be so cavalier. Walmart will not succeed if the ways in which it reduces its costs end up destroying any willingness to pay for buyers (see Sears for a recent example). In other words, Walmart's leaders need to understand what their customers care about. Similarly, the different benefits that *The Economist* creates for its readers cannot be sustainable if the costs required are way too high.

Our focus in this chapter has been on the challenges involved in generating strategy arguments in which the critical element is developing a theory of consumer appeal. For any firm pursuing a perceived quality advantage, such a theory is essential, because the firm's putative advantage rests on being able to create a higher level of willingness to pay than its rivals. We close this chapter with a number of observations about the process of developing such arguments.

First, while the notion of developing a theory of consumer appeal may seem daunting at first, we suggest that one way get to traction is to start with an image of the ideal customer type for the firm's product. In the case of *The Economist*, we did this with the notion of busy, important people, or BIPs. Note that the notion of a BIP is a caricature and a stereotype and conceals a lot of diversity among the kinds of people who find the publication appealing. But our goal is not to provide an exhaustively detailed and accurate picture of the firm's customer segments; the goal is to get the ball rolling on our theory of consumer appeal. To do that we need an image of the customer, and the BIP caricature delivers on that. The reason it does, we suspect, is that our caricature is a crude way of articulating our not-yet-developed theory of consumer appeal, generated through a mix of intuition and observation.

It would be natural—and correct—to worry about too heavy a reliance on caricatures such as the BIPs, if only because different people may imbue the caricature with different meanings. But as we saw in this chapter, one advantage of the formalization process is that it can bring those diverse understandings out in the open. So, in formalizing, we first articulated an argument in which the important characteristics of BIPs was their busyness, or lack of time. Further thought led us to the notion that BIPs will also tend to be highly educated and perhaps have a taste for intellectually challenging material. And so on: we moved past the caricature not through data, but through rigorous thought. The benefit is that in the end, our arguments depend on statements about general characteristics of consumers (their busyness, their level of education) that move beyond the caricature and form the basis for a deeper understanding of the appeal of the firm's product.

Second, strategy arguments for perceived quality strategies will typically be more complex and difficult to develop than arguments for low-cost strategies. While it does not have to be so, a PQ strategy usually will be more complicated for no other reason than the need to contain a theory of consumer appeal that will, particularly when the firm targets individual consumers, rely heavily on a variety of claims about consumer psychology, culture, and social structure. Such insights are all the province of social scientific theories that many executives are less familiar and comfortable with than the economics of cost drivers in a production process. Moreover, as with *The Economist*, the theory of value may take several theoretical premises to even get the basics right. The theory may also be complex because it is self-referential, meaning that one part depends on the other parts. In *The Economist* case, we saw this with the two key argument branches of intrinsic appeal and status appeal.

Third, in the process of developing the formal arguments, we encountered uncertainty about the appropriate connectors between premises. The problem is that while we think all the causes listed in the premises are contributors to the conclusion, we simply do not know how important each of them is, and whether or not any of them could generate the conclusion by itself. In the rendering presented here, we took a conservative route on the subarguments and assumed their premises are all connected with AND connectors, except for the highest-level distinction between content and status. Formally, this decision makes it harder to generate the intermediate conclusions, because all the premises in a subargument must be true. Practically, this decision may make the reasons behind the success of *The Economist* look more difficult to manage (given the many factors in the premises) and easier to undermine (all that is needed is to make one premise false) than is actually the case. The decision also carries implications for any assessment of premise consequentiality discussed in chapter 6. As a result, the formalization raises many useful questions for the analyst to study and grapple with.

Finally, because of the need for a theory of value and the added complexity this brings, we suggest that it may be more difficult to figure out and analyze a perceived quality strategy—even (or perhaps especially) one's own. It would not be surprising to us if a perceived quality strategy takes ten times as many iterations to complete as the argument for a low-cost strategy. Consider what this means. In a perceived quality firm, the leadership team will need to spend significantly more of their time on strategy formulation and implementation and monitoring. They may need more staff involved to get a full set of per-spectives, given the more intangible nature of many of the assessments. Above all, a perceived quality firm needs strong leadership, with leaders who will guide the team in developing the strategy and who will insist that they persist until it is acceptable. The leaders must believe in the process and their people. Failing at this effort—i.e., failing to understand why customers might want the product—will not bode well for the future.

KEY TAKEAWAYS

- Organizations differ in whether their fundamental value creation orien-tation tilts toward lowering costs (LC) or increasing perceived quality in the eyes of their customers (PQ). It is generally easier to formulate and assess strategy arguments for LC strategies, because the main mechanisms for reducing costs (such as economies of scale) are well understood and operate across market contexts and because costs are highly measurable. Arguments for PQ strategies prove more challenging, because they are more likely to be idiosyncratic to the organization and its context and because true consumer preferences are more difficult to discern.

- Strategy arguments for PQ advantages require developing a theory of cus-tomer preferences or a set of explicitly stated claims about how a product or service drives up willingness to pay for different types of customers. A useful starting point for doing so is to imagine the ideal customer type for the organization's product or service. Generate this image through a mix of intuition and observation, and then combine it with scholarly and lay theories of the psychology and sociology of consumer behavior.

PART V

Conclusion

CHAPTER 10

||||||||||||||||||||||||||||||||||||||||||||||||||||||||||||||||||||||||||||||||||||||||||||||||||||||||||||||||||||||||||||||||||||||||||||||||||||||||||||||||||||
||||||||||
The Pillar of Strategy

VISION AND DISCOVERY

Widely heralded as the world's greatest living architect, Frank Gehry designed such iconic works as the Guggenheim Museum in Bilbao, MIT's Stata Center, and the Walt Disney Concert Hall in Los Angeles. Gehry's strikingly unusual and creative design for the Bilbao Guggenheim led the father of modern architecture, Philip Johnson, to break down in tears upon first visiting it late in life.

Gehry's buildings stand as unique artistic accomplishments; they also fundamentally transform urban landscapes and draw crowds of tourists from around the world. People often call Gehry the greatest living architect—a so-called starchitect.

The public reveres Gehry in large part because his *vision* is considered creative and compelling. Anyone who has seen his iconic structures marvels at their unusual forms, defying not only architectural conventions but, seemingly, the laws of physics. The architecture critic Herbert Muschamp wrote in the *New York Times* that:

> [Gehry] has shown that even in architecture, a form notoriously resistant to creativity, it is possible not only to realize a personal vision but also to gain wide public support for it. . . . No one since [Frank Lloyd] Wright has gone further than Mr. Gehry in asserting architecture's capacity to effect relationships among individuals in modern democracy. With Mr. Gehry, unity arises from the articulation of differences among the parts. Both

approaches are organic . . . it is the human relationship: the couple, the group, the community, the observer and the observed.[1]

In the world of business, people accord Steve Jobs a similar status. Indeed, no strategic leader has been more highly celebrated in recent decades than Jobs, the cofounder and two-time CEO of Apple. He has become the modern standard against which CEOs are judged. As with Gehry, commentators laud Jobs for the vision and creativity that imagined the iPod, iMac, iPhone, and their successors. His biographer Walter Isaacson wrote in the *Harvard Business Review*:

> In 2000 he [Jobs] came up with the grand vision that the personal computer should become a "digital hub" for managing all of a user's music, videos, photos, and content, and thus got Apple into the personal-device business with the iPod and then the iPad. In 2010 he came up with the successor strategy—the "hub" would move to the cloud—and Apple began building a huge server farm so that all a user's content could be uploaded and then seamlessly synced to other personal devices.[2]

Jobs' compelling vision frequently gets mentioned when people talk about the design elegance of Apple's products.

But a very different kind of story gets told about the strategic success of Honda Motor Company in the 1960s. First with its motorcycles and then its cars, Honda was originally heralded for a prescient strategy that initially used low-cost entry products to build economic scale, which subsequently facilitated movement into higher-margin profitable segments.[3] That is, Honda first developed economies of scale and leveraged them upward into ever-expanding more lucrative markets. But that was not its intention in entering the United States—or, indeed, anything close to its original strategy. Honda's success is now widely seen as a story of emergent strategic *discovery*.

As Richard Pascale documents in the *California Management Review*, "In the view of Honda's start-up team, this [strategy] was an innovation they backed into—and reluctantly. It was certainly not the strategy they embarked on in 1959."[4] As Pascale reports, the plan at entry was to sell Honda's larger motorcycles, targeting the same market served by Harley-Davidson and others. But quality problems emerged with these vehicles as they were tested in the rougher, longer-range American highway market. Local executives worked night and day to address the quality issues and convince buyers to buy Honda's big bikes despite the unfamiliar brand, but to no avail.

In the midst of this crisis, Honda serendipitously arrived at the strategy of selling small bikes to college students, which became the foundation of its long-term success in the United States. Honda's local executives had brought some 50cc bikes for their own use, but did not plan on selling them in the United States. They would ride them around Los Angeles, where they were based, and would take longer rides to work off their frustrations from the stalled sales process. Consumers began to ask about the bikes, and the local executives began to experiment with various ideas, to the point of ignoring—even directly contradicting—the directives of their Japanese bosses. These activities allowed them to learn and to adapt to the American market, as they discovered a way to break through with a novel product to a new audience. The experimentation included the popular advertising campaign "You Meet the Nicest People on a Honda," which was controversial within the company, because some thought it presented the wrong image and would antagonize buyers of conventional motorcycles. Accordingly, the success of Honda rests not on executive vision, as with Gehry and Jobs, but instead on emergent strategic discovery. Honda successfully embarked on a route of experimentation and discovery after its original plans did not pan out.

REASONED ANALYSIS

These two different stories about success—vision and discovery—reflect what many people think strategy is and how a great strategy gets formulated. Yet in our view, both stories are incomplete and potentially very misleading as depictions of a successful strategy-making process. Despite their insights, each story ignores—and thereby deflects attention from—the crucial role of logical argument and the reasoned analysis underpinning it. To put it bluntly: without reasoned analysis, neither vision nor discovery will lead to strategic success. Consider again these two stories of vision and discovery.

Vision Reconsidered

In many experts' eyes, Frank Gehry's greatness arises from his ability to marry his creative vision with a deep understanding of a project's location, its physical materials, and the principles of engineering. The marriage enjoins intuition and reason. Reason is essential, because architects are hired to build buildings, not just dream about them. Without the analytical reasoning of modern engineering, the architect's vision would only exist on paper or in small-scale models. Indeed, Gehry's pursuit of his vision often bumped up against the limits of what was buildable; it was not until Gehry and his partners made fundamental innovations in modeling software that Gehry's vision could be realized. The technological breakthrough allowed Gehry "to take the liberties with form he had always dreamed of, fashioning models out of sensuously pleated cardboard and crushed paper-towel tubes."[5]

A similar misperception can be seen in popular understandings of great strategic leaders in the business world. Like starchitects, strategic leaders receive popular acclaim and celebrity for the vivid pictures they sketch of the future, not for the careful, systematic thinking that enabled them to make that future a reality.

Although Steve Jobs was lauded for the vision and creativity that imagined the iPod, iMac, iPhone, and their successors, it was meticulous analysis and carefully reasoned arguments that turned radical ideas into an enduring franchise and a dominant strategic product position. Ignoring these facts would be like celebrating Frank Gehry for the beauty of his sketches of the Guggenheim and ignoring the engineering required to keep the structure upright. Without keen analytical reasoning, the iPod might well have been a struggling computer company's swan song, rather than the seeds of the iPhone revolution.

Producing great strategy is, like creating great architecture, exceedingly difficult. Truly great strategists can, like Gehry, envision radically novel combinations, embracing tensions, trade-offs, and big bets that most people do not even comprehend. Only by embracing these contradictions can the strategist generate something revolutionary. Yet these very features typically make the visionary's proposals seem crazy, at least until their success has been proven. Just as Gehry needs to convince his patrons that his structure will stay upright before breaking ground, the ambitious strategist needs to convince employees, investors, and other stakeholders to join him or her in moving forward.

Like architecture, good business strategy melds intuition with reason; it demands an inspiring, novel vision on the one hand, and a convincing argument buttressed by rigorous analysis on the other. Yet the strategist's task is arguably harder. Architects like Gehry turn to the principles and formulas of structural engineering (and related disciplines) to determine what they can build. These formulas are tried and true and universally accepted. An architectural vision that passes their test is feasible: you may not find the building attractive, but it will stay upright.

But as any executive will tell you, strategy can be disconcerting, because often there appear to be no formulas that guarantee success, no background disciplines providing support. For many, strategy seems hopelessly subjective and idiosyncratic, as if there are no objective, universal criteria by which to judge a strategic proposal. Topics like finance and accounting, by contrast, come across as robust and reliable: once you enter the right numbers in the spreadsheet, the answer it spits out squelches debate. For strategy, there is no spreadsheet. Instead, the strategy process can seem like an endless exercise in filling out boxes in a framework.

Can we make strategy more disciplined and structured? We certainly think so. Doing so requires embracing the notion that the strategist's vision ultimately must be expressed as a strategy argument—a set of reasons that a particular combination of resources, activities, and external conditions allow the firm to create and capture value. As Richard Rumelt observes in *Good Strategy, Bad Strategy*, strategizing is akin to scientific theorizing:

> The problem of coming up with a good strategy has the same logical structure as the problem of coming up with a good scientific hypothesis. . . . A good scientist pushes to the edge of knowledge and then reaches beyond, forming a conjecture—a hypothesis—about how things work in that unknown territory. . . . In the same way, a good business strategy deals with the edge between the known and the unknown.[6]

The ultimate value of any hypothesis—in science or in strategy—only becomes obvious after empirical testing, a comparison of its predictions against the reality of the world. But experimentation and testing consume time and money, so scientists only test theories if they meet a minimal standard of logical coherence. As we have emphasized throughout this book, this criterion is the standard of logical validity: Does the conclusion of the strategy argument follow necessarily from its stated assumptions? Not everyone who talks a good talk—or expresses a compelling vision—can deliver the goods. Whether one can deliver often depends on whether one can articulate a valid strategy argument for how the vision will be accomplished. So, when considering strategic proposals, assessments of logical validity should occupy the driver's seat. Without rigorous, logically valid strategy arguments, mainly good luck and fortune separate the strategic genius from the raving lunatic. A vision untethered from reality and logic remains only a passing thought and eventually floats away.

In our experiences with executives, this ideal of strategy is not always achieved (or even approached) in most firms. Leaders at all levels place far too much weight on vision and goals, at one extreme, and facts and numbers, at the other. Far too often they neglect the critical role of a strategy argument in building a bridge between the two. Without this bridge, most executives feel more comfortable on the safer ground of what they already know to be true, or what the facts and numbers tell them. They stick to safe incremental proposals, rather than pursuing a bold vision, because they have not done the work of spelling out what needs to be true for them to achieve their vision. In other cases, executives simply take the leap, relying on their gut instincts to choose between competing goals and opportunities rather than rigorously debating the means through which a vision will be achieved, and the critical assumptions upon which the firm's success relies. Sometimes this works, because good fortune shines upon them. But in many more cases, the same leaders abandon their bold new initiative at the first sign of trouble because they lack a clear understanding of the logic by which they might ultimately succeed. The end result is frustration with the strategy process and disillusionment with the leadership.

In addition to providing a criterion for evaluating strategic proposals, a good strategy argument is the foundation for translating a vision into coherent action. A strategy argument is not the same as an operational plan, no more than an architectural blueprint is a theory of physics. Yet all too often in firms, executives move straight from endorsing a particular vision to breaking it down into an operational plan—a series of smaller and smaller nested goals that add up to the outcome desired, akin to Russian matryoshka dolls. There is comfort (and some wisdom) in this process, because it breaks a hard problem down into smaller, more tractable problems. But the comfort of quickly moving from vision to tactics in an operational plan can be deceptive. Don't get us wrong: establishing subgoals is a very important part of the process—but only once a clear strategy argument has been articulated. Just as there is no guarantee that a carefully drafted blueprint obeys the laws of physics, there is no certainty that a well-defined operational plan enacts a logic of success that makes any sense. The best way to ensure that the strategy is coherent is to articulate and examine the argument's structure explicitly.[7]

Sustained success in guiding a business or organization, like success in creating a building that will stand the test of time, may be easier with an inspiring visionary like Jobs or Gehry at the helm. But no matter who leads, sustained success requires having a clear and valid strategy argument, one that is well communicated throughout the organization.

Discovery Reconsidered

The discovery story of companies like Honda says that strategic success depends not so much on a singular commitment to a strategic insight as on the ability of leaders to adapt to events as they unfold. Via a similar emergent discovery process, in 1984 Disney CEO Michael Eisner arrived at the now heralded strategy of building movies, television series, theme parks, Broadway shows, live events, products, and services around animated characters the company created and owned.[8]

As documented by James B. Stewart in *DisneyWar*,[9] in Eisner's early days as CEO, building strategy around animated characters was the last thing he and the Disney board of directors had in mind. At the time of his hiring, Eisner "had been talking about shutting down animation"[10] and "considered abandoning animation altogether."[11] Instead, he "was far more interested in reviving Disney's live-action film and television divisions, businesses he knew well from his stint at Paramount."[12] Eisner only let the animation unit survive because Roy Disney, who had been central to his appointment as CEO, considered it a key part of the company. Eisner put Jeffrey Katzenberg in charge of animation, told him his main job was to keep Roy happy (apparently for political reasons more than anything), and refused to give him much budget for proposed projects.[13] Eisner's attitude toward animation slowly began to change following the unexpected success of *Oliver & Company* (the animated adaptation of *Oliver Twist*) and the release of *Snow White* on videotape, which sold a remarkable three million units. These events "slowly began to convince Eisner that animation, as Roy [Disney] had always maintained, might indeed be the heart of the company."[14] Any doubt was erased with the release of *The Little Mermaid* in 1989, which opened to rave reviews and smashed box office records for an animated movie. Eisner boosted the animation budget and accelerated the animators' production schedule, expecting a new feature every twelve to eighteen months rather than the traditional four-year schedule. As a result, Disney under Eisner experienced spectacular sustained success.

As Eisner's experience shows, winning strategies often arise through an iterative process of formulating plans, experimenting, learning, and revising one's approach in response to unexpected outcomes. Great strategies sometimes emerge over time with action, become clearer in the process, and then are "discovered." Frank Gehry recognizes the role of chance and experimentation in his designs, especially as they evolve from the first model. Even Steve Jobs did not originally anticipate the spectacular success of the iPod, which was originally introduced as part of a (ultimately unsuccessful) plan to revive the fortunes of the Macintosh computer.[15]

Embracing the strategy discovery lesson to the extreme, Silicon Valley evangelists preach the virtues of start-ups being able to "pivot" when their initial strategies fall short of expectations or fail. But in celebrating the leaders who successfully pivoted from a failing business model to the hot new thing, many lose sight of the countless entrepreneurs who pivoted from one failure to the next. Stories of emergent strategic discovery may be inspiring, but we usually only hear the stories about the winners.

Using discovery as an approach to strategy, or a whole-hearted embrace of pivoting, carries two dangers. One risk lies in abandoning a great strategy too soon. Rich Fairbank launched Capital One as a credit card company with a fundamentally new approach to risk assessment and customer acquisition. But initial attempts to implement the strategy generated large losses, and it took two years of red ink before the company found success. Capital One would not come to occupy its dominant position in the industry had Fairbank decided to pivot after six months and pursue a different strategy.[16] The other danger of pivoting lies in chasing fads, reorienting company investments and activities in response to the latest hot thing, only to discover that the initial promise was ephemeral. Surely not a good way to lead an organization!

Both of these dangers follow from the nature of pivoting, which involves using market performance as the ultimate criterion for assessing a strategy.

Accordingly, if performance is poor, people conclude that the strategy is poor; if performance is good, people conclude that the strategy is good. But this is a flawed logic. Do not misunderstand us: we are firm believers that a great strategy will likely lead to superb performance. But that is very different from inferring that good performance is due to a good strategy. While a good (or great) strategy substantially increases the likelihood of good performance, it does not follow from this belief that good performance is necessarily due to a good strategy. Conversely, a period of poor performance does not necessarily mean the firm has a bad strategy. Why?

Firm performance comes from a variety of sources, and not all of them can be traced back to the firm's strategy. While we have only one empirical record of performance, we have several or many plausible explanations, including strategy, industry or market effects, and random or idiosyncratic effects (luck). As all high school algebra students learn, there generally is no unique solution to a problem that has more unknowns than equations. With so many variables potentially affecting a firm's performance, it is incredibly difficult to determine empirically if a firm has a successful strategy or not. As a result, it is impossible to draw any conclusions about the quality of a strategy by looking at short-run performance.

Instead, the firm's performance record should be used to update our beliefs about the firm's logic of success. Discovery comprises an essential part of strategic leadership because it is about learning or updating what we believe to be true. But effective learning requires clarity about our initial reasoning—our strategy arguments. Critical thinking and logical argument are required to sort out why firms succeed and fail. An understanding of failure—or success— can only be achieved by articulating an explanation for that outcome, i.e., a credible argument for why the strategy failed or succeeded. Interpreting the feedback from the market through the lens of a strategy argument is critical not only to understanding what was wrong about the initial strategy, but also what was right. Revising a story paves a surer route to a successful pivot than abandoning it altogether and making up a totally new story.

William Barnett makes this point forcefully when he says, "We often 'learn' without logic, and so we often walk away from great ideas."[17] By this, he means that much supposed learning is in fact fallacious. Sure, we often draw conclusions from an experience and behave differently going forward, but the conclusions we draw are frequently erroneous. For example, Barnett points out that when the Apple Newton failed, many concluded that there was no market for smart handheld devices; of course, as we now know that was far from the truth. Ditto for the late 1990s conclusion that internet search was not a viable business after the struggles of Lycos, AltaVista, Excite, Magellan, InfoSeek, and others. What if Google founders Larry Page and Sergey Brin had taken that message to heart?

Mistaken learning occurs for many reasons, including cognitive bias, faulty information, and superstition. However, mistaken learning almost always involves an absence or failure of clear and coherent strategy arguments. The scientist marks his progress by formulating theoretical insights, testing them against empirical reality, and revising them. Similarly, the strategic leader wins by translating her intuitions about what it will take to succeed in the market into a strategy argument, subjecting that explanation to the test of the market, and reformulating the strategy argument to improve performance in light of market feedback. In both cases, logical assessment holds together the process of developing, testing, and evaluating the explanation. In other words, the process of discovery must be guided by a clear strategy argument, so that leaders know what needs to be changed (and how) and what should be kept the same.

Effective strategic discovery requires clarity about the strategy argument, because it allows leaders to identify the critical assumptions underpinning the proposed course of action. These are the assumptions about the firm's capabilities, resources, or market conditions that need to be true for the strategy to succeed, without which the plan falls apart. Knowing what must be true for the strategy to succeed gives executives two advantages in the discovery process. First, it helps to identify the critical metrics that should be tracked as a means of assessing strategic health. Second, it helps signal when pivoting is warranted: when one's belief in a critical assumption can no longer be maintained.

The executives in charge at Honda and Disney deserve ample credit for being strategically agile during the periods described earlier. They learned from their experiences and adapted when they saw strategic paths that looked more promising than their original plans, even when those new paths involved activities they had originally wanted to eliminate. While we have no personal insight into the process of strategic discovery used in either of these firms (other than what has been written), we assert confidently that the learning process surely would have been facilitated by the existence of clear strategy arguments, along with the identification of critical assumptions. In the case of

Honda's initial entry strategy, a critical initial assumption that proved false was that U.S. motorcycle buyers would consider a Japanese bike comparable to a Harley-Davidson. In the case of Eisner's original decision to move Disney past animation, the critical assumption was that the popular appeal of full-length animated features had passed.

The leaders of Honda and Disney justifiably received ample praise after they found the right strategies. It takes remarkably clearheaded prescience to see early signs of potentially huge success, great personal courage to be willing to invest heavily in these early signs, and remarkable self-confidence and composure to back away from your own publicly favored high-profile plan when it flounders along without really failing. But successful strategic discovery occurs not merely because of highly able executives; it also has its roots in the skills of logical strategy argumentation.

LOGICAL ARGUMENT AS THE PILLAR OF GREAT STRATEGIC LEADERSHIP

What lessons should we draw from Gehry, Jobs, Honda, and Disney? Taken together their experiences show that great strategy is neither simply about articulating a compelling vision and sticking to it, nor about simply responding intuitively to events as they happen. Strategic leaders need to balance commitment and agility. Strategies are necessarily dynamic and contingent, but to be effective foundations for organizational decision making, they must also have a stable pillar that supports wise choices. That pillar is a well-crafted, logically coherent strategy argument that explains how the organization's activities and resources combine with external conditions to generate sustainably successful outcomes. In fact, we do not think we exaggerate when we claim that great strategy is strong logical argument—nothing more, nothing less.

Accordingly, strategic leadership involves using the pillar of logical argument in formulating, assessing, and revising an organization's strategy. It is about identifying the environmental and other conditions that are true—or need to be true—for the organization to succeed. It is about specifying how the firm interacts with those conditions to operate and gain an advantage over competitors. It is about how the various parts of the firm's organizational structure and practices intersect to coordinate and control the flow of work.

And it is about distilling these insights into a formal representation of the firm's logic of success, one that can be shared and debated among the firm's decision makers.

Few strategic advisors today tell executives they should think more about logic! So, we do not doubt that our general advice differs from the preconceptions most executives have when they think about how to tackle strategic challenges. Likewise, we recognize that suggesting that an executive facing an uncertain situation should behave like a scientist formulating and evaluating a scientific theory will be regarded by some as unusual and perhaps even downright bizarre advice.

Our retort is twofold. First, executives routinely embrace the power of disciplined reasoning in many other realms of business and life, for example, when they apply financial models to project future earnings. If disciplined reasoning is appropriate here, it is surely essential in the realm of strategic decision making. Second, is there really a viable alternative? The widespread frustration of executives with the current state of strategy in most firms would suggest not.

Note that when viewing strategy as an argument, the traditional separation of strategy and execution becomes untenable. This is because execution is how the discoveries are made that lead to improvements. An initial strategic plan may be formulated by top leadership, but those tasked with execution can do a much better job if they do not see the plan as truth set in stone (especially when it quickly becomes clear that it is not), but as a provisional hypothesis subject to revision and improvement. In doing so, decision makers throughout the company contribute to the discovery of a better strategy.

As the Honda and Disney cases illustrate, the plan only constitutes the beginning. Strategic leadership entails the ongoing process of adjustment to unforeseen opportunities and threats. As Cynthia Montgomery notes in *The Strategist*, "No matter how carefully conceived, or how well implemented, any strategy put into place in a company today will eventually fail if leaders see it as a finished product."[18] Yet for many executives, their firms' strategies are viewed as finished products, even when they can see that the reality has changed. No wonder they lack confidence. Changing this attitude requires, of course, that executives throughout a firm be comfortable with formulating and assessing strategy arguments and that an organization has a culture and processes that support constructive argumentation.

Viewing strategy as argument also promises to make strategic debates within the firm more productive and more conducive to confidence in the strategy. This is because the language of formal arguments revolves around assumptions or premises and around determining whether the conclusion follows from the assumptions as stated. In a fight, a common way in which an opponent will try to defeat your preferred course of action, for example, is to point out that you are relying on assumptions that may not be true. But the core to thinking about strategy as argument is to recognize that all strategy arguments rest on assumptions! Strategy always involves making bets on what is going to happen and what is going to work in the future. The important thing is to be clear about what those assumptions are, and then to assess how consequential they are.

Accepting that a strategy should be assessed in the first instance in terms of whether the logic is internally coherent creates a space for rivals to hear one another out. That space is created by realizing that neither party can reach a logical conclusion without making assumptions and that one cannot assess a conclusion before understanding what assumptions have gone into constructing the argument. Such recognition allows the opposing parties to hear each other out "for the sake of argument," even when they do not share the same intuitions about the right conclusion. If only one party can construct a valid argument without making clearly unrealistic assumptions, then it is clear whose conclusion should be endorsed. If both of them can, then they have still made progress, because now they can isolate the assumptions about which they disagree. This shifts the dialogue from yelling "Option A is better than option B!" to focusing on "what has to be true" for each option to be the better option.

Neither vision nor discovery is sufficient for strategic success; both the drive of a clear vision and the insights of learning from experience are strengthened through the pillar of clear and coherent strategy arguments. Without a clear and valid strategy argument, the strategy-making process collapses in confusion, false starts, and misguided investments. With a valid argument, leaders and their teams will be positioned to improve the quality of their strategic decision making, to act as one, and to learn the right lessons from their experiences. Equipped with the system of activities presented in this book, executives will be prepared to lead their teams to build and develop great, winning organizations.

KEY TAKEAWAYS

- Popular views of what makes a great strategic leader hold either of two contradictory images. For some, greatness comes from the possession of a unique vision and insight, while for others, it arises from the ability to pivot and discover abundant opportunities. Both accounts are incomplete. Without reasoned analysis, neither vision nor discovery alone will lead to great strategy.

- Great strategy melds intuition with reason. It offers a novel, inspiring vision of the future supported by the pillar of rigorous, logically valid strategy arguments. Without this pillar, only good luck and fortune separate the strategic genius from the raving lunatic.

- Leaders often discover great strategies as they fail initially and then uncover unexpected opportunities. But pivoting from one strategy to another at the first sign of resistance is no safe road to great strategy. Only through the discipline of a well-reasoned strategy argument can leaders avoid the twin dangers of abandoning a great strategy too soon and chasing fads that prove ephemeral.

- Great strategic leadership depends on using logical argument to formulate, assess, and revise an organization's strategy. Recognizing logical argument as the pillar of great strategy breaks down the distinction between strategy and execution. Decisions in organizations always follow *some* logic of action; the challenge for leaders involves making sure that logic is consistent and coherent.

PART VI

Appendices

APPENDIX A

||||||||||||||||||||||||||||||||||||||||||||||||||||||||||||||||||||||||||||||||||||||||||||||||||||||||||||||||||||||||||||||||||||||||||
||||||||||
Terminology

The goal of this book is to strengthen executive skills in formulating and assessing strategy arguments. By strengthening these skills, an executive will be in a better position to improve his or her organization's strategy when it is inadequate and to sustain it in the face of change when it is successful.

Given their central roles in the book, we devote some explicit attention in this appendix to our use of the term "logic" and associated terms such as "argument," "strategy," "strategy argument," "strategic logic," "strategy map," and "strategic plan." While perhaps dry and seemingly overwrought at times, these definitions should prove useful as a guide and provide clarification for the reader. We try to be consistent in our usage throughout, and because our usage varies with respect to some others' usages, it is worth being explicit, even at the cost of boredom.

To begin, we distinguish between a *strategy* and a *strategy argument*. As social scientists, strategy for us is about actual behavior, while a strategy argument is about the choices made or planned in an attempt to ensure strategic success. While fundamental, this distinction between choices and outcomes is far from obvious and is not necessarily easy to comprehend. Indeed, almost every widely used textbook or source we consulted conflates the two ideas.

For instance, consider the way IMD professor Michael D. Watkins defines strategy: "A business strategy is a set of guiding principles that, when communicated and adopted in the organization, generates a desired pattern of decision making."[1] Or consider the thoughtful management authors A. G. Lafley and Roger Martin: "Strategy is an integrated set of choices that uniquely positions the firm in its industry so as to create sustainable competitive advantage and superior value relative to the competition."[2] Even Michael Porter leans in this direction when he writes, "Strategy is the creation of a unique and valuable position, involving a different set of activities."[3]

Because a plan is essentially an argument with an action list and a timetable, these definitions fail to draw the lines between behavioral reality—what is really happening or happened in the market—and what decisions made or will make for success, including future plans for intended success. As we discuss in chapter 10 with respect to Honda and Disney, success and even strategy sometimes come about because of unexpected fortuitous events, and we do not want to ascribe all outcomes to a plan.

The distinction becomes vivid when we ask whether a firm or organization always has a strategy, be it unintended, implicit, inconsistent, or even ignored. Think of a group of friends who casually form a corporate entity to monetize the products of their individual but unconnected hobbies, because one of the spouses thought it might help recover some of the costs of the hobbies and provide a tax deduction. The traditional approach to strategy— coming from old business policy ideas—would likely state unequivocally that this disorganized company does not have a strategy.[4] But more modern behavioral approaches to strategy, from which the important insights about the emergent aspects of strategy come, would insist that this company—and indeed every company—has a strategy, whether the people inside it know or not and whether the strategy provides any advantage or not. In this view, an organization's strategy is its actual behavior—the way it competes with other organizations and the way it draws resources from its market and other environments—however meager and ineffective those attempts may be. The definition intentionally incorporates the views of Henry Mintzberg and others about what they call "emergent strategy": a set of actions, or behavior, consistent over time that constitute "a realized pattern [that] was not expressly intended" in the original planning of strategy.[5]

In this view, we separate behavioral reality about what a firm does and the consequences of those actions from normative ideas about what a firm might or should do to be effective in competing and extracting resources. By contrast, many analysts want to say a firm does not have a strategy if it does not have a well-reasoned or coherent plan or the plan does not engender success. Similarly, if the firm fails, they would likely say it failed because it did not have a strategy. In such a case, while we may agree that the firm failed because the strategy was ill-conceived or poorly executed, we would insist that it still had a strategy, just likely a bad strategy and perhaps a poor or inadequate strategy argument.

Of course, the goal is to craft great strategies, effective ones that convey advantage in competition and market resource extraction. That's where the strategy argument comes in. A simple way to think about the difference is that the strategy clues us in to the real set of reasons why the firm succeeds (or fails), and the strategy argument is the set of reasons you think causes the firm to succeed (or fail). This may seem confusing at first, so let us define terms in more detail.

An organization's *strategy* is the way in which its resources and activities combine with external conditions to allow it to prosper economically (or fail to do so). In this definition, strategy is the set of firm actions and market positions, coupled with the systematic underlying reasons why the firm is successful (or a failure) in generating economic returns. Strategy in this sense is not directly observable and is not a simple reflection of the leader's intentions. Importantly, in this view, every firm has a strategy, whether it is successful or not, whether it is consistent and coherent or not, and whether its leaders are aware of how it works or not.

A *strategy argument* is a representation or articulation of how the firm's resources and activities combine with external conditions to allow you to create and capture value. An *argument* is defined as a set of reasons offered with the aim of persuading others that an action or idea is good or bad. Accordingly, a strategy argument is the set of reasons someone—usually the executive in charge—offers to persuade others that a particular combination of resources, activities, and external conditions allow the firm to create and capture value. It is the story the leaders (or someone else) tell about why the firm performs as it does. Some strategy arguments are better than others. In part this is a question of empirical accuracy. It may or may not be a correct story or an accurate representation of the true, unobservable story. Of course, we want it to be as correct as possible. But a more fundamental starting point is that it be a logical argument.

A *logical argument* is a particular kind of argument, namely an argument that passes the test of logic. We define logic as reasoning conducted or assessed according to strict principles of validity. *Validity* in this usage means that the premises do indeed imply the conclusion, and the chain of reasoning makes sense and is logical, as discussed in chapter 3. A logical argument is one that is valid (but not necessarily sound, in the sense that the premises are true). Not all arguments that are offered are logical arguments. But all good strategy arguments are logical arguments.

We define a *strategic logic* or a *logic of success* as a strategy argument that is logical, i.e., that meets the conditions of validity. A strategic logic is a subset of all strategy arguments, because not all strategy arguments are logically valid. There may be competing strategic logics or logics of success. In other words, we may try to explain a firm's success in creating and capturing value by developing different logically valid strategy arguments. In that case, deciding among them is a question of the empirical truth of the arguments, i.e., the truth of each argument's premises.

A *strategy map* is a visual representation of a strategy argument, as illustrated in chapter 2. Developing a strategy map is often a useful first step in articulating a strategy argument, but typically a strategy map is not sufficient to assess whether a strategy argument is logically valid. However, a strategy map may also be useful as a means of communicating the strategy argument, once its validity has been assured.

A *strategic plan* is a set of actions and investments derived from a strategy argument. It is what translates a strategy argument into action, with the chosen behaviors being consistent with the reasoning of the strategy argument.

APPENDIX B

||||||||||||||||||||||||||||||||||||||||||||||||||||||||||||||||||||||||||||||||||||||||||||||||||||||||||||||||||||||||||||||||||||||||||||||
|||||||||||
Dissecting Strategy

A PRIMER

WHY THIS APPENDIX?

The book provides a flexible system of activities for formulating and assessing the arguments that form the core of strategy theories. For those less familiar with strategy theory, this appendix provides a brief review of the core issues in business strategy, a primer of sorts.

We use Southwest Airlines to illustrate how to conduct a high-level analysis of a company's strategy. We build on concepts frequently used in strategic analyses (albeit at times with different labels): value creation, value capture, and competitive advantage. We use many of the concepts in the book, where we illustrate how to use them in actually conducting analyses and formulating strategy, using logical reasoning and other tools.

The goal of this appendix is to introduce and explain the key concepts that go into a strategy argument, not to show or elaborate the process of developing or using it. Still, the framework alone should be useful both for diagnosing why a firm succeeds (or not) and when it is important to understand why another organization (perhaps a rival) is winning or losing.

DISSECTING A STRATEGY ARGUMENT

We advocate a simple definition of strategy, as explained in appendix A: an organization's *strategy* is the way in which its resources and activities combine with external conditions to allow it to prosper economically (or not). We emphasize economic prosperity, because this is the fundamental responsibility of any strategic leader, whether the organization is a for-profit, a social enterprise, or a nonprofit. In the latter cases, even when organizations do not seek to maximize their profits, they must secure sufficient economic resources to keep the lights on and to do the work that needs to be done to accomplish the organization's broader mission.[1]

A strategy argument is a theory of firm performance: it is a set of claims about how the firm's resources and activities (will) combine with external conditions to allow it to prosper economically. What determines how economically prosperous a firm is? If we start from an accounting perspective, a simple way to think about this is to imagine the firm as a bundle of transactions. In each transaction, the firm combines a set of inputs from suppliers (including the labor of employees), transforms them in some way, and then sells the resulting product or service to a buyer. The firm's prosperity is a function of how much money it makes in each of these transactions (price minus cost, or $P - C$), times the number of transactions (quantity or Q). This gives us the basic accounting identity, profit = $Q*(P - C)$.

Ultimately, a strategy argument is an explanation for how the firm generates profits. In constructing strategy arguments, however, it is useful to break the problem of generating profits down into two components: *creating value* and *capturing value*.[2] Value creation refers to the *potential* profits that arise as the firm transforms inputs into a product or service that customers want. One driver of differences in economic performance is that some firms create more value in this transformation process than others: they do more with the same inputs than other firms, much as a master chef can create more delicious meals with the ingredients in our kitchen pantries than we can. We define value creation as follows:

- A firm creates value when buyers are willing to pay more (directly or indirectly) for the firm's goods and services than the suppliers' opportunity cost of the required inputs.

Notice that this definition introduces two concepts that were not included in our previous "accounting" definition of profits: (1) the buyers' willingness to pay and (2) the suppliers' opportunity cost. A simple way to think about each of these concepts is to imagine what buyers and suppliers are thinking when they are contemplating a transaction with the producer. When looking at the producer's product, the buyer is (implicitly) asking "How much utility or benefit will I get from this product?" and then translating that perceived utility into a dollar value. Therefore, the *willingness to pay* is the maximum dollar amount the buyer would part with in order to acquire the product or service. The *supplier's opportunity cost* is determined by a similar thought process, but here the supplier is asking "Why should I sell my input to this producer, as opposed to some alternative?" To induce the supplier to provide the input, the firm has to pay at least as much as the supplier could get from the alternative. That is, the supplier's opportunity cost is the hypothetical lowest price at which the supplier is indifferent between selling to the producer versus the alternative. Creating value is about increasing the difference between these two quantities. Colloquially speaking, value creation enlarges the size of the pie.

Creating value is a necessary but not sufficient condition for economic prosperity: a firm that creates value does not necessarily capture that value. For example, Virgin America was adored by its customers, but was never sustainably profitable, and eventually sold itself to Alaska Airlines. In our assessment, Virgin America succeeded in creating value for its customers, but was not able to capture enough of that value to sustain itself in the face of competition from Southwest, JetBlue, and others. Similarly, many software engineers develop apps for the iPhone that people love, but they are not sustainably profitable unless they address the challenges to capturing value. These include Apple's control of the App Store, the threat of imitation from other developers, or the integration of their differentiating features into Apple's next version of the iOS operating system.

If value creation is about the size of the pie, then value capture is about how the pie gets divided. In our hypothetical transaction, there are three kinds of actors: buyers, the producer, and the suppliers. Therefore:

- A firm captures value to the extent that it appropriates the value that it has created, rather than the value being claimed by buyers or suppliers.

At its simplest, this idea comes down to the ability of the buyers to pay less than their willingness to pay, and the ability of the suppliers to charge more than their opportunity cost. Any difference between willingness to pay and price is value captured by the buyer, and any difference between actual input cost and supplier opportunity cost is value captured by the suppliers. What is left over is value captured by the producer.

The ability of the firm to capture value is determined by the structure and dynamics of the competitive environment. Industry analysis, the workhorse of strategic analysis for the past forty years, is centrally concerned with these issues. When buyers have bargaining power, for example, they can force prices below their willingness to pay; similarly, a supplier with bargaining power can force costs for its input above its opportunity cost. Buyers may capture value even in the absence of any bargaining power as competition among existing firms, the existence of substitutes, or the threat of entry drive down prices. To generate profits, firms need to find ways to overcome these obstacles to capturing value.

The distinction between creating and capturing value constitutes the core of the strategy identification process. If a firm sustainably makes a profit, then it must both create and capture value. Identifying a firm's logic of success amounts to clarifying how these two conditions come to be true. In other words, we need to construct an argument for how the firm created value, as well as an argument for how it succeeds in capturing value. Alternatively, if we want to understand why a firm has not succeeded, then we need to isolate where one (if not both) of these processes broke down.

When we are trying to understand a firm's success (or failure), a lot of different competing yet plausible explanations will often surface initially. Identifying a firm's strategy involves detective work. It is an iterative process of documenting critical facts, identifying potential explanations, and then eliminating possible explanations until you are satisfied that you have the best available explanation. A large part of the process involves gathering all of the relevant information—facts about how the firm works (its business model), as well as about the market environment in which it operates. The most difficult and challenging part, however, comes in making sense of how all these different elements fit together—in settling on the most plausible account for the firm's success, or lack thereof. This is where the logical reasoning skills we develop in the book play a critical role.

We illustrate strategy identification by returning to the case of Southwest Airlines and the factors that drove its remarkable run of profitability.[3]

CASE STUDY: SOUTHWEST AIRLINES

The main features of Southwest's business model are widely familiar, thanks to the company's success and extensive discussions of the model in the media and business cases. Southwest pioneered the concept of a low-price, no-frills airline. Starting from its home base in Dallas, Texas, Southwest focused on frequent short-haul flights, often between cities two hundred to three hundred miles apart, such as Houston, San Antonio, and Dallas. Often, Southwest flies into secondary airports in major metropolitan areas (e.g., San Jose or Oakland instead of San Francisco), although in recent years its presence in major airports has expanded. Unlike the major domestic carriers such as United, American, and Delta, which devoted substantial resources to building a hub-and-spoke network, Southwest developed a point-to-point network and did not create major hubs. Southwest only flies one type of airplane, the Boeing 737, while other airlines typically fly multiple planes from both Boeing and Airbus (and McDonnell Douglas before that). The airline is known for its efficient operations, with short gate turnaround times and lower staffing levels than other airlines. Southwest is proudly no-frills, with no meal service on flights except soft drinks and pretzels (earlier, peanuts), but with friendly, no-nonsense customer service. Passengers cannot reserve specific seat assignments on a flight; instead, passengers choose the seat they want as they board the plane. In addition, Southwest does not participate in the major ticket reservation systems, so tickets have to be purchased directly through Southwest. The company's passengers can only go where Southwest flies: passengers cannot book a single ticket that includes both a Southwest flight and a flight on another airline. At the same time, Southwest has historically been aggressive with its pricing, often offering, for example, $49 fares on routes where rivals charge hundreds of dollars.

Describing a company's business model in this way typically stops short of explaining *how* the various pieces of a firm's strategy—customers, value propositions, channels, etc.—all fit together. To put it differently, many accounts of successful businesses leave the logic of success as an open exercise for the reader. As a result, it can be difficult to identify the critical assumptions (about customers, the market, competition, etc.) that have to hold for the firm to succeed. This would not be so much of a problem if it were limited to external accounts of a firm's strategy. Yet as discussed in chapter 1, the lack of confidence executives express in their firms' strategies suggests that many executives lack a clear understanding of their firms' logic of success. And, if they do not understand *how* their firms create value, they are unlikely to make good decisions. The analysts criticizing Southwest's CEO Gary Kelly in chapter 1 were pushing him to introduce policies designed to capture more value from the firm's customers. They argued that these actions would increase profits. While it is likely the case that these fees would increase margins on each transaction, they might also negatively affect value creation. In short, Kelly needed to be clear whether charging for advance seat assignments (for example) threatened Southwest's ability to create value. This requires a clear picture of how Southwest creates value.

Value Creation at Southwest

The core of Southwest's entrepreneurial insight, starting with the founder Herb Kelleher, was the discovery of ways to create value while serving air passengers with relatively low levels of willingness to pay. Successful firms generally adopt one of two orientations toward value creation: either a *low-cost* (LC) approach or a *perceived quality* (PQ) approach.

Recall that value is created by increasing the gap between two variables: the buyer's willingness to pay for the firm's product or service and the supplier's opportunity cost of providing the inputs. The two value creation orientations correspond to focusing on one of these variables. When firms pursue a low-cost strategy, they focus on reducing the opportunity cost of the inputs needed per transaction, for example, by using fewer inputs per transaction or by using less expensive inputs. By contrast, when a firm adopts a perceived quality orientation, it concentrates its efforts on increasing the willingness to pay of buyers. Examples would include introducing technical features that create a lot of utility for the customer (such as making a smartphone waterproof) or crafting an image or reputation for the product that the customer values (such as Apple's branding efforts).

Southwest Airlines is a canonical example of a firm with a strong and consistent low-cost orientation. Its approach involved finding ways to deliver air travel to customers more efficiently—i.e., using fewer inputs per transaction—than rival airlines. Why? Southwest's passengers typically show a lower willingness to pay. Particularly when it started, Southwest appealed to two primary customer segments that were not served by other airlines.

278

The first was a certain kind of business traveler—not high-powered corporate executives, but salespeople, product support engineers, and small business owners. In other words, Southwest appealed to business travelers lower on the corporate totem pole, with smaller expense accounts, who needed to get from (say) San Antonio to Dallas with some regularity, perhaps because they had a sales route and needed to meet with customers. Second, Southwest also appealed to a certain type of leisure traveler; again, not someone going on a lavish European vacation, but instead someone going to visit family or friends for a christening, memorial service, birthday party, or the like. Southwest would appeal to the recent college graduate living in Dallas and returning home to visit his family in San Antonio for his parent's anniversary or the young couple in a long-distance relationship.

Particularly at the time of Southwest's founding, both of these customer segments were unlike the customers of full-service airlines like United or American. Southwest's customers in these segments are only interested in a limited number of destinations, typically in the same region, and have little need to be able to go anywhere in the country. They just want to get from point A to point B regularly. Because regional flights are short, customers care less about in-flight amenities like meal service or video entertainment. Instead, it seems reasonable to assume that these customer segments want to maximize frequency (so as not to be late for the meeting or party, but also not have to get there so early that time is wasted), safety, and reliability, while they want to minimize the time spent traveling, as well as any discomfort, fatigue, and stress. Most importantly, their willingness to pay is limited relative to the customers of full-service airlines. The regional salesperson is allocated a limited travel budget, and the recent college graduate doesn't have a lot of discretionary income, perhaps because he is paying off his student loans. In fact, when Southwest was first starting, their limited budgets meant that these customers rarely if ever would fly between San Antonio and Dallas, given the prices charged by existing full-service airlines. Instead, they would drive, take the bus, or stay at home and use the phone instead. (For this reason, the customers targeted by low-cost airlines like Southwest were sometimes referred to as the "sofa trade," because these airlines get people up off their couches.)

Given these realities, Southwest adopted a low-cost orientation; the primary goal was not to try to introduce features or services that would increase the willingness to pay of the regional salesperson. Part of the entrepreneurial insight of cofounder and CEO Herb Kelleher was not only in identifying the customer segments for whom regional air travel would be appealing, but also in imagining that it was possible to serve these customers at sufficiently low cost to create value.

Southwest's ability to create value rested on two insights. The first had to do with the cost structure of airlines and the fact that it is a business with high fixed costs. It costs (almost) the same to fly an empty seat from San Antonio to Dallas as it does to fly with a passenger in that seat. As a result, capacity utilization is key to the firm's average costs—you want every flight to be as full as possible, even if the passenger filling that otherwise empty seat generates very little revenue. Accordingly, Southwest focuses on maximizing capacity in a number of different ways. Route selection is key: flying between cities that see lots of travel back and forth is important. This fact is one reason why Southwest originally focused on routes between cities such as San Antonio and Dallas, which are close enough (275 miles) and populous enough that many sales representatives have reason to travel between the two cities. Southwest's emphasis on quick gate turnaround times and frequent flights meant that planes spent more time flying as opposed to sitting on the ground, further increasing capacity utilization. (Herb Kelleher was reputed to have observed that people did not pay to sit in a plane on the ground.) Adopting a point-to-point route structure, rather than a hub-and-spoke network, reduced time spent on the ground, because planes do not have to wait as often for other planes to land with transferring passengers.

Another key aspect of Southwest's approach involved reducing variable costs. One way was to simply not offer things that their customers didn't care that much about, such as in-flight meal service or assigned seating. More generally, Southwest focused on efficient operations through a number of distinctive practices and routines. Southwest's reliance on a single type of airplane—Boeing 737s—reduced operational complexity and maintenance costs and made it easier to substitute one plane for another if needed. In addition, workers at Southwest had relatively broad job descriptions (compared to other airlines), which meant that they could perform a number of different jobs required to get the plane ready for takeoff. Similarly, Southwest created a strong sense of teamwork and loyalty to the company, which not only reduced turnover and improved effort levels, but also enabled the rapid gate turnarounds.

Some of the ways Southwest sought reduced costs implied trade-offs in the firm's ability to satisfy different types of customers. For example, trying to maximize capacity utilization by building a regional, point-to-point network meant that the same resources could not be used to build a national route network. Similarly, Southwest reduced operational complexity, and hence variable costs, by not offering product features such as in-flight meal service or advance seat assignments that a high-level executive might demand. But note that these choices had little if any impact on Southwest's ability to appeal to its chosen customer segments. The regional salesperson did not care about a national route network and was perfectly happy with peanuts on an hour-long flight. Possessing a deep understanding of what drives willingness to pay of your customers can greatly reduce costs, as it allows you to drop product and service offerings that do not matter.

To this point we have argued that there was a set of customers for whom Southwest's product creates a willingness to pay that exceeds Southwest's average costs. We constructed this argument by first making a set of assumptions about what drove the willingness to pay for Southwest's product, based on what we think we know about its customers, and then making a set of assumptions about how Southwest was able to reduce its costs sufficiently to serve these customers.

The fact that Southwest, as a sustainably successful company, demonstrated profitable demand for its offerings is empirical evidence that it did (and does) in fact create value. We might therefore be tempted to take this as proof that our argument is correct. But this would be a mistake—there is a difference between knowing that a firm creates value and knowing how it creates value. Our argument is fundamentally about *how* Southwest creates value, and this argument rests on assumptions that might ultimately be wrong.

Even though it does not quantify the value created, note that the argument developed gives us a framework for thinking about the strategic challenges the analysts posed to Gary Kelly in chapter 1. Advance seat assignments, for example, will increase operational complexity and likely lower efficiency. The airline would have to provide customers with individual boarding cards with assigned seats, rather than asking passengers to stand in a line based on their order of arrival. Similarly, personnel would have to be available to accommodate passengers who wish to change their seat assignment. Software systems would need to be upgraded.

All of these changes would increase the opportunity costs per transaction. If these increases are not met with a corresponding (or greater) increase in the willingness to pay of buyers, then Southwest's potential profits will decline, because less value will be created. Some customers may be willing to pay more for advance seat assignments, but as noted in chapter 1, many longtime Southwest passengers accustomed to the old system may lower their willingness to pay because they do not want to change their behavior.

Value Capture at Southwest

To gain a better understanding of how a firm captures value, let's step back and characterize the challenges that any firm faces in doing so. Let's start with a simple question: If the firm itself does not capture the value it creates, where does it go?

When creating value, a firm comprises part of a value chain: it transforms inputs that it acquires from a set of suppliers into a mix of products or services that are subsequently purchased by a range of buyers. Value chains can be very complex, with a long set of intermediate steps between raw materials and a product in the consumer's hands, or they can be relatively simple. Whatever the complexity of the value chain, however, thinking about the basic Supplier → Producer → Buyer structure makes it clear that the value that the firm creates can go to any of three different actors in the value chain: the firm's suppliers (or their suppliers), the firm itself, or the firm's buyers (or their buyers). Constructing a value capture argument is therefore a two-stage process. First, we need to identify the challenges that a firm faces in capturing value, or the forces that might allow buyers or suppliers to capture the value created by the firm. Second, to the extent that such obstacles have been identified, we need to explain how the firm overcomes the potential for buyers or suppliers to capture value.

Consider suppliers first. The main issue to contemplate is their potential bargaining power or ability to charge a producer more than their opportunity cost of providing the input. For Southwest, three types of suppliers are of particular concern from a value capture perspective: labor unions, aircraft manufacturers, and airports. Southwest approaches each in unique ways.

Consider labor unions. Contrary to what many believe, Southwest is heavily unionized—it is the most heavily unionized U.S. airline—with above average salary levels for its workers.[4] The unionized workers, including pilots and flight attendants, perform critical roles. Combined with Southwest's distinctive work practices and long training times, these roles give the unions substantial bargaining power. As a result, Southwest's labor unions capture some of the value the company creates. Rather than fight to weaken the unions' powers, Southwest has historically worked with the unions, mainly to create flexible work rules for the cross-utilization of workers. For instance, pilots at Southwest will help clean a plane to get it ready for takeoff, something that work rules at other airlines generally prohibit. This flexibility creates value, because it results in higher worker productivity. The way we see it, Southwest allows the unions to capture some of the pie in order to grow the size of the pie.

Southwest's approach to the supplier power of aircraft manufacturers is similar. Over the course of Southwest's history, the manufacturers of commercial jets have consolidated; currently there are only two major suppliers, Boeing and Airbus. Aircraft manufacturers thus hold some power, although the two suppliers compete intensely for orders from airlines. Most airlines attempt to reduce the power of these manufacturers by buying from both companies, thereby making the threat to buy from the other company more credible. Because Southwest only flies Boeing 737s, it has actually *increased* the potential for Boeing to capture value, because Boeing is effectively a monopoly supplier.

As with labor unions, however, the argument can be made that Southwest's strategy weighs this loss of value against the efficiency benefits it gains from only operating with one type of plane. Each aircraft type flown by an airline creates some fixed costs, in the form of training for personnel and the need to maintain inventories of spare parts. A single type of plane reduces overhead costs. In addition, when a plane needs to be taken out of service on short notice due to maintenance issues, airlines typically cannot substitute a different type of plane because of different passenger capacities, seating arrangements, etc. A single type of plane again helps to reduce time spent on the ground. In short, the argument is that by allowing Boeing to capture some value, Southwest is able to create more value.

Finally, airports control a critical and scarce resource for any airline: landing rights. As a result, airports can capture some of the value created by airlines, particularly in cities with higher levels of demand. Southwest has historically overcome this obstacle through positioning, in two ways. First, by flying between cities with less demand, Southwest negotiates landing rights with airports that have less supplier power, and who may in fact be eager to welcome Southwest. Second, Southwest for many years would serve major metropolitan areas through secondary airports, thereby avoiding the airports with the most supplier power. For example, it would serve the Boston area through airports in Rhode Island and New Hampshire. The argument in this case is that Southwest's route selection reduces the bargaining power of airports.

We turn now to the ability of buyers to capture value. There are two primary channels through which buyers may capture value from the producer: buyer power and price competition. Just as suppliers try to charge more than their opportunity cost, buyers try to pay less than their willingness to pay. When prices are low relative to the buyer's willingness to pay, the buyer captures more of the value of the firm's product or service. This will happen if there is extensive price competition or if the buyers have bargaining power over the firm.

If we apply these ideas to Southwest, two key conclusions stand out. First, because even the largest customers (e.g., corporations) account for only a small share of Southwest's volume, buyer bargaining power is not a major obstacle to capturing value. Nobody sits down and haggles with Southwest about what it should cost to fly from Dallas to Houston, and if they tried, the airline would politely dismiss them. Another part of the value capture argument is therefore in place: buyer power is not a threat.

Buyers do capture value from Southwest through price competition. Indeed, a major challenge to capturing value in the airline industry in general is the competitive intensity of the industry. Price competition among firms increases to the extent that one firm's (potential) buyers can find other firms that satisfy the same value proposition (in which case we call them rivals), or close to the same value proposition (substitutes), and to the extent that buyers can easily switch between the offerings of different firms.

Consider the major airlines with hub-and-spoke networks (such as United, American, Delta). If you want to fly between two major cities in the United States, you can typically choose any of these airlines. They are typically not highly differentiated from one another—the experience of flying on United is not that different from the experience of flying on American or Delta. Hence customers do not differ in their willingness to pay for different airlines, and the airlines compete on price. Moreover, switching costs are low: if you flew United between San Francisco and New York last time, but American offers you a much better price this time, you could easily switch.

Given these features of the industry, airlines have historically engaged in waves of price wars and intense competition. The major hub-and-spoke airlines try to reduce the extent of competition in a number of different ways. Frequent-flier programs, for example, are attempts to create switching costs for the customer. Focusing on business travelers, who are typically less sensitive to prices because their companies are paying, is another way these airlines mute price competition. Since the 2008 financial crisis, the airline industry has consolidated, which many analysts think has reduced price competition.[5]

Given that price competition is a real obstacle to value capture for Southwest, how would we explain the airline's ability to report superior profits consistently? What is the argument? Southwest responds to the challenges of price competition among airlines in two ways. Historically, the first and simplest way Southwest responded to the threat of competition was to position itself to avoid it: in other words, to go where there was no, or little, competition. Both through its choice of customer segments and its choice of markets, Southwest positioned itself in such a way that the intensity of competition was reduced. As in Walmart's initial decision to introduce discount retailing in rural America, while Kmart, Target, and other discount retailers focused on the rapidly growing suburbs, Southwest used the design of its route network to reduce competitive intensity. It chose to offer shorter regional flights on routes that either were not served or were poorly served by the major airlines, which focused on building national, long-haul networks. For full-service national airlines operating hub-and-spoke networks, for example, the route between San Antonio and Dallas was not a high priority, if they served it at all. Our argument is that Southwest's route structure helped it capture value in two ways. First, it reduced the number of firms it was competing with on those routes, reducing the choices available to customers. Second, the full-service airlines often had less incentive to compete aggressively on price, because the routes Southwest focused on were a small part of their business.[6]

Southwest's competitive positioning did not entirely eliminate competition from other airlines or from substitutes like buses or driving. In general, attempts to avoid competing head-to-head are rarely entirely successful, either because viable (if imperfect) substitutes continue to exist or because other firms enter the market. Competition therefore remains a major obstacle to value capture for Southwest. How does it overcome this obstacle?

In general, the ability of firms to overcome threats from competition—and thereby reduce the extent to which buyers capture value—depends on whether they possess what we call a *value creation advantage*. A firm has a value creation advantage when it generates a greater wedge between buyer willingness to pay and supplier opportunity costs than its competitors do for a given transaction. By creating more value than its competitor(s), the share of the value captured by the firm (as opposed to what is captured by the buyer) can be greater. In other words, the firm can be more profitable than the competition at any given price. Alternatively, the firm with a value creation advantage may choose to pass some of that advantage along to buyers (in the form of lower prices), and thereby win greater market share.

Firms generally achieve a value creation advantage by focusing either on driving down costs for a given level of willingness to pay (a low-cost advantage) or by increasing the buyer's willingness to pay at a given level of producer cost (a perceived quality advantage). Although it may seem oversimplified, we follow economics-based applications of strategy in advocating that executives and analysts consider as sustainable mainly these two generic kinds of value creation advantages—low cost (LC) and perceived quality (PQ).

Many executives resist this constraint, arguing resolutely that their firms try to be both low cost and high perceived quality at the same time. There is no doubt about it: leaders of virtually every firm would like to increase willingness to pay and lower opportunity cost simultaneously. However, if a firm is performing efficiently with a given technology, there is almost always a trade-off between cost and perceived quality. A Mercedes is more expensive to build than a Kia; the Ritz-Carlton is more expensive to run than a Motel 6. If Mercedes is an efficient producer, then it could lower its costs by replacing the wood trim with plastic trim—but we suspect that the willingness to pay of its buyers would decrease as a result.

The cost–quality trade-off is why the notion of a value creation orientation is important: it tells you how the firm will try to win when it faces competition. Because almost all firms face competition of some sort, we feel strongly that when trying to formulate a strategy argument, one should start by determining whether the firm pursues a low-cost (LC) or a perceived quality (PQ) advantage. As noted earlier, Southwest improved its ability to capture value by pursuing a relentless low-cost advantage. Many aspects of Southwest's operations were devoted to improving capacity utilization: its planes spent more time in the air and had fewer empty seats than those of its rivals. Southwest's work practices resulted in substantially higher labor productivity than other airlines. For example, Southwest flew more available seat miles per worker than other major carriers; in 2004, by this measure "the productivity of Southwest employees was 45 percent higher than at American, despite the substantially longer flight lengths and larger average aircraft size of the network carrier."[7] Similarly, as described earlier, Southwest reduced costs by removing features that its customers had limited willingness to pay for.

Southwest's sustained low-cost advantage allowed it to build a strong, self-reinforcing position in the market. Because it created more value than its competitors, Southwest could pass along some of that advantage to its customers in the form of lower prices. While this allowed some customers to capture more value, it also increased the demand for Southwest to include customers with lower willingness to pay. The resulting increase in passenger volume meant that more seats were filled, which reduced average costs further. Furthermore, a history of aggressive low pricing helped establish Southwest's reputation in the market as a low-price leader, which was particularly important, because potential passengers had to book directly from Southwest.

Discussion

In this appendix, we have used the example of Southwest Airlines to illustrate the core building blocks of a strategy argument. As noted at the outset, a strategy argument is a proposed explanation for why a firm prospers economically or profits. A good strategy argument, in our view, has three major components.

First, a good strategy argument provides a clear explanation for how the firm creates value. This involves explaining how different aspects of the firm's business model allow it to transform inputs that have a certain opportunity cost into a product or service that generates a higher willingness to pay among buyers. In a value creation argument, the emphasis is not, primarily, on the amount of value created, but rather on giving insight into what the firm does to make the whole greater than the sum of the inputs. This requires not only describing key elements of the firm's business model—such as distinctive capabilities, unique resources, and the drivers of willingness to pay of the firm's customer segments—but also constructing a narrative about how these different pieces fit together to generate value.

Second, a good strategy argument contains a clear statement of the firm's value creation orientation, or intended value creation advantage. Is the firm low cost (LC) or perceived quality (PQ)? How can you tell? It is not always easy, but a place to start is to ask how the firm would react if it faced an increase in competition. A perceived quality firm, such as the Ritz-Carlton, generally responds to increased competition by trying to drive up the willingness to pay of its buyers; Motel 6 responds by trying to drive down its costs. A firm that is consistently able to deliver higher willingness to pay for a given cost has a PQ orientation; one that can consistently deliver a given willingness to pay for a lower cost has an LC orientation. Generic competitive advantage is often going to be a good way to get started in making a strategy argument logical and reaping the many benefits of that formulation.

Third, a strategy argument must have a clear explanation for how a firm succeeds in capturing value. The argument must contain two components. First is the identification of the obstacles to value capture or the forces that might allow suppliers or buyers to capture the value created by the firm. In our discussion of Southwest, we emphasized buyer and supplier power as well as competition from established rivals. The second component of the value capture argument explains how the firm's business model and strategic choices minimize or overcome those threats.

To conclude, we want to recognize the obvious. Almost surely, Southwest's CEO Gary Kelly holds a different mental model of his firm's strategy than the exact one we have developed here; if nothing else, we would hope that his model is more attuned to the current competitive situation of the company. But ultimately, the mental model serves as the basis for deciding whether or not to follow the lead of other airlines, for example when they introduce baggage fees. This is true whether or not the mental model is correct (i.e., captures the true logic of success), and whether or not the model is explicitly articulated in the CEO's mind or only implicit. Obviously, we think you will be better off if the model is correct and explicitly articulated.

NOTES

PREFACE

1. Richard P. Rumelt, *Good Strategy, Bad Strategy* (New York: Crown Business, 2011).
2. The theorem is attributed to Pythagoras, but some question its provenance. Our comments apply to the originator, whoever that person may have been.

1. ARGUING FOR ORGANIZATIONAL ADVANTAGE

1. Brian Summers, "Why Wall Street Isn't Happy with Southwest's 43 Straight Years of Profits," *Skift*, August 16, 2016, https://skift.com/2016/08/16/why-wall-street-isnt-happy -with-southwests-43-straight-years-of-profits.
2. Details about Pedro Earp and his strategic dilemma can be found in Robert E. Siegel and Amadeus Orleans, "AB InBev: Brewing an Innovation Strategy" (Stanford Graduate School of Business Case E643, Stanford, Calif.: Stanford Graduate School of Business, 2017).
3. Brewers Association, "Craft Brewer Volume Share of U.S. Beer Market Reaches Double Digits in 2014," press release, March 16, 2015, https://www.brewersassociation. org/press-releases/craft-brewer-volume-share-of-u-s-beer-market-reaches-double -digits-in-2014.
4. Siegel and Orleans, "AB InBev," 10.
5. Details about Ellie Fields and her strategic dilemma can be found in Amir Goldberg, Robert Siegel, and Matt Saucedo, "Tableau: The Creation of Tableau Public" (Stanford Graduate School of Business Case E632, Stanford, Calif.: Stanford Graduate School of Business, 2018).
6. Goldberg, Siegel, and Saucedo, "Tableau," 1.
7. To be more precise for those versed in the details of logic, we advocate the use of first-order propositional logic and associated tools.

8. Strategy&, "The Strategy Crisis: Insights from the Strategy Profiler," 2019, https://www.strategyand.pwc.com/gx/en/unique-solutions/cds/the-strategy-crisis.pdf. Also see Paul Weinland and Cesare Mainardi, *Strategy That Works* (Boston: Harvard Business Review Press, 2016).

9. Dan Lovallo and Oliver Sibony, "The Case for Behavioral Strategy," *McKinsey Quarterly*, January 2010.

10. Cynthia Montgomery, *The Strategist: Be the Leader Your Business Needs* (New York: Harper Business, 2012), 11.

11. Gary P. Pisano, *Creative Construction: The DNA of Sustained Innovation* (New York: Public Affairs, 2019), 25. To be clear, Pisano means that without a strategy every issue has to be actively debated when it is challenged. The reason a strategy allows an executive like Kelly to forgo the debating process during urgent times is only because he has already done it many, many times and knows his positions and conclusions well.

12. Summers, "Why Wall Street Isn't Happy with Southwest's 43 Straight Years of Profits."

13. Glenn R. Carroll and Anand Swaminathan, "Why the Microbrewery Movement? Organizational Dynamics of Resource Partitioning in the US Brewing Industry," *American Journal of Sociology* 106, no. 3 (2000): 715–762.

14. Pisano, *Creative Construction*, 171–172.

15. For readers interested in specific theories of strategic success, we suggest the following texts: Jay B. Barney and William S. Hesterly, *Strategic Management and Competitive Advantage* (Upper Saddle River, N.J.: Prentice Hall, 2010); Pankaj Ghemawat, *Redefining Global Strategy: Crossing Borders in a World Where Differences Still Matter* (Boston: Harvard Business Review Press, 2007); Charles W. Hill, Gareth R. Jones, and Melissa A. Schilling, *Strategic Management Theory: An Integrated Approach* (Boston: Cengage Learning, 2014); Michael A. Hitt, R. Duane Ireland, and Robert E. Hoskisson, *Strategic Management Cases: Competitiveness and Globalization*, 10th ed. (Boston: Cengage Learning, 2012); W. C. Kim and Renée Mauborgne, *Blue Ocean Strategy: How to Create Uncontested Market Space and Make the Competition Irrelevant* (Boston: Harvard Business Review Press, 2005); A. G. Lafley and Roger L. Martin, *Playing to Win: How Strategy Really Works* (Boston: Harvard Business Review Press, 2013); Michael E. Porter, *Competitive Strategy: Techniques for Analyzing Industries and Competitors* (New York: Simon & Schuster, 2008); Garth Saloner, Andrea Shepard, and Joel M. Podolny, *Strategic Management* (New York: Wiley, 2001); David J. Teece, Gary Pisano, and Amy Shuen, "Dynamic Capabilities and Strategic Management," *Strategic Management Journal* 18, no. 7 (1997), 509–533. See also appendix B in this book.

2. MAPPING STRATEGY

1. Michael Lewis, *The New New Thing* (New York: Norton, 2000), 99.

2. We use Healtheon's early history here to exemplify the power of a visual model. Healtheon's subsequent history may be debated as successful or not, which is beside

the point we wish to make here. In any event, it may be worth noting that we doubt that the Healtheon team continued to develop the strategy beyond this simple model in the ways that we advocate in this book.

3. Our notion of strategy maps builds on the work of John Bryson, Fran Ackermann, Colin Eden, and others. See John M. Bryson, Fran Ackermann, Colin Eden, and Charles B. Finn, *Visible Thinking: Unlocking Causal Mapping for Practical Business Results* (New York: Wiley, 2004); Fran Ackermann and Colin Eden, *Making Strategy: Mapping Out Strategic Success*, 2nd ed. (Los Angeles: Sage, 2011); John Bryson, Fran Ackermann, and Colin Eden, *Visual Strategy: Strategy Mapping for Public and Nonprofit Organizations* (New York: Wiley, 2014).

4. Our usage of the term "strategy map" should not be confused with that of Robert S. Kaplan and David P. Norton, *Strategy Maps* (Boston: Harvard Business School Press, 2004). They use the term to refer to a diagram based on the "balanced scorecard" approach to strategy, which involves assessing things from four varied perspectives.

5. Daniel Hajek, "The Man Who Saved Southwest Airlines with a '10-Minute' Idea," *National Public Radio's All Things Considered*, June 28, 2015, https://www.npr.org/2015/06/28/418147961/the-man-who-saved-southwest-airlines-with-a-10-minute-idea.

6. Charles O'Reilly III and Jeffrey Pfeffer, "Southwest Airlines (A)," (Stanford Graduate School of Business Case HR1A, Stanford, CA: Stanford Graduate School of Business, 1995), 5.

7. MIT Global Airline Industry Program, "Airline Industry Overview," accessed February 15, 2018, http://web.mit.edu/airlines/analysis/analysis_airline_industry.html.

8. Bryson and coauthors similarly define a "causal map" as "a word-and-arrow diagram in which ideas and actions are causally linked with one another through the use of arrows. The arrows indicate how one idea or action leads to another." Bryson et al., *Visible Thinking*, 3.

9. See, for example, Scott Page, *The Model Thinker: What You Need to Know to Make Data Work for You* (New York: Basic, 2018). Also see Charles A. Lave and James G. March, *An Introduction to Models in the Social Sciences* (Lanham, Md.: University Press of America, 1993).

10. This synopsis draws on Stephen P. Bradley and Pankaj Ghemawat, "Wal-Mart Stores, Inc." (Harvard Business School Case 794–024, Boston: Harvard Business School Publishing, 1994 [revised 2002]). There are many other accounts of the success of Walmart, and most of them agree on the primary factors behind the company's dramatic success.

11. To start an analysis, we almost always suggest that the most important step involves explaining the basis of an organization's *competitive advantage*: why the organization wins. Identifying and analyzing the competitive advantage a firm possesses is sometimes a difficult part of strategy analysis but it is also, we would suggest, the most useful claim to be able to articulate explicitly in propositional logic. Adopting this approach means leaving the analysis of goals and the like until later.

12. For discussion of the distinction between resource advantages and capability advantages, see Garth Saloner, Andrea Shepard, and Joel M. Podolny, *Strategic Management* (New York: Wiley, 2001).

13. Furthermore, not every assumption about the firm needs to be an assumption about the firm's superiority. What matters is the overall outcome, and a firm needs only to differ in a number of key ways to have an advantage.

14. Note that in these examples "data analytics skills" appear in two clusters. That's okay! Ideas can have multiple implications.

3. LOGIC FOR STRATEGY

1. This story was popularized by Karl Weick in multiple venues, first in an article in 1982. Robert J. Swieringa and Karl E. Weick, "An Assessment of Laboratory Experiments in Accounting," Supplement, *Journal of Accounting Research* 20 (1982): 56–101, https://doi.org/10.2307/2674675. It has subsequently been claimed that Weick failed to attribute the story to a poem by Miroslav Holub. Miroslav Holub, "Brief Thoughts on Maps," *Times Literary Supplement*, February 4, 1977, 118.

2. Anton Troianovski and Sven Grundberg, "Nokia's Bad Call on Smartphones," *Wall Street Journal*, July 18, 2012, https://www.wsj.com/articles/SB10001424052702304388004577531002591315494.

3. Ina Fried, "These People Thought the iPhone Was a Dud When It Was Announced 10 Years Ago," *Vox*, January 9, 2017, https://www.vox.com/2017/1/9/14215942/iphone-steve-jobs-apple-ballmer-nokia-anniversary.

4. Logicians since Aristotle have called these arguments with implicit premises *enthymemes*.

5. Scott Gilbertson, "iPhone First Impressions: Not Worth the Money," *Wired*, June 29, 2007, https://www.wired.com/2007/06/iphone-first-im.

6. Denying the antecedent fallacies take the following form: Premise 1: If X, then Y. Premise 2: Not X. Conclusion: Not Y. We discuss different forms of invalid arguments later in this chapter (see table 3.1).

7. "Antennagate" refers to the brief period in 2010 when rumors spread in the press that holding the iPhone 4 in your hand in a particular way blocked its antenna and led to dropped calls. Apparently users complained and watchdog *Consumer Reports* would not recommend the phone as a result.

8. As noted, we letter and number the premises uniquely as an accounting device, simply to keep track of the different formalizations—they play no calculative role, although *W* stands for Walmart.

9. We return to this issue of diagramming connectors in chapter 6.

10. We tend to use AND connectors between premises by default, unless we think the argument clearly holds without them, i.e., depends on one or a few identifiable premises. Our justification is that we would rather be confidently right than narrowly correct in most cases. In engineering, the equivalent practice might be

using materials with greater wind or force tolerance than theoretically needed to, say, build a bridge or a building for a particular place with known specific environmental risks.

11. Many texts are available that review basic principles of logical argumentation. An easy to read book is Raymond S. Nickerson, *Reflections on Reasoning* (Hillsdale, N.J.: Erlbaum, 1986).

12. Note that soundness is a characteristic of an argument as a whole, not the truth of individual premises or conclusions.

4. ARGUING IN ORGANIZATIONS

1. Dom Knight, "Brevity Is the Soul of Twitter. We Don't Need 280 Characters to Say That," *Guardian*, September 27, 2017, https://www.theguardian.com/technology /commentisfree/2017/sep/27/brevity-soul-twitter-280-characters.

2. Fred Jacobs, "6 Reasons Why I Hate Twitter's New 280 Character Limit," *Jacobs Media Strategies* (blog), November 9, 2017, https://jacobsmedia.com/6-reasons-hate -twitters-new-280-character-limit.

3. "Why Did Twitter Change Their Character Limit to 280 Characters?," Dictionary .com, accessed March 12, 2020, https://www.dictionary.com/e/fierce-debate-twitters -280-characters.

4. Aliza Rosen and Ikuhiro Ihara, "Giving You More Characters to Express Yourself," *Twitter* (blog), September 26, 2017, https://blog.twitter.com/official/en_us/topics /product/2017/Giving-you-more-characters-to-express-yourself.html

5. Alexis C. Madrigal, "Twitter's 280-Character Tweets Are Fine," *Atlantic*, September 27, 2017, https://www.theatlantic.com/technology/archive/2017/09/twitters-testing-280 -character-tweets/541221.

6. Gary P. Pisano, *Creative Construction: The DNA of Sustained Innovation* (New York: Public Affairs, 2019), 172.

7. Patty McCord, *Powerful: Building a Culture of Freedom and Responsibility* (Silicon Guild, 2017), 52–53.

8. Hugo Mercier and Dan Sperber, "Why Do Humans Reason? Arguments for an Argumentative Theory," *Behavioral and Brain Sciences* 34, no. 2 (2011): 65.

9. David Moshman and Molly Geil, "Collaborative Reasoning: Evidence for Collective Rationality," *Thinking and Reasoning* 4, no. 3 (1998): 231–248.

10. Mercier and Sperber, "Why Do Humans Reason?," 72.

11. Massimo Garbuio, Dan Lovallo, and Oliver Sibony, "Evidence Doesn't Argue for Itself: The Value of Disinterested Dialogue in Strategic Decision Making," *Long Range Planning* 48, no. 6 (2015): 361–380.

12. Adam Bryant, "Honeywell's David Cote, on Decisiveness as a 2-Edged Sword," *New York Times*, November 2, 2013, https://www.nytimes.com/2013/11/03/business /honeywells-david-cote-on-decisiveness-as-a-2-edged-sword.html.

13. Garbuio, Lovallo, and Sibony, "Evidence Doesn't Argue for Itself," 375.

14. Fran Ackermann and Colin Eden, *Making Strategy: Mapping Out Strategic Success*, 2nd ed. (Los Angeles: Sage, 2011), 15.

15. John M. Bryson, Fran Ackermann, and Colin Eden, *Visual Strategy: Strategy Mapping for Public and Nonprofit Organizations* (New York: Wiley, 2014), 3.

16. Phillip M. Fernbach et al., "Political Extremism Is Supported by an Illusion of Understanding," *Psychological Science* 24, no. 6 (2013): 939–946, Supplemental Materials, p. 2.

17. Ackermann and Eden, *Making Strategy*, 7.

18. Alaric Bourgoin, François Marchessaux, and Nicolas Bencherki, "We Need to Talk About Strategy: How to Conduct Effective Strategic Dialogue," *Business Horizons* 61, no. 4 (2018): 587–588.

19. Bourgoin, Marchessaux, and Bencherki, "We Need to Talk About Strategy," 588.

20. Bourgoin, Marchessaux, and Bencherki, "We Need to Talk About Strategy," 592.

21. Matt Rosoff, "Jeff Bezos: There are 2 Types of Decisions to Make, and Don't Confuse Them," *Business Insider*, April 5, 2016, https://www.businessinsider.com/jeff -bezos-on-type-1-and-type-2-decisions-2016-4.

22. Ackermann and Eden, *Making Strategy*, 10.

23. At Amazon, the tagline apparently is "Have Backbone, Disagree and Commit."

24. McCord, *Powerful*, 60.

25. Steven Sande, "Steve Jobs's Story of the Stones," *Engadget*, November 11, 2011, https:// www.engadget.com/2011/11/11/steve-jobss-story-of-the-stones.

26. Bryce G. Hoffman, *American Icon: Alan Mullaly and the Fight to Save Ford Motor Company* (New York: Currency, 2012).

27. Michael Arena, *Adaptive Space: How GM and Other Companies Are Positively Disrupting Themselves and Transforming Into Agile Organizations* (New York: McGraw-Hill, 2018), 9.

28. Arena, *Adaptive Space*, 9.

29. Richard M. Cyert and James G. March, *A Behavioral Theory of the Firm* (2nd ed., New York: Wiley-Blackwell, 1992).

30. Eric Newcomer, "In Video, Uber CEO Argues with Driver Over Falling Fares," *Bloomberg*, February 28, 2017, https://www.bloomberg.com/news/articles/2017-02-28 /in-video-uber-ceo-argues-with-driver-over-falling-fares.

5. ARGUING ABOUT AN UNCERTAIN FUTURE

1. Cadie Thompson, "Your Car Will Become a Second Office in 5 Years or Less, General Motors CEO Predicts," *Business Insider*, December 12, 2016, https://www.business insider.com/gms-mary-barra-interview-2016-12.

2. Jeff Goodell, "The Rolling Stone Interview: Steve Jobs," *Rolling Stone*, December 25, 2003, https://www.rollingstone.com/music/music-news/the-rolling-stone-interview -steve-jobs-233293.

3. Thomas Ricker, "First Click: Remember When Steve Jobs Said Even Jesus Couldn't Sell Music Subscriptions?," *The Verge*, June 8, 2015, https://www.theverge.com/2015/6/8 /8744963/steve-jobs-jesus-people-dont-want-music-subscriptions.

4. Calculations from Recording Industry Association of America (RIAA), U.S. Sales Database, accessed March 7, 2019, https://www.riaa.com/u-s-sales-database.

5. Apple Inc., "iTunes Now Number Two Music Retailer in the US," press release, February 26, 2008, https://www.apple.com/newsroom/2008/02/26iTunes-Now -Number-Two-Music-Retailer-in-the-US.

6. Hannah Karp, "Apple iTunes Sees Big Drop in Music Sales," *Wall Street Journal*, October 24, 2014, https://www.wsj.com/articles/itunes-music-sales-down-more-than -13-this-year-1414166672.

7. Hannah Karp and Alistair Barr, "Apple Buys Beats for $3 Billion, Tapping Tastemakers to Regain Music Mojo," *Wall Street Journal*, May 28, 2014, https://www.wsj.com /articles/apple-to-buy-beats-1401308971.

8. Karp and Barr, "Apple Buys Beats for $3 Billion."

9. Sarah Mitroff, "Beats Music Review: Music Streaming Done Right," *CNET*, July 7, 2015, https://www.cnet.com/reviews/beats-music-review.

10. Ben Popper and Micah Singleton, "Apple Announces Its Streaming Music Service, Apple Music," *The Verge*, June 8, 2015, https://www.theverge.com/2015/6/8/8729481 /apple-music-streaming-service-wwdc-15.

11. Ewan Spence, "Apple Music Has Failed," *Forbes*, October 5, 2015, https://www.forbes .com/sites/ewanspence/2015/10/05/apple-music-failure.

12. More formally, by falsifying premise A3, we have only rejected a specific strategic argument; there are likely other valid arguments that would support the conclusion that Apple Music will grow more rapidly than rivals.

13. It is worth noting that when Apple entered into video streaming in 2019, in competition with Netflix, Disney, Hulu, etc., its initial pricing was much lower than pricing for rival services. Avie Schneider, "Apple Launches Video Streaming Service for $4.99 a Month," *National Public Radio Technology*, September 10, 2019, https://www .npr.org/2019/09/10/759500972/apple-launches-video-streaming-service-for-4-99-a -month.

14. Emily Blake, "Spotify Says Tidal's 'Lemonade' Exclusive Is Bad for Everyone," *Mashable*, April 24, 2016, https://mashable.com/2016/04/24/spotify-beyonce-tidal.

15. Chance Miller, "Jimmy Iovine Slams Free Music Services, Talks Exclusivity Deals in New Interview," *9To5Mac*, May 5, 2017, https://9to5mac.com/2017/05/17/jimmy-iovine -free-music-interview.

16. Parker Hall, "Apple Music vs. Spotify: Which Service Is the Streaming King?," *Digital Trends*, March 5, 2019, https://www.digitaltrends.com/music/apple-music-vs -spotify.

17. We would be surprised if executives at established streaming firms totally missed the role of defaults, and the remarkable growth of Apple Music should not be interpreted as meaning that they did. Even if they did recognize the issue, it is something that seems quite difficult to respond to effectively.

18. Cynthia Montgomery, *The Strategist: Be the Leader Your Business Needs* (New York: Harper Business, 2012), 130.

6. FORMULATING STRATEGY

1. Clayton M. Christensen, *The Innovator's Dilemma* (Boston: Harvard Business School Press, 1997).

2. Clayton M. Christensen and Michael B. Horn, "Innovation Imperative: Change Everything," *New York Times*, November 1, 2013, https://www.nytimes.com/2013/11/03 /education/edlife/online-education-as-an-agent-of-transformation.html.

3. Barack Obama, "Obama's Economics Speech at Knox College," *New York Times*, July 24, 2013, https://www.nytimes.com/2013/07/25/us/politics/obamas-economics-speech -at-knox-college.html.

4. The experience with San Jose State University led Thrun himself to declare, "We don't educate people as others wished, or as I wished. We have a lousy product." Soon after, Udacity pivoted to focus on vocational education. Max Chafkin, "Udacity's Sebastian Thrun, Godfather of Free Online Education, Changes Course," *Fast Company*, November 14, 2013, https://www.fastcompany.com/3021473/udacity -sebastian-thrun-uphill-climb.

5. Reihan Salam, "Online Education Can Be Good or Cheap, but Not Both," *Reuters .com*, July 26, 2013, http://blogs.reuters.com/reihan-salam/2013/07/26/online-education -can-be-good-or-cheap-but-not-both.

6. Steven Johnson, *Farsighted: How We Make the Decisions That Matter the Most* (New York: Riverhead, 2018).

7. Paul C. Nutt, *Why Decisions Fail: Avoiding Blunders and Traps That Lead to Debacles* (San Francisco: Berrett-Koehler, 2002). See also Chip Heath and Dan Heath, *Decisive: How to Make Better Choices in Life and Work* (New York: Crown Business, 2013).

8. We are simplifying radically by characterizing the divergence phase as a single-stage process.

9. As this suggests, self-filtering can be a delicate balance, as it may involve considerations of external consistency (e.g., the truth of premises about the future) that can therefore drive out good, outside-the-box ideas. To avoid this, one rule of thumb is to not reject valid ideas because the empirical premises (i.e., claims about future facts) seem too fanciful. If, on the other hand, formulating a valid argument requires stating theoretical premises for which exceptions can easily be identified, self-filtering is more acceptable.

10. A. G. Lafley and Roger L. Martin, *Playing to Win: How Strategy Really Works* (Boston: Harvard Business Review Press, 2013), 191. Lafley and Martin emphasize the need for emotional commitment to a strategic option, in addition to an intellectual commitment. This kind of emotional buy-in is ultimately important for successful execution, but firms are unlikely to be served well if it is allowed to be an independent criterion. Unlike the logical validity that forms the basis for intellectual or rational commitment, there is no objective basis for evaluating whether something is deserving of emotional commitment.

11. Lafley and Martin, *Playing to Win*, 188.

12. For example, if the probability that each premise will be true individually is 75 percent, and there are four premises joined by AND statements, then the joint probability is $0.75^4 = 32$ percent.

13. Although identifying criticality of premises in this way seems relatively straightforward, the example is deceptive, because it is often difficult to know what the appropriate connector is—uncertainty often exists about whether AND or OR is more credible. In chapter 9, we review an example about *The Economist*'s appeal to consumers as a social status good, in which such uncertainty about the better connector exists (at least in our eyes). Of course, one could assess the argument both ways, for both AND and OR connectors, and compare the results, but even this effort may not yield a clear resolution.

14. Readers may notice that the criticality of the teamwork assumption depends on the structure of the arguments supporting the two intermediate conclusions. Obviously, there might be other reasons, independent of teamwork, to conclude that Southwest has higher capacity utilization and lower variable costs. However, if we restrict ourselves to the argument represented by figure 6.3, teamwork is a critical assumption.

15. Lafley and Martin, *Playing to Win*, 198.

7. COMMUNICATING STRATEGY

1. Ryan Felton, "Why Mark Fields Was Fired," *Jalopnik*, May 22, 2017, https://jalopnik.com/why-mark-fields-was-fired-1795431562.

2. Felton, "Why Mark Fields Was Fired."

3. Felton, "Why Mark Fields Was Fired."

4. Phil LeBeau, "Ford Investors 'Want Some Comfort' from CEO Jim Hackett as Shares Drop to Six-Year Low," *CNBC*, October 9, 2018, https://www.cnbc.com/2018/10/09/ford-investors-want-some-comfort-as-shares-drop-to-six-year-low.html.

5. Christina Rogers, "Ford's New CEO Has a Cerebral Style—and to Many, It's Baffling," *Wall Street Journal*, August 14, 2018, https://www.wsj.com/articles/fords-new-ceo-has-a-cerebral-styleand-to-many-its-baffling-1534255714?mod=searchresults&page=1&pos=5.

6. Ford Motor Company, "Ford Statement on Business Transformation," Press release, November 26, 2018, https://media.ford.com/content/fordmedia/fna/us/en/news/2018/11/26/ford-statement-on-business-transformation.html.

7. Rogers, "Ford's New CEO Has a Cerebral Style."

8. Rogers, "Ford's New CEO Has a Cerebral Style."

9. Paul Weinland and Cesare Mainardi, *Strategy That Works* (Boston: Harvard Business Review Press, 2016).

10. Walmart, Inc., "Wal-Mart Stores, Inc. Enterprise Strategy," accessed March 13, 2020, https://stock.walmart.com/investors/our-strategy.

11. In *Good Strategy, Bad Strategy* (New York: Crown Business, 2011), Richard Rumelt lists four hallmarks of bad strategy: 1. Fluff (gibberish); 2. Failure to Face the Challenge (ignoring the obvious obstacles to achieving goals); 3. Mistaking Goals for Strategy (listing of objectives and treating them like plans); and 4. Bad Strategic Objectives (an elaboration of goals). We focus here on confusion with goals because we believe it is the most pervasive problem.

12. Rumelt, *Good Strategy, Bad Strategy*, 5–6.

13. Elon Musk, "The Secret Tesla Motors Master Plan (Just Between You and Me)," *Tesla Inc.*, August 2, 2006, https://www.tesla.com/blog/secret-tesla-motors-master-plan -just-between-you-and-me.

14. Musk, "The Secret Tesla Motors Master Plan."

15. Roche, "Our Strategy," accessed March 14, 2020, https://www.roche.com/about/our -strategy.htm.

16. Noel Tichy and Ram Charan, "Speed, Simplicity, Self-Confidence: An Interview with Jack Welch," *Harvard Business Review*, September–October 1989.

17. Arthur Plotnik, *The Elements of Editing: A Modern Guide for Editors and Journalists*, (New York: Macmillan, 1982), 31.

18. Zūm, "Overview of Zūm Services," accessed March 22, 2020, https://ridezum.com /our-services.html.

19. Dectar, "Introducing Dogise—On-Demand Dogwalkers App," accessed March 15, 2020, https://www.dectar.com/dogwalkers-app.

20. Patagonia, "Don't Buy This Jacket, Black Friday, and the New York Times," accessed March 22, 2020, https://www.patagonia.com/stories/dont-buy-this-jacket-black-friday -and-the-new-york-times/story-18615.html.

21. Zūm, "Our Story Begins with Our Mission," accessed March 22, 2020, https://ridezum .com/our-story.html.

8. ELABORATING THE STRATEGY

1. Kim Souza, "The Supply Side: Walmart and Amazon Go Head to Head in Private-Label Push," *Talk Business and Politics*, March 21, 2018, https://talkbusiness.net/2018/03 /the-supply-side-walmart-and-amazon-go-head-to-head-in-private-label-push.

2. Nika Kabiri and Leslie Helm, "The Rise of Amazon's Private Label Brands," *Seattle Business*, January 2018, https://seattlebusinessmag.com/business-operations/rise -amazons-private-label-brands.

9. PERCEIVED QUALITY STRATEGIES

1. Details about *The Economist* can be found in Felix Oberholzer-Gee, Bharat Anand, and Lizzie Gomez, *"The Economist"* (Harvard Business School Case 9-710-441, Boston: Harvard Business School Press, 2010).

2. "Why Are *The Economist*'s Writers Anonymous?," *The Economist*, September 5, 2013, https://www.economist.com/the-economist-explains/2013/09/04/why-are-the -economists-writers-anonymous.

3. In looking at the formulated argument, we can see one place where it might be made more precise, namely, the connection between BIPs' perception of superior content and overall market judgment about content. Clearly, BIPs are only a part of the market. However, because they are the primary target of the newspaper, we think the argument properly captures the core of the strategy and wonder whether further refinement is worth the payoff. (Our inside informant essentially said that the magazine was unclear about this matter too, when he told us that no one really understood what made their "secret sauce" work so well.) So, we made a judgment call to stop here for now, recognizing the limitation. We also leave it as an exercise to the reader to construct similar arguments for the other drivers of intrinsic appeal that we identified in figure 9.3.

4. However, this is how we originally connected them in our strategy map in figure 9.3. This shows how moving from a map to a syllogism can change your thinking, or at least force you to confront issues that the map did not.

5. A skeptic might argue that marketing cannot, in the long run, convince people of something that has no basis in reality. In other words, people will not believe the *Economist*'s high-status claims if there are no high-status readers (BIPs) of the magazine. Such a skeptic could modify our argument here by introducing a dependency on premise ESA3* in the marketing subargument. While such an argument seems plausible, we do not explore it here for the sake of brevity.

10. THE PILLAR OF STRATEGY

1. Herbert Muschamp, "Architecture Review; Gehry's Vision of Renovating Democracy," *New York Times*, May 18, 2001, https://www.nytimes.com/2001/05/18/arts/architecture -review-gehry-s-vision-of-renovating-democracy.html.

2. Walter Isaacson, "The Real Leadership Lessons of Steve Jobs," *Harvard Business Review*, April 2012.

3. The original Honda story, widely promoted by the Boston Consulting Group, goes as follows. Honda entered the U.S. market with a clear market opportunity in mind: to appeal to a large and growing set of middle-class consumers. These customers were put off by both the price and the image associated with the large, muscular motorcycles offered by Harley-Davidson and other American and British producers. Honda, in this telling, combined this consumer insight with a plan to emphasize market share as a means of ensuring a low-cost production position. The company's first product was a small, lightweight 50cc motorcycle that it could sell in volume to build scale and gain experience; the low capital cost of production would allow Honda to move down the experience curve quickly and reap strong economies of scale. As Honda's production ramped up, it built a production-oriented labor force that with experience soon became very efficient.

4. Richard T. Pascale, "Perspectives on Strategy: The Real Story Behind Honda's Success," *California Management Review* 36 (Spring, 1984): 47–72.

5. Matt Tyranor, "Architecture in the Age of Gehry," *Vanity Fair*, August 2010, http://www.vanityfair.com/culture/2010/08/architecture-survey-201008.

6. Richard P. Rumelt, *Good Strategy, Bad Strategy* (New York: Crown Business, 2011), 242–243.

7. Moreover, in their eagerness to define timelines, assign responsibilities, and create key performance indicators, leaders too often lose sight of the fact that there may be several different ways of defining the relevant subgoals. Any sufficiently ambitious vision of the future allows for several different ways to achieve it, and it is extremely unlikely that these various paths are equally efficient or effective. Surely, being strategic means in part choosing a better path to a goal.

8. As with the original Honda story about strategy, the Disney success story of Eisner is often told retrospectively as one of vision and planning. As conventionally taught, the lesson to be learned from Eisner's turnaround is that he recognized the critical role of animation and animated characters in tying together the company's many diverse businesses. Disney has built a multifaceted business empire woven together at the core by its animated characters, which they control and own in entirety. The strategy was always there, to some extent, because Walt Disney fostered animation and considered Mickey Mouse the center of his kingdom. By this view, Eisner quickly embraced and elaborated this strategy and pushed it into all the businesses, driving the unifying theme to become so prominent and profitable.

9. James B. Stewart, *DisneyWar* (New York: Simon & Schuster, 2006).

10. Stewart, *DisneyWar*, 55.

11. Stewart, *DisneyWar*, 104.

12. Stewart, *DisneyWar*, 73.

13. When employees complained that Katzenberg's management efforts ran up against "hallowed Disney traditions" (69), "Eisner seemed amused by the turmoil." Later, when Eisner remodeled the Disney studios and associated office space, he forced the animators to move several miles away to "a dreary, nearly windowless warehouse in Glendale" (73). To the animators and others, the relocation decision sent a clear signal "since Walt's office had always been in the animation building at the heart of the studio" (73). The outcome was predictable. "The move was demoralizing . . . the animators concluded that their days were probably numbered . . . they had so little work to occupy them that they passed the time with chair races, cell-sliding contests and Trivial Pursuit games" (74). Key animation personnel left the company. Quotes from Stewart, *DisneyWar*.

14. Stewart, *DisneyWar*, 93–94.

15. The idea was that the iPod (and other features of Apple's "digital hub") would drive sales of Macintosh computers because it only worked on Apple's proprietary operating system. It was not until after Apple made the iPod and iTunes available on Microsoft Windows and adopted a new strategy for the Macintosh line that sales improved. See William P. Barnett and Debra Schifrin, "The Rise of Apple" (Stanford Graduate School

of Business Case SM260, Stanford, Calif.: Stanford Graduate School of Business, 2016).

16. Victoria Chang and Garth Saloner, "Capital One Financial Corporation: Setting and Shaping Strategy" (Stanford Graduate School of Business Case SM135, Stanford, Calif.: Stanford Graduate School of Business, 2005).

17. William P. Barnett, "Learning Without Logic," *Bill Barnett on Strategy* (blog), February 15, 2017, http://www.barnetttalks.com/2017/02/learning-without-logic.html.

18. Cynthia Montgomery, *The Strategist: Be the Leader Your Business Needs* (New York: Harper Business, 2012), 13.

APPENDIX A. TERMINOLOGY

1. Michael D. Watkins, "Demystifying Strategy: The What, Who, How and Why," *Harvard Business Review*, September, 2017, https://hbr.org/2007/09/demystifying -strategy-the-what.

2. A. G. Lafley and Roger L. Martin, *Playing to Win: How Strategy Really Works* (Boston: Harvard Business Review Press, 2013), 14.

3. Michael E. Porter, "What Is Strategy?," *Harvard Business Review*, November–December 1996, https://hbr.org/1996/11/what-is-strategy.

4. From a totally different context, we see as a parallel comment the claim that a particular person, say your aunt Georgia, has "no personality." Of course, she has a personality, as all people do. The comment about no personality connotes that Georgia has no obviously distinct or engaging or memorable personality, just as a comment about no strategy implies no obviously distinct or unique or successful strategy.

5. Henry Mintzberg, *The Rise and Fall of Strategic Planning* (New York: Free Press, 1994), 25.

APPENDIX B. DISSECTING STRATEGY

1. To prioritize what we think is most important, we have throughout the book advocated a simpler approach of staying focused on strategic advantages and not worrying too much about goals. A full-blown analysis could bring goals back into the picture, often at the costs of greater complexity in the argument. In such an analysis, the highest-level conclusion we might seek is an answer to questions about how an organization achieves its prespecified long-term goals. To do this, we would first need to know the organization's objective function—what is it trying to maximize? (It could be market share, for instance, or profits, or shareholder value.) Then we would need to explain how the elements of the organization's strategy and its context work together to achieve those goals. This part of the analysis may sometimes be complex and possibly problematic (say the organization wishes to maximize the sustainable profit stream over the next five years and could possibly do it by any of several possible ways based on an identifiable competitive advantage).

2. This conceptualization relies heavily on the work of Adam M. Brandenburger and Harbone W. Stuart, "Value-based Business Strategy," *Journal of Economics and Management Strategy* 5, no. 1 (1996): 5–24; and Garth Saloner, Andrea Shepard, and Joel M. Podolny, *Strategic Management* (New York: Wiley, 2001).

3. Our goal in performing an analysis of Southwest's strategy is to illustrate the strategy identification framework, rather than to provide an original analysis. Our claims about Southwest build on widely popular analyses, including Charles O'Reilly III and Jeffrey Pfeffer, "Southwest Airlines (A)" (Stanford Graduate School of Business Case No. HR1A, Stanford, CA: Stanford Graduate School of Business, 1995); and Michael E. Porter, "What Is Strategy?,"*Harvard Business Review*, November–December 1996, https://hbr.org/1996/11/what-is-strategy.

4. MIT Global Airline Industry Airline Program, "Airline Industry Overview," accessed February 15, 2018, http://web.mit.edu/airlines/analysis/analysis_airline_industry.html.

5. United merged with Continental; American merged with USAir; Delta merged with Northwest.

6. We should note that while the focus on shorter regional routes helped reduce direct competition from other airlines, it increased Southwest's exposure to another obstacle to capturing value by increasing the pressure Southwest felt from substitutes. For cities that are relatively close to each other, such as San Antonio and Dallas, driving, taking a bus, or taking a train are all viable substitutes: if the price of an airplane ticket is too high, the bus will do. By contrast, when United offers a flight between San Francisco and New York, surface-based transportation is a much weaker substitute. The existence of these alternatives limited, to a certain extent, how much Southwest could charge for its flights and hence its ability to capture value.

7. MIT Global Airline Industry Airline Program, "Airline Industry Overview."

REFERENCES

Ackermann, Fran, and Colin Eden. *Making Strategy: Mapping Out Strategic Success*, 2nd ed. Los Angeles: Sage, 2011.

Apple Inc. "iTunes Now Number Two Music-Retailer in the US." Press release, February 26, 2008. https://www.apple.com/newsroom/2008/02/26iTunes-Now-Number-Two-Music -Retailer-in-the-US.

Arena, Michael. *Adaptive Space: How GM and Other Companies Are Positively Disrupting Themselves and Transforming Into Agile Organizations*. New York: McGraw Hill, 2018.

Barnett, William P. "Learning Without Logic." *Bill Barnett on Strategy* (blog), February 15, 2017. http://www.barnetttalks.com/2017/02/learning-without-logic.html.

Barnett, William P., and Debra Schifrin. "The Rise of Apple." Stanford Graduate School of Business Case SM260. Stanford, Calif.: Stanford Graduate School of Business, 2016.

Barney, Jay B., and William S. Hesterly. *Strategic Management and Competitive Advantage*. Upper Saddle River, N.J.: Prentice Hall, 2010.

Blake, Emily. "Spotify Says Tidal's 'Lemonade' Exclusive Is Bad for Everyone." *Mashable*, April 24, 2016. https://mashable.com/2016/04/24/spotify-beyonce-tidal.

Bourgoin, Alaric, François Marchessaux, and Nicolas Bencherki. "We Need to Talk About Strategy: How to Conduct Effective Strategic Dialogue." *Business Horizons* 61, no. 4 (2018): 587–597.

Bradley, Stephen P., and Pankaj Ghemawat. "Wal-Mart Stores, Inc." Harvard Business School Case 794–024. Boston: Harvard Business School Press, January 1994 (revised November 2002).

Brandenburger, Adam M., and Harbone W. Stuart. "Value-based Business Strategy." *Journal of Economics and Management Strategy* 5, no. 1 (1996): 5–24.

Brewers Association. "Craft Brewer Volume Share of U.S. Beer Market Reaches Double Digits in 2014." Press release, March 16, 2015. https://www.brewersassociation.org/press-releases /craft-brewer-volume-share-of-u-s-beer-market-reaches-double-digits-in-2014.

REFERENCES

Bryant, Adam. "Honeywell's David Cote, on Decisiveness as a 2-Edged Sword." *New York Times*, November 2, 2013. https://www.nytimes.com/2013/11/03/business/honeywells-david-cote-on-decisiveness-as-a-2-edged-sword.html.

Bryson, John M., Fran Ackermann, and Colin Eden. *Visual Strategy: Strategy Mapping for Public and Nonprofit Organizations*. New York: Wiley, 2014.

Bryson, John M., Fran Ackermann, Colin Eden, and Charles B. Finn. *Visible Thinking: Unlocking Causal Mapping for Practical Business Results*. New York: Wiley, 2004.

Carroll, Glenn R., and Anand Swaminathan. "Why the Microbrewery Movement? Organizational Dynamics of Resource Partitioning in the US Brewing Industry." *American Journal of Sociology* 106, no. 3 (2000): 715–762.

Chafkin, Max. "Udacity's Sebastian Thrun, Godfather of Free Online Education, Changes Course." *Fast Company*, November 14, 2013. https://www.fastcompany.com/3021473/udacity-sebastian-thrun-uphill-climb.

Chang, Victoria, and Garth Saloner. "Capital One Financial Corporation: Setting and Shaping Strategy." Stanford Graduate School of Business Case SM135. Stanford, Calif.: Stanford Graduate School of Business, 2005.

Christensen, Clayton M. *The Innovator's Dilemma*. Boston: Harvard Business School Press, 1997.

Christensen, Clayton M., and Michael B. Horn. "Innovation Imperative: Change Everything." *New York Times*, November 1, 2013. https://www.nytimes.com/2013/11/03/education/edlife/online-education-as-an-agent-of-transformation.html.

Cyert, Richard M., and James G. March. *A Behavioral Theory of the Firm*. 2nd ed. New York: Wiley-Blackwell, 1992.

Dectar. "Introducing Dogise—On-Demand Dogwalkers App." Accessed March 15, 2020. https://www.dectar.com/dogwalkers-app.

Felton, Ryan. "Why Mark Field Was Fired." *Jalopnik*, May 22, 2017. https://jalopnik.com/why-mark-fields-was-fired-1795431562.

Fernbach, Phillip M., Todd Rogers, Craig R. Fox, and Steven A. Sloman. "Political Extremism Is Supported by an Illusion of Understanding." *Psychological Science* 24 no. 6 (2013): 939–946.

Ford Motor Company. "Ford Statement on Business Transformation." Press release, November 26, 2018. https://media.ford.com/content/fordmedia/fna/us/en/news/2018/11/26/ford-statement-on-business-transformation.html.

Fried, Ina. "These People Thought the iPhone Was a Dud When It Was Announced 10 Years Ago." *Vox.com*, January 9, 2017. https://www.vox.com/2017/1/9/14215942/iphone-steve-jobs-apple-ballmer-nokia-anniversary.

Garbuio, Massimo, Dan Lovallo, and Oliver Sibony. "Evidence Doesn't Argue for Itself: The Value of Disinterested Dialogue in Strategic Decision Making," *Long Range Planning* 48, no. 6 (2015): 361–380.

Ghemawat, Pankaj. *Redefining Global Strategy: Crossing Borders in a World Where Differences Still Matter*. Boston: Harvard Business Review Press, 2007.

Gilbertson, Scott. "iPhone First Impressions: Not Worth the Money" *Wired*, June 29, 2007. https://www.wired.com/2007/06/iphone-first-im.

Goldberg, Amir, Robert Siegel, and Matt Saucedo. "Tableau: The Creation of Tableau Public." Stanford Graduate School of Business Case E632. Stanford, Calif.: Stanford Graduate School of Business, 2017.

Goodell, Jeff. "The Rolling Stone Interview: Steve Jobs." *Rolling Stone*, December 25, 2003. https://www.rollingstone.com/music/music-news/the-rolling-stone-interview-steve -jobs-233293.

Hajek, Daniel. "The Man Who Saved Southwest Airlines with a '10-Minute' Idea." *National Public Radio's All Things Considered*, June 28, 2015. https://www.npr.org/2015/06/28/418147961 /the-man-who-saved-southwest-airlines-with-a-10-minute-idea.

Hall, Parker. "Apple Music vs. Spotify: Which Service Is the Streaming King?" *Digital Trends*, March 5, 2019. https://www.digitaltrends.com/music/apple-music-vs-spotify.

Heath, Chip, and Dan Heath. *Decisive: How to Make Better Choices in Life and Work*. New York: Crown Business, 2013.

Hill, Charles W., Gareth R. Jones, and Melissa A. Schilling. *Strategic Management Theory: An Integrated Approach*. Boston: Cengage Learning, 2014.

Hitt, Michael A., R. Duane Ireland, and Richard E. Hoskisson. *Strategic Management Cases: Competitiveness and Globalization*. 10th ed. Boston: Cengage Learning, 2012.

Hoffman, Bryce G. *American Icon: Alan Mullaly and the Fight to Save Ford Motor Company*. New York: Currency, 2012.

Holub, Miroslav. "Brief Thoughts on Maps." *Times Literary Supplement*, February 4, 1977.

Isaacson, Walter. "The Real Leadership Lessons of Steve Jobs." *Harvard Business Review*, April 2012.

Jacobs, Fred. "6 Reasons Why I Hate Twitter's New 280 Character Limit." *Jacobs Media Strategies* (blog), November 9, 2017. https://jacobsmedia.com/6-reasons-hate-twitters -new-280-character-limit.

Johnson, Steven. *Farsighted: How We Make the Decisions That Matter the Most*. New York: Riverhead Books, 2018.

Kabiri, Nika, and Leslie Helm, "The Rise of Amazon's Private Label Brands." *Seattle Business*, January 2018. https://seattlebusinessmag.com/business-operations/rise-amazons -private-label-brands.

Kaplan, Robert S., and David P. Norton. *Strategy Maps*. Boston: Harvard Business School Press, 2004.

Karp, Hannah. "Apple iTunes Sees Big Drop in Music Sales." *Wall Street Journal*, October 24, 2014. https://www.wsj.com/articles/itunes-music-sales-down-more-than-13-this-year -1414166672.

Karp, Hannah, and Alistair Barr. "Apple Buys Beats for $3 Billion, Tapping Tastemakers to Regain Music Mojo." *Wall Street Journal*, May 28, 2014. https://www.wsj.com/articles /apple-to-buy-beats-1401308971.

Kim, W. C., and Renée Mauborgne. *Blue Ocean Strategy: How to Create Uncontested Market Space and Make the Competition Irrelevant*. Boston: Harvard Business Review Press, 2005.

Knight, Dom. "Brevity Is the Soul of Twitter. We Don't Need 280 Characters to Say That." *The Guardian*, September 27, 2017. https://www.theguardian.com/technology/commentisfree /2017/sep/27/brevity-soul-twitter-280-characters.

REFERENCES

Lafley A. G., and Roger L. Martin. *Playing to Win: How Strategy Really Works*. Boston: Harvard Business Review Press, 2013.

Lave, Charles A., and James G. March, 1993. *An Introduction to Models in the Social Sciences*. Lanham, Md.: University Press of America, 1993.

LeBeau, Phil. "Ford Investors 'Want Some Comfort' from CEO Jim Hackett as Shares Drop to Six-Year Low." *CNBC*, October 9, 2018. https://www.cnbc.com/2018/10/09/ford-investors -want-some-comfort-as-shares-drop-to-six-year-low.html.

Lewis, Michael. *The New New Thing*. New York: Norton, 2000.

Lovallo, Dan, and Oliver Sibony. "The Case for Behavioral Strategy." *McKinsey Quarterly*, January 2010.

Madrigal, Alexis C. "Twitter's 280-Character Tweets Are Fine." *The Atlantic*, September 27, 2017. https://www.theatlantic.com/technology/archive/2017/09/twitters-testing-280-character -tweets/541221.

McCord, Patty. *Powerful: Building a Culture of Freedom and Responsibility*. Silicon Guild, 2017.

Mercier, Hugo, and Dan Sperber. "Why Do Humans Reason? Arguments for an Argumentative Theory." *Behavioral and Brain Sciences* 34, no. 2 (2011): 57–111.

Miller, Chance. "Jimmy Iovine Slams Free Music Services, Talks Exclusivity Deals in New Interview." *9To5Mac*, May 17, 2017. https://9to5mac.com/2017/05/17/jimmy-iovine-free -music-interview.

Mintzberg, Henry. *The Rise and Fall of Strategic Planning*. New York: Free Press, 1994.

MIT Global Airline Industry Program. "Airline Industry Overview." Accessed February 15, 2018. http://web.mit.edu/airlines/analysis/analysis_airline_industry.html.

Mitroff, Sarah. "Beats Music Review: Music Streaming Done Right." *CNET*, July 7, 2015. https://www.cnet.com/reviews/beats-music-review.

Montgomery, Cynthia. *The Strategist: Be the Leader Your Business Needs*. New York: Harper Business, 2012.

Moshman, David, and Molly Geil. "Collaborative Reasoning: Evidence for Collective Rationality." *Thinking and Reasoning* 4, no. 3 (1998): 231–248.

Muschamp, Herbert. "Architecture Review; Gehry's Vision of Renovating Democracy." *New York Times*, May 18, 2001.

Musk, Elon. "The Secret Tesla Motors Master Plan (Just Between You and Me)." *Tesla Inc.*, August 2, 2006. https://www.tesla.com/blog/secret-tesla-motors-master-plan-just -between-you-and-me.

Newcomer, Eric. "In Video, Uber CEO Argues with Driver Over Falling Fares." *Bloomberg*, February 28, 2017. https://www.bloomberg.com/news/articles/2017-02-28 /in-video-uber-ceo-argues-with-driver-over-falling-fares.

Nickerson, Raymond S. *Reflections on Reasoning*. Hillsdale, N.J.: Erlbaum, 1986.

Nutt, Paul C. *Why Decisions Fail: Avoiding Blunders and Traps That Lead to Debacles*. San Francisco: Berrett-Koehler, 2002.

Obama, Barack. "Obama's Economics Speech at Knox College." *New York Times*, July 24, 2013. https://www.nytimes.com/2013/07/25/us/politics/obamas-economics-speech-at-knox -college.html.

Oberholzer-Gee, Felix, Bharat Anand, and Lizzie Gomez. "*The Economist.*" Harvard Business School Case 710–441. Boston: Harvard Business School Publishing, 2010.

O'Reilly, Charles, III, and Jeffrey Pfeffer. "Southwest Airlines (A)." Stanford Graduate School of Business Case No. HR1A. Stanford, Calif.: Stanford Graduate School of Business, 1995.

Page, Scott. *The Model Thinker: What You Need to Know to Make Data Work for You.* New York: Basic Books, 2018.

Pascale, Richard T. "Perspectives on Strategy: The Real Story Behind Honda's Success." *California Management Review* 36 (Spring, 1984): 47–72.

Patagonia. "Don't Buy This Jacket, Black Friday, and the New York Times." Accessed March 22, 2020. https://www.patagonia.com/stories/dont-buy-this-jacket-black-friday-and-the-new -york-times/story-18615.html.

Pisano, Gary P. *Creative Construction: The DNA of Sustained Innovation.* New York: Public Affairs, 2019.

Plotnik, Arthur. *The Elements of Editing: A Modern Guide for Editors and Journalists.* New York: Macmillan, 1982.

Popper, Ben, and Micah Singleton. "Apple Announces Its Streaming Music Service, Apple Music." *The Verge*, June 8, 2015. https://www.theverge.com/2015/6/8/8729481 /apple-music-streaming-service-wwdc-15.

Porter, Michael E. 1996. "What Is Strategy?" *Harvard Business Review*, November–December 1996. https://hbr.org/1996/11/what-is-strategy.

——. 2008. *Competitive Strategy: Techniques for Analyzing Industries and Competitors.* New York: Simon & Schuster, 2008.

Recording Industry Association of America (RIAA). U.S. Sales Database. Accessed March 7, 2019. https://www.riaa.com/u-s-sales-database.

Ricker, Thomas. "First Click: Remember When Steve Jobs Said Even Jesus Couldn't Sell Music Subscriptions?" *The Verge*, June 8, 2015.

Roche, Inc. "Our Strategy." Accessed March 14, 2020. https://www.roche.com/about/our -strategy.htm.

Rogers, Christina. "Ford's New CEO Has a Cerebral Style—and to Many, It's Baffling." *Wall Street Journal*, August 14, 2018. https://www.wsj.com/articles/fords-new-ceo-has-a -cerebral-styleand-to-many-its-baffling-1534255714?mod=searchresults&page=1&pos=5.

Rosen, Aliza, and Ikuhiro Ihara. "Giving You More Characters to Express Yourself." *Twitter* (blog), September 26, 2017. https://blog.twitter.com/official/en_us/topics/product/2017 /Giving-you-more-characters-to-express-yourself.html.

Rosoff, Matt. "Jeff Bezos: There Are 2 Types of Decisions to Make, and Don't Confuse Them." *Business Insider*, April 5, 2016. https://www.businessinsider.com/jeff-bezos-on -type-1-and-type-2-decisions-2016-4.

Rumelt, Richard P. *Good Strategy, Bad Strategy.* New York: Crown Business, 2011.

Salam, Reihan. "Online Education Can Be Good or Cheap, but Not Both." *Reuters.com*, July 26, 2013. http://blogs.reuters.com/reihan-salam/2013/07/26/online-education-can-be -good-or-cheap-but-not-both.

Saloner, Garth, Andrea Shepard, and Joel M. Podolny. *Strategic Management.* New York: Wiley, 2001.

REFERENCES

Sande, Steven. "Steve Jobs's Story of the Stones." *Engadget*, November 11, 2011. https://www
.engadget.com/2011/11/11/steve-jobss-story-of-the-stones.

Schneider, Avie. "Apple Launches Video Streaming Service for $4.99 a Month." *National
Public Radio Technology*, September 10, 2019. https://www.npr.org/2019/09/10/759500972
/apple-launches-video-streaming-service-for-4-99-a-month.

Siegel, Robert E., and Amadeus Orleans. "AB InBev: Brewing an Innovation Strategy." Stanford Graduate School of Business Case E643. Stanford, Calif.: Stanford Graduate School
of Business, 2017.

Souza, Kim. "The Supply Side: Walmart and Amazon Go Head to Head in Private-Label
Push." *Talk Business and Politics*, March 21, 2018. https://talkbusiness.net/2018/03/the
-supply-side-walmart-and-amazon-go-head-to-head-in-private-label-push.

Spence, Ewan. "Apple Music Has Failed." *Forbes*, October 5, 2015. https://www.forbes.com
/sites/ewanspence/2015/10/05/apple-music-failure.

Stewart, James B. *DisneyWar*. New York: Simon & Schuster, 2006.

Strategy&. "The Strategy Crisis: Insights from the Strategy Profiler." 2019. https://www.strategy
and.pwc.com/gx/en/unique-solutions/cds/the-strategy-crisis.pdf.

Summers, Brian. "Why Wall Street Isn't Happy with Southwest's 43 Straight Years of
Profits." *Skift*, August 16, 2016. https://skift.com/2016/08/16/why-wall-street-isnt-happy
-with-southwests-43-straight-years-of-profits.

Swieringa, Robert J., and Karl E. Weick. "An Assessment of Laboratory Experiments in
Accounting." Supplement, *Journal of Accounting Research* 20 (1982): 56–101. https://doi
.org/10.2307/2674675.

Teece, David J., Gary Pisano, and Amy Shuen. "Dynamic Capabilities and Strategic Management." *Strategic Management Journal* 18, no. 7 (1997): 509–533.

Thompson, Cadie. "Your Car Will Become a Second Office in 5 Years or Less, General Motors
CEO Predicts." *Business Insider*, December 12, 2016. https://www.businessinsider.com
/gms-mary-barra-interview-2016-12.

Tichy, Noel, and Ram Charan. "Speed, Simplicity, Self-Confidence: An Interview with Jack
Welch." *Harvard Business Review*, September–October 1989.

Troianovski, Anton, and Sven Grundberg. "Nokia's Bad Call on Smartphones." *Wall Street
Journal*, July 18, 2012. https://www.wsj.com/articles/SB10001424052702304388004577531
002591315494.

Tyranor, Matt. "Architecture in the Age of Gehry." *Vanity Fair*, August 2010. http://www
.vanityfair.com/culture/2010/08/architecture-survey-201008.

Walmart, Inc. "Wal-Mart Stores, Inc. Enterprise Strategy." Accessed March 13, 2020, https://
stock.walmart.com/investors/our-strategy.

Watkins, Michael D. "Demystifying Strategy: The What, Who, How and Why." *Harvard Business Review*, September 2017. https://hbr.org/2007/09/demystifying-strategy-the-what.

Weinland, Paul, and Cesare Mainardi. *Strategy That Works*. Boston: Harvard Business Review
Press, 2016.

"Why Are *The Economist's* Writers Anonymous?" *The Economist*, September 5, 2013. https://
www.economist.com/the-economist-explains/2013/09/04/why-are-the-economists
-writers-anonymous.

"Why Did Twitter Change Their Character Limit to 280 Characters?" Dictionary.com. Accessed March 12, 2020. https://www.dictionary.com/e/fierce-debate-twitters-280-characters.

Zūm. "Our Story Begins with Our Mission." Accessed March 22, 2020. https://ridezum.com/our-story.html.

——. "Overview of Zūm Services." Accessed March 22, 2020. https://ridezum.com/our-services.html.

INDEX

business process review. 117
Busy Important People (BIPs), for *The Economist*, 238–240, 242, 244–249, 299
buyer power, at Southwest Air, 264, 274–276, 278, 281–282, 284–288
buy-in, 97, 101–102, 109, 121, 163, 296n10

Cabify, 125
capabilities, organizational, 49, 51, 156, 262, 287; at Ford, 126, 128; at Roche, 186; at Tesla, 185
Capital One, 260, 301n6
Carroll, Lishan Nan, v
car-sharing, 126. *See also* ride-sharing services
Cash, Aaron, xvii
CAT. *See* critical analytical thinking
Caterpillar, xvi
case discussion, typical, xii; of Southwest, 37
cellular phone technology, 67–70
CFRA Research, 179
Chabot, Christian, 6
Chafkin, Max, 296n4
challenge: of capturing value, 275, 282; choice, 156, 158; of convergence phase, 158; of doing strategy, 89; executive examples of strategy, 3–7, 12–19; facing automakers, 126–127; filtering, 155, 159, 162; learning, 158, 170
Chang, Patricia, v, xvii
Chang, Victoria. 301n16
Charan, Ram, 298n16
choice challenge, in strategy formulation, 156, 158
choosing, among strategic options, 113, 154, 258
Christensen, Clayton, 148, 296n1, 2
Clark, Jim, 33–35
clichés, xiv, 191–192
clustering ideas, 51–53, 55, 91
common sense, 207–208

communicating, strategy, 178–202, with strategy maps, 188; within the organization, 197–199
competitive advantage, 44, 61, 90, 270, 273, 288, 291n11, 301n1; at Apple, 140; at Southwest Air, 14, 38, 40; sustainable, xiv, 24; at *The Economist*, 225, 247; theories of, xiv, 24; at Walmart, 72
conceit, central, 175
conclusion: xii, 8; in argument, 8, 68–71, 74; intermediate, 77–78; in mapping, 54–57; multiple, 45–47; as starting point in argument, 44–47, 90
confidence, lack of among executives, 10, 29
confirmation bias, 98–100, 109
consequent, affirming the, 87, 60
consequentiality of premises: defined, 151; implications for argument, 157, 164–165, 168, 177; implications for strategic action, 157, 169–170
consumer surplus, 135, 137, 144
consumer appeal, theory of, 248–249
consumer preferences, theory of, 238
convergence phase, 152–155, 157–158, 160, 174, 176–177; as three distinct sub-phases, 154
Cook, James, xvii
Copenhagen, 203–204
Corona, 5
Cote, David, 101, 293n12
Coursera, 148–149
craft beer, 4–5, 14–17
critical analytical thinking (CAT), xvi–xvii
cross-docking, at Walmart, 43, 50, 52, 58–59, 205
Cruise, 178
culture, organizational, 106, 115, 181
Cyert, Richard M., 294n29

Daimler, 129
Dallas, 277, 279–280, 284–285, 302